THE
SOWREYS

THE
SOWREYS

A unique and remarkable record of
one family's sixty-five years of
distinguished RAF service

Air Commodore
Graham Pitchfork MBE, BA, FRAeS

Foreword by
Professor Sir Laurence Martin Kt

Grub Street • London

Published by
Grub Street
4 Rainham Close
London
SW11 6SS

Copyright © Grub Street 2012
Copyright text © Air Commodore Graham Pitchfork 2012
Copyright foreword © Professor Sir Laurence Martin 2012

British Library Cataloguing in Publication Data

The Sowreys : a unique and remarkable record of one
   family's sixty-five years of distinguished RAF service.
   1. Sowrey family. 2. Great Britain. Royal Air Force—
   Biography. 3. Air pilots, Military—Great Britain—
   Biography.
   I. Title
   358.4'00922'41-dc23

ISBN-13: 9781908117311

Cover design by Sarah Driver
Typeset by Sarah Driver
Edited by Sophie Campbell

Printed and bound by MPG Ltd, Bodmin, Cornwall

Grub Street Publishing only uses
FSC (Forest Stewardship Council) paper for its books.

This book is dedicated to The Sowrey Family

Remembering in particular Jimmy
'Who failed to return'
24 June 1941

By the same author

Men Behind the Medals

The Buccaneers

Men Behind the Medals – A New Selection

Shot Down and on the Run

Shot Down and in the Drink

Royal Air Force – Day by Day

The RAF's First Jet Squadron

The Battle of Britain Story

CONTENTS

FOREWORD

Professor Sir Laurence Martin Kt

This is an unusual book about a remarkable family, six members of which, in two generations, served with distinction in the RAF, spanning the greater part of its history. Five reached very senior ranks, won an AFC each, with many other decorations, and made great contributions to the evolution of the service. The sixth never attained seniority, for he made the greatest contribution possible, his life, in combat over North Africa.

That just two generations could span most of the RAF's duration reminds us of what a young service it still is in the perspective of military history. It is, of course world renowned but perhaps too much of its fame rests on the role of the 'Few' in saving their country and the world from a dreadful tyranny. The story of the Sowreys embraces that heroic era but also recalls, not only, other major episodes in the development of the RAF – such as the first battles over the Western Front, air policing in Iraq, rearmament in the thirties – but also affords glimpses of actions less often recalled even by those generally familiar with RAF history. Some of these were seminal, such as night fighting against Zeppelins and Gothas, pioneering efforts at coordinated air defence that were developed so vitally for the Battle of Britain. Some were tragic, as was the forgotten role of the RAF in resistance to the post-Great War Irish rising. Some had a comic dimension, as when a handful of aircraft were posted to interwar Shanghai, using the racecourse as a runway and compelled to fit operations around race meetings and golf tournaments.

Other episodes in the Sowrey story are less forgivably neglected: the invention by Bill Sowrey, in the unlikely arena of early World War II operations against the Italians in East Africa, of what we would now call close air support, integrating air and ground forces, presaging the 'cab rank' tactics employed in the Allied advance after D-Day. Less glamorous but no less vital were contributions to the training of aircrew in both World Wars, the encouragement of 'air-mindedness' in the ranks of potential recruits, and the adaptation of the RAF post-1945 to the entirely new climate of nuclear deterrence and of conflict without war.

It was only in the last of these phases that I had the fortune, as the academic advisor to the National Defence College, to meet and even work a little with the last remaining Sowrey in the RAF, the second Freddie Sowrey, when he became commandant. I knew nothing of his family then but could not fail to appreciate the experience and dedication that I now know characterised the whole band of brothers. His career had embraced combat in the earlier stages of the war and a wide range of command and staff appointments. My own RAF experience was as a lowly, conscripted officer shortly after the war but even that service with men who had served before and during the war had taught me that the RAF itself was something of a family, concerned with welfare of the whole as well as their immediate responsibilities. The younger Freddie now had to carry that spirit, which the Sowreys had consistently embodied, into a very new era.

The earlier Sowreys had been largely absorbed, beyond flying, in matters of technology and tactics. In the post-1945 era these still mattered but had to be set in a new context of deterrence of conflict without combat in which military strategy can only be effective if closely set in its political context. The younger Freddie grasped that lesson firmly. The NDC was an ideal platform from which to reflect this but the same insight informed his many other appointments.

Now the context is changing again. The threat is no longer so clear, technology evolves with daunting speed and social change is rapid and confused. Partly for these very reasons the resources available to the RAF are shrinking just as the problems become, if perhaps not more dangerous, more complicated and uncertain. We must hope the Royal Air Force rises to these challenges as successfully as it did to those it faced in the lean years between the wars. Those seeking inspiration to undertake this task could well find it in the record of dedication, loyalty, and courage recorded in this volume.

ACKNOWLEDGEMENTS

Writing this book about the remarkable Sowrey family has been immensely stimulating, rewarding and enjoyable. My thanks go to many people who have helped bring the project to fruition.

First I want to thank Professor Sir Laurie Martin for his eloquent foreword, which sets the perfect tone for what follows, and for his advice.

Without the enthusiastic support of Sir Freddie Sowrey, writing this book would have been very difficult. He has never spared himself to travel to London to meet me in the RAF Club and when I have visited his lovely home he and his wife Ann have been wonderful hosts offering me a warm welcome and generous hospitality. He has given me access to his records, personal papers, letters, logbooks and photographs in addition to allowing me to tape record his memories and views. He has checked all the chapters and offered corrections together with additional invaluable comments and anecdotes. I also thank Sir Freddie's son and daughter, Peter and Susan. The whole Sowrey family have given me great assistance and I am very grateful to the Countess Fortescue for her hospitality and patience and for allowing me access to her grandfather's and father's logbooks, diaries and photographs. Elizabeth 'Boof' Edge, Heather Sowrey, Lorna Sowrey, Mandy Sowrey, Carol Sowrey Thorpe and Gavin Stewart have all been a great help in offering advice and lending me notes and photographs.

Much of the military research has been carried out at the Joint Services Command and Staff College, Watchfield, where the head librarian, Chris Hobson MBE, gave me a very great deal of help and advice and full access to the college's excellent library where he allowed me to spend many hours. I am also grateful to the Air Historical Branch where the head of the branch, Sebastian Cox, and Graham Day have been most helpful.

At the RAF Museum, Hendon, Air Vice-Marshal Peter Dye OBE, the director, and Peter Elliot have responded to all my requests and allowed me access to the Sowrey Archive which is lodged at the museum. I am also indebted to the keeper of the National Archives at Kew where I consulted a wide variety of sources, the major documents being listed in the bibliography. Tim Pierce at the RAF College Cranwell library could not have been more helpful and Diana Manipud helped me at King's College London. I also thank Air Vice-Marshal Nigel Baldwin CB, CBE and Air Vice-Marshal Tony Mason CB, CBE for their valuable advice.

Anne Barrett at Imperial College, London, Dr Reg Bryan at the Tangmere Military and Aviation Museum, Tim Kershaw at the Jet Age Museum, Group Captain 'Min' Larkin CBE, Halton Aircraft Apprentices Association, Wing Commander Paul Moss and Flight Sergeant Barry Dobson of 8 Squadron, Squadron Leader N. Short at the Central Flying School, David Walsh at Tonbridge School, Squadron Leader Richard Willis and Sergeant Mark Brewster at RAF Northolt have all provided valuable information and help.

Many individuals have given me specialist advice and I want to thank them all. Group Captain Chris Morris OBE and Wing Commander Jeff Jefford MBE have been an immense help providing much information and checking parts of the narrative. Others who have made significant contributions are Eric Absolon, Bill Brown DFC, Julie Burgess, Phil Butler, Peter Green, Alastair Goodrum, Norman Franks, Trevor Henshaw, Tony Holmes, Wally Kahn MBE, Mike O'Connor, Ray Rimell, John Scott, Peter Stratten, Andrew Thomas and Tony Vivian. I am grateful to all of them.

The great majority of the photographs are from the Sowrey family and the Sowrey Archive at the RAF Museum. I have acknowledged those others that I have been generously loaned.

Finally, I want to thank John Davies, Sarah Driver and Sophie Campbell at Grub Street for all their support in bringing this project to fruition.

ABBREVIATIONS

AAF	Auxiliary Air Force	DAIS	Directorate of Aeronautical Inspection Services
A&AEE	Aeroplane and Armament Experimental Establishment	D Def S	Director of Defence Studies
ADGB	Air Defence Great Britain	DFC	Distinguished Flying Cross
AFC	Air Force Cross	DGP	Director General of Production
AID	Aeronautical Inspection Directorate	DSO	Distinguished Service Order
AMDP	Air Member for Developmental and Production	EFTS	Elementary Flying Training School
AOC	Air Officer Commanding	ETPS	Empire Test Pilots' School
APC	Armament Practice Camp	FAI	Fédération Aéronautique Internationale
ATS	Air Training Section	FTS	Flying Training School
BCATP	British Commonwealth Air Training Plan	GCA	Ground Control Approach
BEF	British Expeditionary Force	GCI	Ground Control Interception
BEM	Medal of the Order of the British Empire	GOC	General Officer Commanding
		GOC-in-C	General Officer Commanding-in-Chief
BT	Bomber Transport	HMS	Her Majesty's Ship
CAS	Chief of Air Staff	HMT	Her Majesty's Transport
CBE	Commander of the Order of the British Empire	IAF	Indian Air Force
CENTO	Central Treaty Organisation	IDC	Imperial Defence College
CFI	Chief Flying Instructor	IISS	International Institute for Strategic Studies
CFS	Central Flying School		
CGS	Central Gunnery School	IRA	Irish Republican Army
COSSEC	Chiefs of Staff Secretariat	IRBM	Intermediate Range Ballistic Missile
DAI	Director Aeronautical Inspection	ITW	Initial Training Wing

JSSC	Joint Service Staff College	RAFO	Reserve of Air Force Officers
LDV	Local Defence Volunteer	RAFVR	Royal Air Force Volunteer Reserve
MAP	Ministry of Aircraft Production	RASC	Royal Army Service Corps
MBE	Member of the Order of the British Empire	RCAF	Royal Canadian Air Force
		RFC	Royal Flying Corps
MC	Military Cross	RIC	Royal Irish Constabulary
MOD	Ministry of Defence	RNAS	Royal Naval Air Service
MU	Maintenance Unit	R/T	Radio Telephony
NATO	North Atlantic Treaty Organisation	SAAF	South African Air Force
NCO	Non-Commissioned Officer	SACEUR	Supreme Allied Commander Europe
NDC	National Defence College	SAM	Surface-to-Air Missile
NTS	Night Training Squadron	SASO	Senior Air Staff Officer
OC	Officer Commanding	SDF	Shanghai Defence Force
OCU	Operational Conversion Unit	SFTS	Service Flying Training School
OTC	Officer Training Corps	TAF	Tactical Air Force
OTU	Operational Training Unit	UAS	University Air Squadron
PAI	Pilot Attack Instructor	UDI	Unilateral Declaration of Independence
PEG	Programme Evaluation Group		
POW	Prisoner of War	UKPMD	United Kingdom Permanent Military Deputy
PSO	Personal Staff Officer		
QFI	Qualified Flying Instructor	USAF	United States Air Force
RAAF	Royal Australian Air Force	USAAF	United States Army Air Force
RAE	Royal Aircraft Establishment	WAAF	Women's Auxiliary Air Force
RAFGSA	Royal Air Force Gliding & Soaring Association		

Chapter One

THE SOWREY FAMILY

From the end of the seventeenth century, a large branch of the Sowrey family was established in the area around Leeds in Yorkshire. William Sowrey had married Ann Rigg at Hawkshead on 16 June 1688 but their six children, the youngest named John, were all baptised in Armley near Leeds. Their eldest son Francis, born on 3 October 1696, married Elizabeth in St Peter's Church, Leeds in 1729 and their five offspring were all born in Armley. During the next two centuries, numerous Sowrey boys were given the names William and John and born into large families, many of them cloth makers, and they too all lived in the Leeds area. However, in December 1860, Joseph, the youngest of seven children, married Ann Benton from Wolverhampton and they chose to settle in the town. He became a licensed victualler and ran the Boot and Star in Wolverhampton. The eldest of their children was John William Sowrey born on 6 January 1862.

Aged twenty-seven, John married Susan Maria Chambers from Dersingham in Norfolk in 1889. She was seven years his junior and a year after their marriage the first of their six children, Cissy, was born. On 19 January 1892, their eldest son John was born at South Hamlet, Gloucester and eighteen months later, on 25 August 1893, Frederick, named after one of his uncles, was born at Kingsholm, Gloucester. William, also born in Kingsholm, arrived a year later on 8 August 1894 and over the next six years two daughters were added to the family. Two years after the arrival of the youngest daughter Joan, the family suffered a sad loss when the eldest girl Cissy died in 1904 aged fourteen.

The Boot and Star at Wolverhampton.

John senior, an intelligent man with strong Victorian principles, rose to be the Deputy Chief Inspector of Revenue. Throughout his life his family always referred to him as 'The Governor', an affectionate nickname that members of the family recognise gives an accurate assessment of his character and manner. After his retirement he became a very successful investment consultant but, despite their wartime success, he always regretted that his three sons had not entered the Indian Civil Service.

The three boys were all educated at home by their mother and they then passed on their knowledge to their sisters. Built around the affection of their loving and devoted mother, who was the central figure in their lives for many years, the children established a very close bond and spent most of their childhood in each other's company. With less than three years separating the three brothers, they shared many interests. They had an aptitude for science and engineering with a fascination for anything mechanical, particularly motor cycles and, as they grew older, this fascination extended to cars. During their early childhood, sport did not play a large part in the Sowrey household, study and learning took precedence and discipline was rigidly enforced.

From an early age Freddie was the natural ringleader of his brothers and sisters. He was blessed with an ability to turn his hand to many practical applications, a quality that proved beneficial to other members of the family over the next few years. He was very practical and observant and, after watching a cobbler at work, he bought a knife and an anvil and was soon repairing his brother's shoes.

By the time John was ready to attend school, the family had moved from Gloucestershire and settled at Merton in south-west London and John entered King's College School, Wimbledon in 1904 having gained a Junior Entrance Scholarship. It was an independent school founded in 1829, and the junior division of King's College, University of London. KCS, as it became universally known, had recently moved from its long-established location in London's Strand in order to

Above: 'The Governor' with his sister Annie.
Below: Susan Sowrey, 1913.

Above: The three brothers: John, Fred and William.
Below: John.

expand.

Fred also gained an Entrance Scholarship and joined his elder brother at KCS in 1906 and William – always known as Bill – continued the tradition a year later. Their success, each at the first attempt, reflects great credit on their mother's teaching skills and determination.

In 1909, John gained his matriculation, which completed his schooling, and the following year he moved up to King's College, University of London to take his place in the Natural Science Division of the Faculty of Science. The Sowrey family had a long and distinguished history of service with the Indian Civil Service and it was expected that the brothers would follow this family tradition and John entered King's to prepare for entry into the service. In the summer of 1911 he gained an Intermediate Certificate, Class II in Chemistry.

By the time the boys started to leave school the family had moved to a substantial house and farm in Staines, Middlesex and Yeoveney Lodge became a very happy home full of fun and laughter and a place where the children could entertain their friends. They had enjoyed a very happy childhood. The younger girls idolised their three older brothers and in the difficult years ahead, this family love and mutual loyalty was a great strength to all of them.

Fred was a prefect at KCS and he enjoyed active membership of the school's Scientific Society, which had expanded its interests to include the new and exciting technology of aeronautics. He visited Bisley Shooting Ground on occasions where he became a superb shot, and one year his team managed to win the coveted Ashburton Shield.

He followed elder brother John to King's, London in October 1912 having been awarded a Salter's Company Exhibition and the KCS Maths Scholarship. He too joined the Faculty of Science and after two years he successfully gained a Bachelor of Science intermediate degree. However war intervened before he could complete the three-year course and at the end of the 1914 summer term, he volunteered for service in the army. John had completed his three-year course and passed the civil service examination in April 1914. Bill, who had gained his school matriculation in 1912, was awarded the Edgell Hunt Science Scholarship to King's College specialising in mathematics, chemistry and physics. He followed his brothers into the Faculty of Science and entered the university a year after Fred. His attendance was also interrupted by the outbreak of war and after two years he too withdrew in order to undertake military service.

During their time at university, Fred and Bill served with the Officer Training Corps (OTC) and attended the annual summer camps so were well prepared for entry into the military. As with so many of their generation, they were quick to volunteer and ready to meet the national call to arms.

Fred in 1913.

Chapter Two

ARMY SERVICE

On 5 August 1914, the day that he took over as Minister for War, Field Marshal Earl Kitchener of Khartoum issued orders for the expansion of the army. Contrary to general popular belief that the war would be over by the Christmas of 1914, Kitchener predicted a long and brutal war in which, if timed right, the arrival of an overwhelming force of new, well-trained and well-led divisions would prove a decisive blow against the Central Powers. Kitchener declined to use the existing Territorial Force as the basis for the New Army, as many of its members had volunteered for 'Home Service' only and, in the early days of the war, the Territorial Force was not immediately available to reinforce the regular army. Hence, on 6 August parliament sanctioned an increase of 500,000 men of all ranks.

'Your King and Country need you: a call to arms' was published on 11 August 1914. It explained the new terms of service and called for the first 100,000 men to enlist. This figure was achieved within two weeks. The new infantry battalions would be given numbers consecutive to the existing battalions of their regiment, but with the addition of the word 'Service' after the unit number.

Most of the junior officers came from the university OTCs, which became officer-producing units with some 30,000 passing through the corps. With the war commencing during the summer vacation of 1914, many of these young men were available immediately and they responded to Kitchener's call. Others chose to interrupt their studies and volunteered immediately. Undoubtedly, there was also a strong sense of patriotism and, for many of them, it offered an opportunity for adventure.

John had just completed his studies at King's and he volunteered immediately. Fred had completed two years and he too decided to join Kitchener's New Army. By the end of August, John had been appointed a temporary second lieutenant in the 6th (Service) Bn Queens (Royal West Surrey) Regiment and Fred was appointed a temporary second lieutenant in the 12th (Service) Bn Royal Fusiliers. William had completed a year of his studies and after a further year of study, he also volunteered for service.

John as an officer in the 6th Queen's Regiment.

John joined the 6th Queens just as it was forming at Guildford as part of the 37th Brigade, 12th (Eastern) Division. It soon moved to Purfleet where infantry training was started. The next nine or ten months were taken up by very intensive training and a move to Sandling in late November put the battalion closer to the large range at Hythe for musketry practice. Training continued throughout the winter with brigade marches and visits to the rifle ranges at Ash and at Hythe before the battalion moved to Aldershot in February 1915 for divisional training. John was with the battalion until the end of 1914 when he decided to transfer to the expanding Royal Flying Corps (RFC).

Fred had completed two years with the University of London OTC when he volunteered at the same time as elder brother John. Initially placed on the Infantry General List he joined the 12th Royal Fusiliers in November. The battalion had formed at Hounslow in September and infantry training followed. In early April Fred wrote home from Shoreham to say that he was 'very comfortable'.

Fred commissioned into the 12th Bn Royal Fusiliers.

In the week of 19 June 1915 the battalions of the 24th Division moved to Aldershot for final training. Lord Kitchener inspected the division at Chobham ranges on 19 August and the next day it was the turn of King George V. Orders had just been received to move to France to join the British Expeditionary Force (BEF) and the first units departed one week later.

Fred landed in France on 1 September and sent a card to his mother:

> 'We did not expect to leave for at least a month but yesterday had orders to move off today so we are leaving. This may be rather a shock but do not worry I shall be all right.'

Concentration of the various battalions was completed in the area between Étaples and St Pol on the 4th and the following day, Fred was able to send a longer letter to his mother. He recorded his address as, 'Somewhere in France', with the added note saying 'Use this address!' He commented, 'we had a pleasant crossing'.

It soon became apparent why Fred and his battalion had left in such haste. A combined Anglo-French offensive was to be launched and additional troops were required to form a powerful reserve for what would later be called the Battle of Loos. This left just enough time for Fred to attend the BEF Machine Gun School for a five-day course before returning in time to join the advance to Loos.

Compared with the small-scale British efforts of spring 1915, the Battle of Loos was part of a wider offensive on the German lines and the largest British offensive of the war that had so far taken place. The attack to be launched on 25 September by six divisions from Douglas Haig's First Army was a mighty onslaught, so much so that it was referred to at the time as 'The Big Push'. The attack would see the first use of poisoned gas by the British. It is also famous for the first large-scale use of the units raised under Kitchener's New Army.

Two divisions, the 21st and 24th, the latter including Fred's 12th Royal Fusiliers, were in the vicinity and were earmarked as the reserve, but Sir John French refused to release them to Haig's command before the battle.

Over two days these two divisions had marched sixty kilometres on the French cobbled roads towards the front line. The volunteer battalions were keen but had no real practice in the arts of war save their

Damage caused by the Battle of Loos (Imperial War Museum).

initial training. Like Fred Sowrey's battalion, they had been in France for less than four weeks and were now expected to take on well emplaced and defended German positions.

The battle was preceded by a four-day bombardment but the chlorine gas attack turned out to be a great disappointment. It was released at 5.50 am on the first morning, giving it forty minutes to do its work before the infantry attacked at 6.30. However, much of the gas lingered in no-mans land or drifted back over the British lines.

Despite this setback, the first British assault was a success. The German front line was breached, with the New Army divisions performing well. North of Loos the strong Hohenzollern Redoubt fell to the 9th Division, while further south the village of Loos was captured. Early on the morning of 25 September Haig asked for the reserves to be sent in. French agreed, and ordered the two reserve divisions to join the attack.

Haig needed the reserves because of the nature of the German lines. Having decided to stay on the defensive in the west, and concentrate on winning the war in the east, the Germans had begun to dig in earnest. Part of this preparation involved the creation of an entire second line of fortifications, running as far as three miles behind the first line. This gap made it very unlikely that any Allied attack could break through both German lines, and allowed the Germans to launch their own counterattacks once the Allied assaults ran out of energy.

The two reserve divisions had spent the eve of the battle marching into the Loos valley in the pouring rain to a position six miles from the front line. Progress had been slow and exhausting. Staffs were unfamiliar with the ground; communication trenches were flooded and packed with men and roads and tracks were jammed with transport going in both directions. There were few bridges across shattered trenches, and wire was still stretched across wide areas. Men were carrying extra supplies, equipment, rations and ammunition. By the end of the first day the British had advanced to within 1,000 yards of the German second line to the north of Loos. The reserve divisions were needed to attack this second line of defences still intact, and the 12th Royal Fusiliers marched into action near Vermelles. However, poor communications and poor planning, partly by French and partly by Haig, meant that the reserves were left too far behind to be a useful reinforcement on the first day. They didn't reach the original British lines until the end of the day. On arrival, they were very tired but French sent them forward and they reached the advanced positions facing the enemy's second line early on the morning of the 26th. Once there they were informed that a general attack had been ordered for 11.00 am.

The 21st and 24th Divisions launched their attack in ten columns across the open ground in front of the German second line. They had been given no specific objectives, just an urging to go forward. Largely unaffected by the four-day artillery bombardment, the barbed wire in front of this line was unharmed. The British advanced to the wire taking heavy casualties all the time, and most formations were then forced to retreat to the old German front line, from where they had started that morning.

Formations in the Loos area consolidated their positions and the remnants of 21st and 24th Divisions prepared to withdraw to establish a new line along the eastern face of a ridge, giving a good field of fire. Elements of the 12th Royal Fusiliers, who had been one of the three leading battalions when the 24th Division advanced, remained forward. For the next two days, when they had little or no sleep or rations, they were subjected to heavy shelling. During the night of the 27th, a large German force of the Bavarian Composite Regiment directed a counter attack against the fusiliers and the 7th Northants. After a stiff fight, weight of numbers forced the two exhausted battalions to withdraw under heavy machine-gun fire and regroup along the eastern face of the Hohenzollern Redoubt. A comment in the war diary of one of these lead battalions provides a stark realism of the situation they had faced:

> 'It is regretted that before being launched into such a desperate action steps had not been taken to accustom the men to war conditions.'

The 24th Division's first battle experience resulted in appalling losses, suffering over 4,178 casualties for very little gain. The 12th Royal Fusiliers lost 275 men, including twelve officers. The battalion war diary commented, 'all ranks behaved with great gallantry and coolness'.

The battle continued for another three weeks. When the fighting finally died down, the British front line stood close to the line reached at the end of the first day, although the Germans had recaptured the Hohenzollern Redoubt. British losses at Loos were close to 50,000, with 16,000 dead and 25,000 wounded. The autumn battles of 1915 all ended in a similar tale of Allied failure and heavy losses.

Sir John French was a casualty of the battle. The confusion over the reserves, combined with a determined campaign by Douglas Haig, resulted in his removal as commander of the BEF. On 16 December Douglas Haig was appointed to command the BEF, a post he would hold for the rest of the war.

Immediately after the battle, Fred scribbled a note to his mother and told her, 'we went into action last Saturday and came out Wednesday night. Our men were simply splendid and fought like heroes.'

A few days later he wrote a longer letter. Before giving details of his experiences, he thanked his sister Queenie and his aunts for sending him chocolate commenting, 'it was very acceptable I can tell you after being nearly four days without food and water'. He went on to provide some other details but was unable to comment on casualties. His letter continues:

> 'Well! I expect you have seen all about the great British victory in the papers. I am very proud to say that our regiment was in the thick of it and all the men fought like heroes. We first went into action on Friday 24 Sept, I think it was. It is very difficult to keep count of days and dates out here.
>
> 'We fairly got the devils on the run. They cannot stand the bayonet and give in like children. I managed to take nine prisoners and sent them back under a cpl and two men but they met some Scotsmen coming up and they tried to shoot the lot. They managed to get

one but the others got back and are now safely interned. The "Jocks" as they are called are fine fighters and absolutely refuse to take prisoners. We came out of action last Wednesday and after collecting as many as possible of the men, we went back some distance for a so-called rest which we are enjoying in moving all over the country.

'I hope you are well at home. Please do not worry about me. I am quite all right and have now quite recovered from all strain. It is getting somewhat cold…

'I will write very soon and let you know all news. Good bye. Don't worry we are going to have an easy time now.

> With best love
> Your affectionate son
> Fred'

Like most young and educated sons writing to a worried mother, he was upbeat and made light of some aspects but he displayed an understandable naivety. In a letter to his older brother, John, who he always called 'Onion', and who had just started his flying training, he was a little more forthcoming. He wrote:

'Dear Onion
'Thanks for your letter. I hope you are progressing favourably. I had a letter from home yesterday saying that your leg was giving you rather a lot of trouble and that you had been compelled to undergo another operation. It is rather rotten seeing that you were getting on so well with your flying. I also heard something else about you. Well "congers!" old boy, hope she is nice. I will come and look you up as soon as I get a chance to come home.

'I suppose you have heard about the bloody show we were in. Our casualties have not yet been published I believe. But we now have twelve officers left out of twenty-nine!

'We are now having a good rest refitting etc before starting again, but I do not think we shall ever be in such a show again. The damn snipers are the limit, they are even behind our own lines.

'I have seen a few scraps in the air. The Huns won't stand up to our fellows although they certainly seem to have much better machines. They have some huge brutes with quick firing guns aboard.

'Well! Cheery-ho! Let me know all the news. Hope you will soon be quite fit.

> Yrs affect brother
> Fred'

There are many interesting points in these two short letters. The war had barely been going for a year and, despite the huge losses during the Battle of Loos, there is a note of optimism and no expectation of the carnage that would follow in the next three years. Yet, Fred's own regiment had lost over half its officers in their first engagement and just a few weeks after arriving at the front.

He makes interesting comments about flying and paints an optimistic view about the capabilities of the RFC. Also, despite the devastating scenes he had witnessed and the events he had experienced, he is still able to write with an almost innocent regard to the events and revert to family ribaldry and affection, which is so apparent in all his earlier correspondence. This is graphically illustrated in a letter he wrote on 17 October (in pencil) to his youngest sister Joan:

'My Dearest Little Joan
'Thank you so much for the writing pad it is just the very thing I wanted. The parcel arrived this morning but it did not look much like a parcel. It was very much knocked about and nearly all the walnuts had dropped out. However I enjoyed what there were very

much. I suppose you all helped to make it up so please thank Mam and Queenie for me will you. The biscuits are topping.

'How are you all getting on at home? I hope you are all quite well and fit. How is Onion getting on? I wish he would write and let me know how he is getting on and all about his girl.

'Well good-bye Joannie. Write me one of your nice letters and tell me all the news. Very best love to Mam, Queenie and all of you at home.

Your affectionate Br
Fred

P.S. I am so glad you are looking after little Nip [his dog] and keeping him well.'

Over the next four weeks, the fusiliers returned to the trenches for six-day periods when much of their work was repairing and improving the trenches and sandbagging. Fred contracted jaundice and was brought back to Dover on 11 November and transferred to the 4th Northern General Hospital. He was to spend three months under medical care and on leaving hospital decided he would follow in his brother's footsteps and apply for a transfer to the RFC. On his application form he noted that he had studied science, was keen on his motor cycle and had already managed to fly on one or two occasions.

The third brother, Bill, remained at university to complete his studies before volunteering for army service. He asked to join brother Fred's battalion but was commissioned as a temporary second lieutenant in the 9th (Reserve) Bn Royal Berkshire Regiment on 28 August 1915. The battalion was based at Bovington Camp near Wool. Large numbers of officers and men joined it from time to time and many drafts were sent overseas. Two of Bill's officer colleagues were sent as reinforcements to Gallipoli and they were both dead within a few weeks.

Bill commissioned into the 9th Royal Berkshire Regiment.

After completing his basic infantry training, Bill decided to follow his two brothers into the RFC and he reported to Reading to commence flying training on 9 January 1916.

Chapter Three

ROYAL FLYING CORPS – EARLY DAYS

John was the first of the three brothers to transfer to the RFC. He first applied on 4 November 1914 but there was a long waiting list. On his application he stated, 'considerable experience of motor engineering'. After he had made repeated attempts to bring his entry forward, he finally left his battalion in June 1915 and headed for the Military Training School at Castle Bromwich, four miles east of Birmingham, where he joined the recently-formed 5 Reserve Aeroplane Squadron.

John flew for the first time on 8 July when he was taken up for a ten-minute flight. Over the next few days he flew a number of short sorties with Captain Rodwell when he completed exercises to fly 'straights' and then 'circuits'. After three hours of tuition he was sent solo and after flying 'figures of eight' he had completed his basic training and on 29 July was awarded his Royal Aero Club Certificate (No. 1481).

A week later he was posted to Gosport, the home of the RFC's 5th Wing, where he will probably have been assigned to the resident 13 Squadron. Pending its mobilisation for deployment overseas, the role of a home-based service squadron at this stage of the war was to provide training in what was termed 'higher aviation'. That is to say, bringing a pilot who had qualified for his Royal Aero Club 'ticket' up to the standard required for the award of his RFC flying badge, after which he might remain with the unit or he could be posted to France as a replacement, or to another squadron that had yet to be mobilised.

When 13 Squadron began its operational work-up, its training task, along with surplus equipment and personnel (including John), was passed on to its successor, 22 Squadron, which began to form on 1 September 1915 to take its place. The new unit soon acquired the motley collection of aircraft that were used for training at that time, including an assortment of Blériots, Curtiss JN3s, Shorthorns, Martinsydes and Bristol Scouts and the BE2c.

On 2 September 1915 John was gazetted as a flying officer and transferred to the General List, entitling him to wear his RFC 'wings'. All that was required to be an instructor in those days was that one had to have been recognised as a fully-qualified pilot, so John will probably have begun to pass on what little he knew himself to the new arrivals – such was the primitive state of flying training in 1915-16. At the same time he will have been consolidating his own skills in anticipation of the day when the squadron might move to France.

In February 1916, 22 Squadron started to prepare for operational service, for which it began to re-equip with its operational type, the FE2b. Just as 13 Squadron had done in the previous Septem-

Bill alongside a Bristol Scout (RAF Museum).

ber, 22 Squadron now passed on to other units its collection of training aircraft, part-trained students and qualified pilots who were in excess of establishment. John was amongst the latter, as he had been involved in a motor-cycling accident, which had resulted in a complicated fracture of his right leg. Still on sick leave, on 19 March he was posted to 45 Squadron, which had just begun to form at Gosport to fill the vacuum that was about to be created by the departure of 22 Squadron. He was not passed as medically fit to resume flying until 27 April and a week later he left for Hounslow where he was to join the newly-formed 39 Squadron.

Meanwhile, in January 1916 the other two Sowrey brothers had also transferred to the RFC. Bill reported to the School of Aeronautics at Reading for a ground-based course of instruction that began on the 6th and three weeks later Fred arrived to start his course. By the middle of February Bill had joined 6 Reserve Squadron at Catterick and on 1 April he was awarded his Royal Aero Club Certificate (No. 2757) before going to Beverley to join the newly-formed 47 Squadron, which, apart from carrying out training in 'higher aviation', provided air defence for the Humber ports flying the BE2c. As Bill was completing his initial flying training, Fred arrived at Thetford to commence his with 12 Reserve Squadron.

Fred's flying logbook gives a clear indication of the basic nature of flying training in these pioneer days. On 6 April he had a ten-minute 'joy ride' in a Maurice Farman Shorthorn (7367). After three short flights of 'instruction', which included 'one landing back seat and eight landings front seat', Fred went solo two days after his first flight and with just fifty minutes instruction.

On 23 April he completed his initial flying training and gained his certificate (No. 2838) with just eight hours of flying, which included seventy-five minutes dual instruction. On 5 May he reported to Hounslow where he joined 19 Reserve Squadron, which specifically embraced night flying within its training function and had, until recently, also been responsible for maintaining a number of small detachments that were tasked with the night defence of London, but this obligation had ceased with the formation of 39 Squadron in April.

So, by the end of April, John was already a fully-qualified flying officer, currently holding with 45 Squadron at Gosport while recuperating, but about to join 39 Squadron at Hounslow; Bill was with 47 Squadron at Beverley, where he would gain his 'wings' with effect from 29 May, while Fred was shortly to be posted to Hounslow where he would be gazetted as a flying officer on 17 June. All three of them were destined to become night fighters.

In February 1916 the responsibility for the aerial defence of Great Britain was transferred from the Admiralty to the army. Even before war had been declared, there was considerable concern about the menace posed by the increasing number of German airships. Capable of remaining airborne for twenty-four hours and covering distances of up to 900 miles at high altitude, they had successfully carried many passengers in peacetime. This significant capability had caught the imagination of the civilian population and a certain amount of Zeppelin hysteria had been generated.

In the period leading up to the outbreak of war, the Admiralty had shown a greater awareness of the threat from enemy air attack than the army had. The RFC, whilst providing a modest contribution to air defence, saw the support of the BEF as its primary role. On 3 September 1914, the Cabinet agreed that the Admiralty should assume responsibility for home defence.

The first air attack did not materialise until mid-December and when it did, it was a solitary seaplane,

Fred's Royal Aero Club Certificate.

not an airship, which appeared off Dover and dropped two bombs in the sea. The Admiralty introduced a defence scheme for the London area based on a screen of aircraft between Grimsby and Dover to intercept airships. However, aircraft were few in number, had a very limited performance and pilots were not trained to fly at night. Although some aircraft were employed for air defence they were, on the whole, totally unsuitable. The Admiralty developed an elaborate system of anti-aircraft guns, organising the London gun defences on the lines of the night defence system used in battleships.

The first successful Zeppelin attack occurred on the night of 19/20 January 1915 when two German navy airships dropped some bombs on Great Yarmouth and King's Lynn. However, although further raids were sporadic and ineffective, they had an adverse effect on the morale of the population. Following the kaiser's approval to bomb London, the first attack was carried out on the night of 31 May/1 June when two army Zeppelins targeted the east end of London, killing seven people. A much more damaging attack was mounted on the night of 6/7 June when bombs were dropped on Hull leaving twenty-four dead. This created indignation amongst the population. Mr T. Ferens MP wrote to Mr Balfour, the First Lord of the Admiralty:

> 'Citizens of all classes are in a state of great alarm; the night after the raid a further warning was given and tens of thousands of people trooped out of the city. The screams of the women were distressing to hear. Could you let us have half a dozen aeroplanes?'

There was some consolation on this night as Flight Sub Lieutenant R.A.J. Warneford, attacked the returning Zeppelin (LZ37) over Belgium dropping a string of small bombs as he flew overhead the airship. They split the huge envelope of LZ37 and it went down in flames. Warneford was awarded the Victoria Cross but died ten days later in a crash.

The new series of attacks and public concern prompted a review of the defences when it was decided that guns still had to constitute the main defence, with aeroplanes having only a supplementary role. There was also another debate over which service should be responsible for home defence, with the navy maintaining that this came well down its list of priorities. The main tasks for the RNAS were seen as countering the increasing U-boat threat and operations in support of the High Seas Fleet. The Admiralty urged the War Office to increase its efforts and pressed for the RFC to be assigned the responsibility for home defence. In response, the War Office argued, with some justification, that the demands of the armies in France were increasing and that, as a result, no additional aircraft could be provided for defence over Britain.

On the night of 8/9 September, the Navy Zeppelin L13 penetrated the gun defences and the city of London received its first high explosive bombs resulting in twenty-six deaths and over £500,000 worth of damage. Though fired at by all twenty-six guns, the entire ground defences of the capital at the time, the L13 departed unscathed. Attacks on the capital by one German service or the other now became frequent causing great alarm amongst the civilian population.

A raid on 13/14 October was the most ambitious yet launched against London, and the costliest in casualties. An attempt was made to intercept the raiders before they reached their target, but resources and techniques proved inadequate for the task. RFC squadrons were alerted, following the interception of wireless transmissions, but poor visibility hampered operations and all five Zeppelins, only three of which had actually attacked the capital, escaped.

Notwithstanding the poor results, but spurred on by them, some improvements were introduced. The initial warning system, using policemen, railway staff and the like to pass reports of Zeppelins up the chain of command via their own telephone networks, were enhanced by the addition of military personnel. By early 1916 this had created a screen of observers covering the area from the coast to within thirty miles of London. Behind this were several night landing grounds each manned by two RFC pilots and finally, there was a screen of mobile guns and searchlights on the north-east outskirts of the city.

During 1915 the main anti-Zeppelin armament was the 20-lb high explosive and 16-lb incendiary bombs dropped from above the airship. At the beginning of 1916 explosive darts were issued but it was soon apparent that the machine gun was the most effective weapon. However, the riddling of a gas bag was unlikely to bring a Zeppelin down so incendiary bullets were introduced and finally, the most effective, the explosive bullet.

Later in the year the German Command reorganised the airship force and this, together with poor weather, prevented any attacks so it was not until the last night of January 1916 that another attack was mounted. Nine naval ships crossed the North Sea and headed for Liverpool. Some lost their way but a number dropped their bombs and seventy citizens of Liverpool were killed. Twenty-two defence sorties were flown but none saw any sign of the Zeppelins.

The situation for home defence at the end of January 1916 can best be described as ineffective. There were few aircraft and pilots allotted to the task of defending London and other important objectives. Those aircraft which were available were unsuitable, due to their poor ceiling and inadequate armament. In addition, no attempt had been made to standardise night-flying equipment and armament, the training of pilots, the lighting of landing grounds and there was no co-ordination between the anti-aircraft guns, searchlights and aircraft.

On 16 February, the War Office resumed responsibility for the defence of London, and in the following April for the rest of the country. In anticipation of this change, the War Office on 1 February issued instructions that the twenty BE2cs then dispersed in pairs at ten landing grounds around London should be placed under the control of Major T.C.R. Higgins, the officer commanding (OC) 19 Reserve Squadron at Hounslow.

With a view to co-ordinating the work of the RFC in the London area, the various detachments were grouped into a newly-formed 18th Wing on 25 March. By this time it had become abundantly clear that night fighting was a specialist activity needing a more focused approach to training. This would best be achieved by forming dedicated squadrons for home defence work. The result was the formation, on 15 April, of 39 Squadron with its headquarters at Hounslow. The nucleus of the new unit was provided by elements of the collocated 19 Reserve Squadron, including its various detachments around London. Most of these were closed down and reorganised to create B Flight at Sutton's Farm and C Flight at Hainault Farm. In June the squadron HQ moved to Woodford Green and in August A Flight was deployed to North Weald.

To begin with, the standard equipment for the newly-constituted home defence squadrons, of which

A BE2c, 1914-1915.

39 Squadron was the third, would be various derivatives of the BE2. Designed by the Royal Aircraft Factory before the war, and originally intended as a two-seat reconnaissance aircraft, by the summer of 1915 the BE2c was outclassed on the Western Front. However, its inherent stability, which made it relatively easy to fly at night, meant that it was suitable for attacks against the Zeppelins, and perhaps more importantly, it was available in relatively large numbers. Flying at about 70 mph it had a ceiling of 12,000 feet (although it could take almost an hour to get there) and with some aerodynamic improvements, later derivatives, like the BE2e, had a slightly better performance. Firing incendiary and explosive ammunition from single or twin Lewis guns on flexible mountings, the aircraft was flown as a single-seater.

For a few weeks the newly-formed 39 Squadron attempted to continue to provide, as its predecessor had done, night-flying training whilst also discharging its increasingly high-profile role as an operational unit. It soon became apparent that this was impractical, so the training task passed to 11 Reserve Squadron at Northolt, which became a dedicated school for night flying.

Additional squadrons were assigned to home defence work over the next few months and in July 1916 when they were brought together under the umbrella of the home defence wing which was set up to co-ordinate their activities. By this time the Sowrey brothers were beginning to make their presence felt.

Chapter Four

ZEPPELIN HUNTERS

John's arrival at Hounslow coincided with the shorter summer nights, which caused a temporary halt in Zeppelin raiding. During this lull, the home defence force was built up so that there were, by the beginning of June, a notional eight squadrons assigned to the task, with detached flights operating from twenty-five sites. 'Notional' because less than fifty per cent of the necessary aeroplanes were available so that half of the sites were inactive. Similarly, while this force was backed up by 271 anti-aircraft guns and 258 searchlights for the defence of vulnerable points, this too represented only fifty per cent of the requirement.

While the force was still well under strength, it did begin to receive some of the early production models of the new BE12 single-seater; fifteen of them by 5 June. Developed from the well-tried BE2c, it was 20 mph faster and had a better rate of climb, although, according to some sources, its more powerful 140-hp engine produced a marked swing to port on take-off presenting a more difficult challenge for the inexperienced pilot.

With most flying carried out at night, an interesting debate developed amongst the more experienced pilots. The BE2c aircraft had been selected for night-fighting duties because of its inherent stability but, unlike the FE2b, a possible alternative that had a pusher engine, there was a tendency for the aircraft to swing unless pressure was kept on the rudder bar. One CO thought that stability was unnecessary on clear nights with a moon – weather conditions that could hardly be relied on in Britain. Another raised the issue of disorientation and claimed that the aircraft's engine, rigging and compass 'would tell you that something is wrong'. John Sowrey entered the debate and claimed that it was more important to design an aircraft for night fighting that was directionally stable with the engine on as well as off. He also advocated the development of air-brakes to allow a steep descent without gaining excessive speed – a man ahead of his time.

After spending six weeks with the training squadron at Hounslow where he had built up his flying hours to thirty-six, which included the delivery of a BE2d from Lincoln to St Omer via Farnborough, totalling six hours, Fred joined his brother on 39 Squadron on 17 June. He was appointed to B Flight at Sutton's Farm, later to become famous as RAF Hornchurch. Fred soon established a close friendship with the other five pilots, in particular Lieutenant William Robinson and later with Captain Robert Stammers. They spent a great deal of their off-duty time together.

At the beginning of July, John was promoted to be a flight commander with the rank of temporary captain and on 14 July he left to command a flight of 50 Squadron at Swingate Down near Dover. Throughout the war, all three brothers kept closely in touch with each other. A few days after arriving at Dover, John wrote:

'My dear Freddie

'This is a bloody spot, a b….. aerodrome, he's a b….. squadron commander and he has got a b….. adjutant. In fact the whole show is absolutely (B.H).

'I came down here as an acting flight commander and Fraser as a flying officer. We are both being treated as the rawest of juniors. It's the absolute limit. Hope things will mend soon. Anyhow if they don't there'll be a row when the gazette comes out.'

Ironically, the b….. squadron commander he refers to would be his CO later when he served in France!

What became known as 'The Great Airship Offensive of 1916' commenced at the end of July, some three months after the last Zeppelin raid. Amongst the raiders were the first of the new 'Super Zeppelins', a larger and more powerful airship capable of carrying a maximum bomb load of 9,250 lb.

On the night of 24/25 August four Zeppelins crossed the English coast. Two were the 'Super Zeppelins' L31 and L32 commanded respectively by two of Germany's most competent airship captains, Kapitänleutnant Heinrich Mathy and Oberleutnant zur See Werner Peterson. Twelve Zeppelins had set off but eight had turned back. Mathy crossed the Kent coast and bombed London, killing nine people, with the first bombs to fall on the capital since October 1915. Five aircraft of 39 Squadron took off including Robinson and Fred Sowrey but no sightings were made.

Fred Sowrey (left), William Leefe Robinson, Robert Stammers, Wulstan Tempest.

On the night of 2/3 September the Germans launched the biggest airship raid of the war and the first, and only, time the navy and army combined their efforts. Sixteen airships were involved but not all reached their targets. Sixteen defence sorties by the BE2c squadrons were launched and these included John and Fred but both suffered engine troubles and had to land early. A number of airships were held by searchlights but initially there were no successful engagements by aircraft.

William Robinson, whose Lewis guns were armed with the new Brock and Pomeroy ammunition, which included tracer, had taken off from Sutton's Farm to patrol between that landing ground and Joyce Green at 10,000 feet. He was coming to the end of his patrol when he saw an airship caught by two searchlights to the south-east of London. He climbed to 13,000 feet and headed to cut off the departing airship but he lost sight of it as it entered cloud. He was about to return to Sutton's Farm when he saw a dull glow to the north, and he headed in its direction. After fifteen minutes, he closed on the army Schütte-Lanz S.L.11 airship. He made two attacks with his Brock and Pomeroy bullets but saw no effect. With his final drum, he concentrated his fire on the rear of the Zeppelin and this time he saw a red glow start. Very quickly, the whole of the rear part was ablaze and he had to manoeuvre violently to avoid the blazing Zeppelin as it fell. The S.L.11 came down near

Robinson at the wheel of his 'Prince Henry' with Fred. Bowers and Tempest are in the back seats.

the village of Cuffley and there were no survivors.

The effects of this raid were enormous on both sides. It was the first time a Zeppelin had been destroyed in the air by machine-gun fire and the loss of S.L.11 had an overwhelming impact on the German airship service. The effect on the morale of the British people was immense. The event had been witnessed by tens of thousands of people and the huge conflagration was visible for over fifty miles. After many months of suffering the menace and bombing of the apparently invulnerable airship, the British population's feelings exploded in a national wave of near hysterical relief.

Robinson immediately became a national hero and within days was awarded the Victoria Cross. He received over £4,000 in 'prize' money from well wishers, money he used to buy a new 'Prince Henry' Vauxhall car with which he shared many excursions with his great friend Fred Sowrey.

During this period the Sowrey family were able to enjoy a brief period of normality and happiness amongst the tragic and distressing events of the war when they celebrated the marriage of John. An edition of *Flight* magazine reported the occasion:

> 'Captain John Sowrey was on 16 September married at Hythe (Kent) Parish Church to Miss Sybil Audrey Adams of Hythe. A feature of the event was a visit of aeroplanes by brother officers of the bridegroom, and during the ceremony they gave an exhibition of flying over the church and town, looping the loop, spirals etc.'

No doubt the 'brother officers' who entertained the wedding guests were pilots from John's flight based at nearby Dover. Within a few days, the enjoyable interlude of John and Audrey's wedding was only a happy memory as the brothers and their friends returned to

John and Audrey Sowrey's wedding, with Fred as best man.

the reality of war fighting.

Undeterred by the loss of S.L.11, the Germans launched their next raid on the night of 23/24 September when eleven naval airships headed for England. They included four of the latest 'Super Zeppelins' all heading for London after crossing the Belgian coast. L.33 launched an attack on east London during which it suffered a direct hit from an anti-aircraft battery near Bow. In the meantime, four pilots of 39 Squadron had taken off, including Fred Sowrey who set up a patrol near Joyce Green.

Zeppelin L.32 with Petersen in command (F.Moch/DH Robinson/RL Rimell).

Fred had been airborne for almost two hours when he saw the L.33 just after it had been hit, as did his New Zealand friend, Lieutenant Alfred Brandon. Both lost sight of it as it flew out of the searchlight but Brandon found it again and prepared to attack. The Zeppelin had been hit badly and was losing height through a loss of hydrogen gas. Brandon fired a drum of ammunition into the airship but the second drum jammed and he was unable to bring it down. However, despite valiant attempts by the airship's commander, Kapitänleutnant Alois Böcker, and his crew, the airship grounded north of the Blackwater estuary and burnt out. The crew were captured.

Peterson, in command of L.32, approached London from the south-east and dropped his bombs. He was picked up by the searchlights and all three pilots of 39 Squadron spotted him. Fred was flying the most southerly patrol and after a twenty-five-minute chase at 13,000 feet, he was ready to attack with his single Lewis gun. The report he filed describes the action:

'On the night of 23 September 1916 we were ordered to "stand by" about 9 pm. At 11 pm I left Sutton's Farm on BE2c 4112. My orders were to patrol from Sutton's Farm to Joyce Green as high as possible. This I did, reaching the height of 14,000 feet, the greatest height I ever reached on this machine. The weather was very cold and somewhat misty with a thin layer of clouds at 10,000 feet making visibility very poor.

'At 12.45 am I noticed an enemy airship on an easterly direction. I at once made in this direction and manoeuvred into a position underneath. The airship was well lighted by searchlights, but there was not a sign of gunfire. I could distinctly see the propellers revolving, and the airship was manoeuvring to avoid the searchlight beams. I fired at it. The first two drums of ammunition had apparently no effect, but the third one caused the envelope to catch fire in several places; in the centre and the front. All firing was traversing fire along the envelope. The drums were loaded with a mixture of Brock, Pomeroy and tracer ammunition. I watched the burning airship strike the ground and then proceeded to find my flares.'

Brandon, who was still airborne, saw the engagement and the tracers, later reporting that the Zeppelin was being 'hosed with a stream of fire'. The L.32 came down at South Green near Billericay with the loss of Peterson and his twenty-two man crew. The engagement had been witnessed from the ground by thousands of Londoners including Robinson and other pilots of B Flight at Sutton's Farm who all shouted encouragement. When he landed, Fred was concerned that the wreckage might have fallen on houses but a visit to the site put his mind at rest.

After compiling his report, Fred was bundled into Robinson's Vauxhall with other pilots. They were

Remains of L.32 (RAF Museum).

mobbed by local villagers as they headed into the countryside to inspect the wreckage where they again received a hero's welcome. Although it was still the early hours of the morning, the lane leading to the crash site was completely blocked by transport of every type and by streams of pedestrians, many having travelled from London. When Fred and his colleagues tried to get within the half-mile cordon they were told they must have a pass. After a long explanation, they were allowed to drive into the field to see the wreckage. The huge, gaunt metal construction of the Zeppelin attracted crowds of people for days before the German crew were buried with full military honours.

The loss of L.32 and L.33 on this remarkable night proved to be a turning point in the Zeppelin offensive against England. Following on Robinson's achievement, the events proved beyond doubt the great value of the aeroplane in the scheme for home defence. Furthermore, even Germany's most ardent airship supporters started to doubt the effectiveness of the strategic bombing offensive that would later be dubbed 'The First Blitz'. To those in Germany who still harboured the view that the airship campaign could succeed, there was to be another rude awakening a few days later.

On the night of 1/2 October another large force of Zeppelins headed for England. The experienced Mathy in command of L.31 coasted in near Lowestoft and headed south for London. The airship was illuminated by a searchlight and 39 Squadron was ordered to launch aircraft. Near Cheshunt, Second Lieutenant Wulstan Tempest saw the illuminated L.31 and closed in. He was seen by the crew of the airship who jettisoned the bombs as the airship was put into a climb but Tempest achieved a good position. He fired from above then closed underneath near the gondola and emptied his drum of ammunition. The Zeppelin started to glow 'like a Chinese lantern' and the fire spread rapidly. He had to take violent evasive action as the Zeppelin fell at Potters Bar. Tempest returned to his landing ground where he wrecked his aircraft landing in mist. The loss of Mathy was a huge blow to the Germans and the naval airship service which now recognised that the air defences against them were formidable and gaining the upper hand.

The last word on this unique period should be with Fred's son Freddie (later Air Marshal Sir Frederick Sowrey and who will figure a great deal more in this book later). He wrote:

Fred (centre) with squadron colleagues and his BE2c 4112.

> 'The major turning point was barely one month in the late summer of 1916 when, by extraordinary coincidence, three pilots, Robinson, Sowrey and Tempest, from the same flight of the same squadron shot down three raiders in flames within sight and sound of the previously dispirited population of London. The result was electric – the Zeppelin was no longer invulnerable.'

Fred Sowrey and his two colleagues, Alfred Brandon and Wulstan Tempest, were each awarded the Distinguished Service Order (DSO) for their great feats, Fred's being announced on 4 October. The excitement, and the boost to the morale of the civilian population stemming from Robinson's success, had nourished the mood of great patriotism. With three more successes following so soon after, the national press, which was never slow to capitalise on the heroic deeds of the nation's fighting men, had a field day.

There was widespread coverage in the national press and Fred's exploits were shown across the full spectrum of newspapers from *The Times* to the *Daily Mirror*. He also featured in the magazines and journals of the establishment including the *London Illustrated News*. Photography agents clamoured for a sitting and invitations to receptions and parties flooded in. On one occasion, a theatre performance was interrupted and he was invited to stand and receive the acclaim of the audience.

The extensive publicity led to a huge swell of adulation and hero worship. Fred received hundreds of letters from well wishers many asking for his autograph and photographs. The announcement of the award of the DSO generated even more letters of congratulation and it was notable that many of them considered that he should have been awarded the Victoria Cross 'just like Robinson'. One colleague serving in Sowrey's old regiment, the Royal Fusiliers, said it was 'a ruddy shame that you did not get the VC'. There was also considerable lobbying by the public that Fred should receive the same award as Robinson.

Fred's fan mail came from a wide cross section of society. Lord Rosebery wrote in his own hand a formal and correct letter of congratulation. His schoolmasters and university professors wrote to tell him of their great pride and invited him to speak to the pupils. The general public, not least countless young women, sent letters and that of Margery Smythe from County Wexford in Ireland is typical:

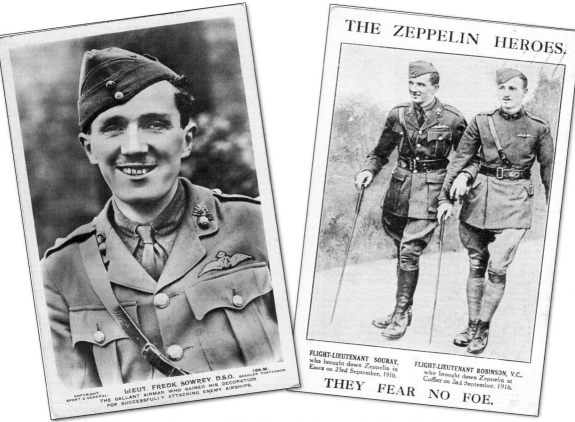

Postcards were published for sale depicting the Zeppelin heroes.

'Dear Lieutenant Sowrey

'I hope you do not mind me writing to you but I wanted you to know that there is at least one "Irish Girl" who has read and re-read with delight and pride the account of your wonderful achievement in bringing down the Zepp.

'I have cut out your photograph from the *Daily Mail* and it now stands framed in an important place in my private den.

'Do write soon and oh! I know you will forgive me.

'Heaps of love and Irish luck
Margery Smythe'

There were many others in a similar vein in addition to letters from Canada, the USA and numerous European countries. Perhaps inevitably, there was no shortage of those which started with introductions such as 'you may remember me and I was wondering if......'

Following Robinson's success, and some generous offers of 'prize money' to those pilots who shot down a Zeppelin, a number of wealthy businessmen wanted to make the same offer to Fred Sowrey. Prominent amongst these was Lord Michelham who offered £1,000 and there were a number of other offers of £500. They wished to make the presentations as soon as Fred's DSO had been announced and the editor of *Flight* magazine asked on 7 October, 'when will the winner of the prizes offered to the first airman to bring down a Zeppelin be declared'. The following week, he raised the issue again but shortly afterwards, the Army Council refused to give permission, since the deeds were performed in the normal course of duty. No doubt they were also conscious of the sensitivity of authorising such gifts following a legitimate act of war, which had resulted in the deaths of many men. So, Fred did not benefit financially in the way that his friend William Robinson had done, although Lord Michelham did make a handsome presentation to Fred once the war was over. However, there were many other forms of recognition afforded to the heroes, not least an extremely hectic social life.

Fred speaks at the presentation of the Zeppelin Cups.

On 16 October, under the heading 'Cups for Airmen Heroes', *The Times* newspaper reported a ceremony in Essex attended by Robinson and Fred Sowrey (Tempest could not be found!). Following Robinson's success and the award of his VC, the inhabitants of the village near Sutton's Farm asked for subscriptions to present him with a cup and over 3,000 donations were received. When Fred repeated the feat a few days later the villagers were unsure how to proceed. The newspaper article commented:

> 'Captain Robinson then wrote the most sportsman-like letter ever received. Having heard the proposal, he wrote: "Since Lieutenant Sowrey has performed a similar deed, I wish him to equally share your gift, whatever it may be."'

As final arrangements for the presentation were being made, Tempest brought down a third Zeppelin so the villagers decided to include him as well and each pilot received a handsome silver cup suitably inscribed.

Sowrey's celebrity status, whilst enjoyable and offering some unique experiences, did not go to his head and he was soon back on duty. However the round of invitations and parties continued. The band of close friends at Sutton's Farm would often jump into Robinson's car and head for the West End, usually ending up in the Café Royal.

The Zeppelins did not return for almost two months and when they did, on the night of 27/28 November, they raided targets in the Midlands and the North. It was another disastrous night with two naval airships destroyed by fighters, one off Lowestoft and the second near Hartlepool. This successful night indicated the progress made in developing the home defence organisation and demonstrated that it offered more than just the defence of London.

With the combat being in the north, the Sowreys were not in action but both were involved the following day when a single LVG aircraft made an audacious daylight bombing attack on London. Fred, flying a BE12, took off from Sutton's Farm and patrolled for three hours but saw nothing. John took off from Bekesbourne, also flying a BE12, but he had to return early with engine trouble. In the event, it was his last operational flight with 50 Squadron and in the New Year he left for Filton to join 62 Squadron but his time there was short. As an experienced night-flying pilot, he left after five weeks to be a flight commander on a new night bombing squadron.

All three Sowrey brothers were deeply interested in mechanical and technical issues, particularly John and Fred. They were passionate about cars and motor cycles and this interest soon started to manifest itself with numerous innovative ideas to modify in-service systems and to improve aircraft and engine efficiency. John developed many proposals for improving engine performance and amongst his suggestions was the development of 'a lubrication system for tappets and rockers in Royal Aircraft Factory 140 engines'. Fred devised a simple system to assist in maintaining smooth turns at night and he later developed this into an 'experimental turn indicator'.

Fred found operating the Lewis gun at night difficult and cumbersome, particularly changing expended drums of ammunition. He also saw the advantage of attacking an enemy from below and he developed a system of coupling two guns together by adapting a standard Admiralty mounting together with a more efficient system of raising them into an upward-firing position. He wrote a detailed paper on his ideas and included a proposal for a better sighting system, which moved parallel to the guns rather than a fixed sight. He arranged for one of his BE12b aircraft to be modified and, in due course, most of his ideas were adopted.

On 1 December, a few days after his unsuccessful patrol, Fred was made a flight commander which involved a promotion to temporary captain and a posting to 37 Squadron which had its HQ at Woodham Mortimer. Fred took command of C Flight at Goldhanger but the winter months were quiet and there was no sign of the Zeppelins.

On 14 February 1917, the youngest Sowrey, William, arrived at Goldhanger to

One of 37 Squadron, B Flight's BE12b with the Lewis gun mounting at thirty degrees.

become the third member of the family to chase Zeppelins. While his brothers had been tackling the airship menace, William had spent the previous nine months flying in support of the BEF. Having already achieved flight commander status, and thus a captaincy, while in France, he had now been appointed to take over C Flight from his brother. They had two weeks together before Fred departed for his next appointment in France. Fred's involvement in the night air defence of Britain came to an end for the time being. As he departed it was announced in the *London Gazette* that he had been mentioned in despatches.

After the disasters of late 1916, the German navy Zeppelin experts sought to regain the initiative by improving the airships. Their main effort was directed towards providing more power and reducing weight, thus enabling the Zeppelins to fly higher and out of range of the guns. The improved 'height climbers' made their first attempt to bomb London in the middle of March 1917 but the five airships were thwarted by the weather.

There was a prompt reaction to this raid by the home defence squadrons. Two Zeppelins came in over Thanet and ten minutes after the first sighting Bill Sowrey was airborne in a BE12a at 10.30 pm and climbing. He saw a Zeppelin (probably L.39) but it was flying at approximately 18,000 feet so was out of his reach. He landed after ninety minutes and within the hour he was airborne again but was unable to make an attack. Although it escaped the guns of the night fighters, L.39 was shot down by French artillery as it neared Compiègne.

It proved to be a busy introduction to home defence for Bill. He wrote to Fred on 20 March:

'My dear old Freddium
    'There has been plenty of excitement lately. Zepp raids at 6.30 am, and so forth. I have beaten my record for one day's flying here seven-and-a-half hours. Raid in the morning, rocket and gun tests after lunch, formation flying in the afternoon and then three-and-a-half hours after the Zepps at night. The blighters did not come this way.
    Billyum'

Above: A BE12 of 37 Squadron (Andrew Thomas).
Below: Zeppelin L.48 in the air (Imperial War Museum).

What he does not mention is the physical effort for such a day. On the anti-Zeppelin sorties he had to climb, at night, to heights of 15,000 feet or more without oxygen, in an open cockpit and in temperatures that could be as low as -15°C. The aircraft was fitted with rudimentary instruments, there was no wireless communication with the ground and the pilot then had to find his landing ground and make a safe landing with the most primitive type of lighting to assist him. All of this represented quite a challenge for the pilots, many of whom had barely 100 hours of experience.

It was not until the night of 23/24 May that the Zeppelins returned. Six of the navy's 'height climbers' set off but adverse winds and heavy cloud prevented them reaching London. Bill took off just before midnight and headed towards the Suffolk coast but thick cloud thwarted his attempts and that of another 37 Squadron pilot. Landing in poor visibility, and with the very rudimentary landing lights available at the time, the propeller and lower port wing of his BE12 were damaged as he came down. Two hours after landing, he took off again and had been airborne for one hour when his engine started to misfire and he made a successful forced landing near Easthorpe.

Four navy Zeppelins set off to raid London on the night of 16/17 June but two were forced to turn back. On board the new, five-engined Zeppelin, the height climber L.48, captained by Kapitänleutnant Franz Eichler, was the recently appointed commander of the Naval Airship Service, Korvettenkapitän Viktor Schütze. The airship crossed the coast near Orford Ness in the early hours of the 17th but engine trouble forced it to descend. It was intercepted by two aircraft which attacked. In the meantime, 37 Squadron had six aircraft at readiness at Goldhanger and Rochford to cover the Essex-Suffolk coastline. Bill was the first to take off at 1.53 am but, within the hour, he was forced to return with engine

The wreckage of L.48 at Theberton (RAF Museum).

trouble just as Pierce Watkins, a Canadian, was taking off and heading for Harwich. A few days later Bill wrote to Fred:

> 'Had to go up in an RE 7 which cut out at 500 feet. I then took up a BE2c (2767) and was about ten miles away from a Zepp when I saw it in flames. I am damned pleased it was 'C' Flight all the same.'

Watkins found L.48 at 12,000 feet and, as he closed from below, he emptied two drums into it without effect. After a long burst with a third drum, however, a fire started in the tail and spread quickly. The Zeppelin came down at Theberton and only three men survived. Later analysis suggested that the three aircraft, acting independently, had accounted for the airship but the War Office gave the credit to Watkins and he was awarded the Military Cross (MC). The destruction of Germany's newest airship was a great boost to the home defence squadrons who had experienced a lean time since the successes of 1916.

This was the last Zeppelin to be shot down over British soil. By July 1917, the German Army Air Service was dissolved and the building programme for the navy was restricted to twenty-five airships, primarily for reconnaissance, although they would mount one or two attacks over the next twelve months. The Zeppelin campaign was now almost finished, but another and more serious bombing assault had been launched by the Germans. A new menace, the Gotha bomber, was starting to make its appearance.

Chapter Five

WITH THE BEF

The first of the three brothers to serve with the RFC in France was Bill. After completing his flying training, he was sent almost immediately to France where, on 26 May 1916, he joined 8 Squadron at La Bellevue on the Doullens to Arras road. The squadron was equipped with the BE2c, a slow, stable aircraft with a poor rate of climb but a good range of 200 miles. Completely outclassed by German aircraft during 1915, when it earned the grim nickname of 'Fokker Fodder', it nevertheless remained the workhorse for observation and aerial photography, defended by more manoeuvrable aircraft that were starting to equip the scout squadrons.

The BE2c's slowness and inherent stability made it a good aircraft in the army co-operation role flying contact patrols and 'shoots' for the artillery during the Battles of the Somme and Arras. Using a basic 'wireless telephone', the two-man crew of pilot and observer were able to direct the fire of their assigned artillery batteries. The aircraft also provided an excellent platform for aerial photography and the squadron had a well-equipped photographic section. Hence, 8 Squadron was in great demand during the preliminary bombardment correcting the artillery's fall of shot, identifying new targets for the gunners and producing hundreds of photographs which were used to create and update trench maps and to show the disposition of German forces.

For some time before the opening of the Somme offensive on 1 July activity in the air had been increasing and the days before the attack proved to be very strenuous. On the 26th 8 Squadron engaged thirteen targets and silenced ten hostile batteries, on one of which two direct hits with twelve-inch howitzers were obtained. In addition, 168 observations were sent by wireless to the heavy howitzers firing at the enemy trenches.

The main attack on 1 July was preceded by a subsidiary attack at Gommecourt on the extreme left of the line, to be carried out by the 46th and 56th Infantry Divisions. Helping them were the aircraft of 8 Squadron, which started taking

A BE2c of 8 Squadron in France (Andrew Thomas).

off shortly after 5 am to work with the guns. To assist other aircraft flying 'contact' patrols, the attacking infantry were to light red flares, but for some unexplained reason they failed to do so and Bill Sowrey and his colleagues could only recognise the troops by the colour of their uniforms. This meant flying very low where their aircraft were subjected to heavy rifle and machine-gun fire. Surprisingly, no aircraft were lost but many were damaged.

From mid morning, the 8 Squadron crews managed to keep in contact despite the problems and were able to drop sketches made of the troop dispositions and movements. The squadron had practised this work before the battle and it paid off handsomely. The commander of the III Corps stated:

> 'In our attack yesterday 8 Squadron did extraordinarily good work. They never once failed us either with regards to getting information or taking photos, and we found that what news they were able to send about the position of our troops was most reliable.'

In the two months that followed the initial attack, the squadron also conducted bombing raids when the aircraft carried two 112-lb bombs. It was usual to send seven or eight machines against road and rail communications and the German landing grounds immediately behind the front in the area around Bapaume. Targets included the railway junction and sidings at St Leger and Boyelles, the enemy aerodrome at Douai, dumps at Croisilles and Coron and enemy rear positions in the Ancre valley. This is an early example of what in modern times became known as 'battlefield air interdiction' and 'offensive counter air'.

It was not only the enemy that posed a threat to the airmen. Aircraft reliability was still a problem and pilots became well versed in making emergency landings. On 14 August, in one of his regular letters to brother Fred, Bill wrote:

> 'Everything as usual. Had another forced landing. One cylinder had cracked on both sides and piston was red hot.'

As he was approaching the end of his time with 8 Squadron, the announcement was made of the award of the Victoria Cross to Robinson. In a letter to brother John dated 14 September, Bill makes an interesting comment, which reflects the feelings of some of the pilots on the front line in France:

> 'My dear old Onion
>   'Many thanks for your letter. I suspect you have been able to see by the papers that there is a hell of a "strafe" going on at present. As the "eyes of the army" you may guess we have had our work cut out. *Voila*!
>   'I was awfully surprised to hear you were getting married so early in the month. I am damned sorry not to be at home but *c'est la guerre*.
>   'Well! Anyhow from here I can again wish you both a damned good time now and even better future.
>   'I suppose you have been worked hard the last few weeks. Robinson did damned well but everybody out here is frightfully sick about the fuss made of him. We have a Nieuport pilot in our wing here who has had fifty-four air fights and brought down twenty-seven Huns and fifteen sausages [balloons]. His machine often comes home riddled with bullets. What does he get? A DSO. Probably each one of his fights requires more skill and courage than is necessary to bring down a blind gas-bag.
>
>   'Well! Cheery-ho old lad
>   Kindest regards to Audrey
>   Yours ever
>   Billyum'

On 29 October, after five months of intense operations in one of the most demanding roles, and when the squadron had suffered heavy casualties, Bill left for 1 Aircraft Depot to await a flight commander vacancy. This occurred on 9 November when Captain Duncan Bell-Irving of 60 Squadron was shot down and wounded. On the 10th, Bill was gazetted as a flight commander and promoted to temporary captain and the following day he reported to Savy to take up his new appointment.

Nieuport 17s of 60 Squadron at Filescamp, near Arras, February 1917 (Andrew Thomas).

60 Squadron had recently disposed of the last of its Moranes, making it the first RFC unit to be fully equipped with the Nieuport 17. The CO was Major Robert Smith-Barry whose innovative approach to flying training would soon lay the foundations of the instructional technique that is still in use today. Some of the RFC's most illustrious pilots served with 60 Squadron, including one of the RFC's greatest aces, Albert Ball, who had recently left for the United Kingdom. Future air marshals Peter Portal, Roderic Hill and Stanley Vincent were serving and Billy Bishop would arrive a few weeks after Bill left the squadron.

Bill faced a difficult situation when he arrived on 60 Squadron, which had developed a reputation as something of an elite scout squadron having enjoyed considerable success. According to one writer his appointment caused 'some upset' as the more experienced scout pilots on the squadron had assumed that one of their own would be appointed as a flight commander rather than 'someone from a BE squadron'.

On 16 November, Bill flew his first patrol. Smith-Barry, whom Bill described as a 'topping fellow', led a patrol including three new pilots. At 12,000 feet, they saw six hostile aircraft with another six flying some 700 feet higher. Smith-Barry fired a red flare and dived on the lower formation. Inevitably, the higher group entered the fight and in the mêlée, one of the hostile aircraft was seen to go down out of control. As the combatants broke away, Bill joined another Nieuport and they were both forced to land for fuel before returning to their aerodrome at Savy, a few miles west of Arras.

Much of 60 Squadron's work over the next few weeks was escorting the FE2bs of 11 Squadron flying photography and reconnaissance sorties. However, the winter of 1916/17 was one of the worst in Europe for many years and this limited flying. As a result, on 18 November, the final offensive of the Battle of the Somme ground to a halt in the snow and mud. Air activity continued, however, and Bill saw some action on 28 November when, along with two other pilots, he obliged the Germans to winch down a kite balloon. And a month later, on 27 December, again in concert with two other pilots, he was credited with driving down a Roland D.I.

The New Year saw little improvement in the weather and there were long periods of inactivity and frustration with most Allied and German squadrons grounded. The cold also affected the air-cooled Le Rhône engines, which proved very difficult to start in the freezing conditions.

By the time Bill was due for a rest in early February, having been on front-line squadrons in France for eight months, he had seen little activity with 60 Squadron. He returned to England and after a pe-

60 Squadron's 1916 Christmas card sent by Bill to Fred.

riod of leave headed for Goldhanger to take over Fred's flight on 37 Squadron.

After completing the handover of C Flight to Bill, Fred had a few days leave before departing for Folkestone and sailing to France on 21 February. He reported initially to HQ RFC at St André-aux-Bois, where he met General Trenchard, before travelling the short distance to Samer, twelve miles south-east of Boulogne. This was the headquarters of the 1st Cavalry Division where he was to act as the RFC liaison officer. A few days later he met the GOC of the division, Major General R. Mullens before setting off on a tour of the various cavalry units.

At the beginning of March he received a touching letter from his mother who was a prolific letter writer to her three sons. She wrote in the vein that so many mothers must have felt at this time:

'My dearest Fred

'It's not pleasant to know you are in France again amidst the shot and shell but let's hope your presence there will hasten the end of the war. John came to spend last weekend here and also called on Friday on his way to London. He is leaving for France early next week I believe.

'Poor old Onion, he is still the same thoughtful and kind boy, ever ready to help and comfort us. I feel so intensely interested in my boys and I want them each to do the very best possible for themselves without feeling they are martyrs.

'I am so glad to hear you like your work; John says you are lucky to have such a soft job. It's nice for Bill to have your "flight". I hope we shall soon see the end of this dreadful conflict.

'Will you let me know when you want things and also whether you live well and if you would like me to send you parcels.

'Please write as often as you can and do please be as careful as you are brave.

Fondest love from all and every good wish
From your
Loving Mother'

Throughout March Fred visited the local aerodromes to familiarise himself with their activities. He planned and then co-ordinated a series of wireless trials between aircraft of 5 Squadron and units of the Cavalry Division. Driving a Singer car or a motor cycle and sidecar, both of dubious reliability, he was also able to visit friends and he took full advantage of any opportunity to do so. Lunches and dinners with high ranking staff officers and tea in Boulogne with his friends were regular routines. Amongst those he visited was his great friend William Robinson who had recently arrived in France. Now a flight commander with 48 Squadron, he was based at La Bellevue some thirty-five miles from Samer.

On 28 March, he paid a visit to his brother John who had also just arrived in France with the RFC's first night-bomber squadron.

Major General Hugh Trenchard, now GOC RFC in France, had always been an advocate of the long-range bombing against Germany but had recognised that the struggle for air superiority above the battlefield had to take precedence over everything else. However, the Air Board decided in early 1917 to form two night-bomber squadrons for service in France and the first of these would be 100 Squadron.

On 20 February John, already an experienced night-flying pilot, joined 100 Squadron which had just begun to take shape at Hingham in Norfolk. The CO was Major M.G. Christie, and John was to be one of his three flight commanders. The squadron was formed from resources and personnel drawn from the home defence squadrons and was equipped with the FE2b, powered by the somewhat unreliable 160-hp Beardmore engine. The FE2 had met with some success when it had been introduced into service as a two-seat fighter in the autumn of 1915 but a year later it was no match for the formidable new Halberstadt and Albatros fighters. While it was clearly no longer able to operate in daylight, the FE's indifferent performance would be of little significance after dark, hence the decision to use the aeroplane as a night bomber. As such, it proved to be quite effective, carrying a reasonable bomb load a relatively long way at 60-70 mph, typically at about 3,000 feet.

The squadron moved to Farnborough to complete its mobilisation. The first elements to leave for France, mainly the heavy transports and workshop lorries, were under the command of John. He travelled at the head of the column in the squadron touring car as the party left for Portsmouth where they embarked for Rouen, arriving on 20 March. The rest of the squadron followed a few days later and the whole unit assembled at St André-aux-Bois on the 27th. The following day twelve FE2bs arrived and were immediately fitted to carry the 25-lb and 112-lb bombs and new equipment included luminous instruments and a watch for their night-flying role.

On 1 April, 100 Squadron left for Izel-les-Hameau, three miles from Savy and ten miles from Arras, where it received four BE2e aircraft, which were equipped in the same way as the FEs. During the afternoon the pilots flew around the local area and towards Arras to become familiar with the landmarks. 100 Squadron was now ready to go into action as the RFC's first night-bombing squadron in France under Trenchard's personal control and the first operation was mounted four days later.

Navigation was made as simple as possible. Most bombing raids took place in moonlight and routes followed straight line features to towns and rivers when possible. A number of lighthouses, which flashed in Morse individual identification numbers, were used. Three miles from le Hameau was No. 5 Lighthouse, an important aid for returning crews.

The squadron's first bombing raid, indeed the RFC's first night-bombing raid, was flown on the night of 5/6 April when the target was the airfield at Douai situated fourteen miles from Arras and about eight miles over the lines. Douai was home to the 'Richthofen Circus', which was becoming the scourge of the RFC scout squadrons.

Many of the later attacks made by the squadron adopted similar procedures and tactics employed on this first raid so it is worth looking at the attack on Douai aerodrome in some detail.

During the afternoon the crews marked their maps, noting the positions of the lighthouses, and studied the route to Douai. The aircraft were bombed up with 20-lb HE and phosphorous bombs with the detonators to be inserted shortly before take-off. Observers carried a Lewis gun, with two drums of ammunition, and two parachute flares.

The first aircraft took off at 10.30 pm with the others following at three-minute intervals. Eleven aircraft took off and John Sowrey had 2/AM Hodson as his observer. Crews headed for No. 5 Lighthouse and then followed the straight St Pol-sur-Ternoise road that took them to Arras. After leaving the town, navigation lights and the downward identification light were switched off. A canal and river were used as check points and the first aircraft took the enemy defences by surprise. It glided down

A FE2b of 100 Squadron prepares for a night-bombing mission.

from 3,000 feet to 500 feet and dropped a phosphorous bomb on one of the hangars which was soon on fire. This provided an aiming point for the following aircraft, which arrived over the next twenty minutes. Some attacked the searchlights with machine guns and as the last aircraft left, two hangars were well alight as well as other buildings.

The aircraft returned on a similar route to find the lighthouse and then headed the short distance to the airfield where flares had been lit. A second raid was mounted later that night and other hangars and buildings were attacked. One crew failed to return from the second sortie. The post-attack report commented:

'First and foremost this raid proved that machines could glide down to a very low altitude and get direct hits on their targets without difficulty or any serious opposition.'

Captain von Richthofen wrote a colourful account of these two raids. He paid tribute to the individual bravery of the pilots and observers and his narrative bears witness to his own sporting instincts. He wrote:

'We were fearfully excited. The Englishman was flying very high. First he circled round the aerodrome and we began to think that he was looking for some other objective. All at once he shut off his engine and came down. At last he was caught in the beam, and the whole aerodrome shouted with surprise, for it was quite an old machine. He was flying straight for us and coming still lower. It wasn't long before the first [bomb] dropped and then there came a rain of small bombs. It was a fine display of fireworks and might have impressed a rabbit. I believe that night bombing has a merely moral effect. We thought it great fun and hoped the British would come over often.'

Richthofen plays down the damage and exaggerates the claims made by the anti-aircraft gunners. He also fails to mention that his unit was forced to evacuate the airfield and move to another aerodrome but one has to accept that he was writing for home consumption.

The results of these two attacks were excellent, with considerable damage inflicted, and they created a degree of shock amongst the German forces.

During the rest of the moonlight period, the squadron provided support during the Battles of Vimy Ridge and Arras and attacked railway junctions and trains together with convoys of troops on roads. Crews were particularly successful against trains. The method of attack was similar to that on airfields. The aircraft would glide down from 3-4,000 feet with the engine throttled back fully followed by a slow approach from the rear of the train up its length, dropping the bombs in a stick before climbing away to drop a parachute flare to observe the results. Some attacks were carried out at 100 feet with the larger bombs released at 500 feet. Considerable damage was inflicted and it was claimed by one source to have, 'a far reaching effect upon the battles being fought'.

Immediately following the successful attack against Douai airfield, John attacked the railway station at Douai on consecutive nights. On the night of 9/10 April six 100 Squadron aircraft were involved. After a very successful sortie, three of the FEs were forced to land, two because of a heavy snowstorm. The petrol tank of John's FE was hit and he was forced to land just inside Allied lines. The night's work had been very successful. The six aircraft had wrecked two trains and derailed another in addition to scoring several hits on Douai station.

John returned to le Hameau later in the morning and shortly after brother Fred turned up on one of his frequent visits. He had heard the distressing news that William Robinson (known as Robin to the family) had failed to return from a patrol.

On receiving this news, Fred entered into a long series of correspondence with Robinson's fiancée, Joan Whipple, whom he knew very well from his Sutton's Farm days. He was also in regular contact with his other great friend of that time, Wulstan Tempest, and with his family all in an attempt to discover Robinson's fate. He drove over to see John on the 14th to discuss the situation and was also able to make regular enquiries in the various local headquarters. He received a letter from Joan in which she expressed 'not much hope for Robin'.

On the 18th, Fred wrote to John:

> 'My Dear Onion
>   'I have had the enclosed message written in German enquiring after Robin. Do you think you could drop it one day when you are over the lines. I should think an aerodrome would be the best place. There is absolutely nothing that will show where it came from. Hope you won't mind.
>   'Cheery-ho! Look after yourself.
>
> Yours ever
> Fred'

The following is a translation of the note written in German.

> To The German Air Service
> From the Royal Flying Corps
>
> 'The Royal Flying Corps send their compliments to the German Air Service and request that they will let them have some news of Captain W.L. Robinson V.C. who was shot down on Friday 6 April.'

John did not fly over the lines for another two weeks so it is not clear if the note was ever delivered but it indicates the lengths Fred was prepared to go to in an effort to discover the fate of his friend. It is also an example of a degree of chivalry that existed between the two air services at the time.

A telephone call every day to the HQ RFC to enquire if there was any news brought no comfort and on the 25th he was told 'there is very little hope'. Then, on the following day he received a telegram from Joan to say that Robinson had been injured and was a prisoner of war. GHQ rang to confirm the news and Fred immediately telephoned John. In his diary he simply wrote 'Damn good'. His mood, and relief, is evident from the entries in his diary. For the next few days, the first entry is 'another topping day' and mention of the letters from home, from Joan and from Tempest together with visits to see John.

With the new moon period, 100 Squadron started operations again on the night of 3/4 May when the railway system was attacked. The squadron operations book shows that John flew without an observer on this raid, and for the remainder of his time with the squadron he flew all his operations solo. He was not the only pilot to fly operations without an observer but it is not entirely clear why. The squadron had four BE2es on charge (although eighteen individual airframes are known to have passed through its hands at various times, at least two of which had actually been reconfigured as single-seaters) a type of aircraft very familiar to John, but there are a number of operations when five or six pilots flew solo, hence some must have been flying the FEs. One explanation could be the need to dispense with the observer in order to save weight and carry a greater number of bombs.

On some operations, a relay of single aircraft flew ahead to the area for attacks and patrolled at 6,000 feet identifying enemy aerodromes that were lit in order to send a wireless message back to the aerodrome. On such operations, the bombing aircraft carried 20-lb bombs and 'as aerodromes light they will proceed to drop a bomb, aiming at the flares, with the observer to fire a few rounds immediately afterwards'. Constant patrols of two bombing aircraft were established in the Lille and Tourcoing areas. There is no direct evidence that John flew these wireless aircraft but he was one of the squadron's most experienced night pilots, and was familiar with wireless from his previous operations.

The 100 Squadron records also refer to a 'Pom Pom' aircraft tasked with extinguishing enemy searchlights. On one or two occasions, John attacked searchlights but it was not indicated if he attacked with bombs or with the 'Pom Pom', a Vickers automatic one-pounder gun mounted in a much modified nose of the FE2b.

On the night of 29/30 May, a force of eight aircraft, including John Sowrey's, attacked trains in the Lille area. Seven were flown without an observer and a total of eighteen 112-lb bombs were dropped. This raid was particularly successful.

The following night an equally successful raid was carried out when one aircraft dropped a 230-lb bomb and twenty 112-lb bombs were also dropped. Eleven crews, including John, flew on this attack. Several pilots reported seeing the 230-lb bomb explode with extreme violence in Orchies, blowing out portions of the structure.

As the Battle of Arras came to an end the Battle of Messines opened on 7

The 'Pom Pom' mounted in the nose of the FE2b.

A Spad VII (Tony Holmes).

June. To provide support, the squadron had moved to Treizennes, an aerodrome between St Omer and Béthune. The bombing operations during May had been a prelude to the opening of the attack by General Plumer's Second Army.

During the moon period of early June, the squadron was flying every night and John flew on five consecutive nights, mostly against the railway system around Lille, Courtrai and Menin. The 230-lb bomb was more widely used and to great effect. One could be carried by FEs with their undercarriage modified to allow the bomb to be positioned under the nacelle.

On the eve of the battle, John's aircraft was one of seven FEs that bombed railways. One 230-lb bomb was dropped on a large supply dump near Comines. The following night, John was out again when the squadron sent out fourteen aircraft to attack Menin station, the Courtrai goods yard and Warneton station. Three 230-lb and four 112-lb bombs were dropped on the latter and a massive explosion occurred which was heard for miles around. Later reports indicated that a train carrying ammunition had been hit.

During the first nine days of June, John flew eight night-bombing sorties before the moon phases prevented further operations. 100 Squadron had made a major contribution to the successful ground operations at Messines.

During this period of night bombing for John, Fred returned to France at the end of May after a period of leave in England and reported to 1 Aircraft Depot near St Omer to wait for an appointment to a scout squadron as a flight commander. He took the opportunity to fly a number of different types of aircraft and he made regular visits to see John who was 'very fit'.

On 14 June Fred joined 19 Squadron commanded by Major W.G.S. Sanday DSO, MC a veteran of the early days of the air war. Based on the aerodrome at Liettres, twelve miles south of St Omer, (and only two miles from John's airfield at Treizennes), the squadron was equipped with the excellent French fighter, the Spad VII. It was powered by a 150-hp Hispano-Suiza engine and was armed with a fixed Vickers gun.

Fred was appointed to command A Flight and he spent the first two days getting familiar with the local area. He took advantage of landing at Treizennes to have lunch with John who telephoned him the following day to say that one of the pilots in brother Bill's Flight on 37 Squadron (Watkins) had shot down a Zeppelin. This was cause for a celebration and Fred wrote to congratulate his younger brother.

After a few sorties, when he was unable to engage the Hun, Fred gained his first success on 17 June. The weather had been poor in the morning but, with a clearance later, he led four other Spads on an evening patrol and attacked a formation of six hostile aircraft and shot down an Albatros DIII. One of his pilots failed to return. His diary entry indicates how he, and many colleagues, had become hardened by war:

> 'Dud morning. Standing by finishing off tennis court. Opening game played in afternoon, Young and self versus Major and Hagon. We lost. Patrol at 6 pm. Scrap over Houthulst forest. First Hun down! An Albatros.'

The first few days of July brought little action for the pilots of 19 Squadron but this was not the case for the night bombers. The moon period at the beginning of the month was a period of intense operations for John and his fellow aircrew of 100 Squadron. After a few raids against the railway system early in the month, the squadron concentrated the bulk of its efforts against airfields, a pattern that would continue for the next two months, using the 230-lb bomb and 112-lb bombs. John continued to fly without an observer on all his operations.   During July he attacked six airfields when a number of hangars were destroyed. One report suggested that over thirty aircraft had been destroyed in one hangar at Heule aerodrome, twelve miles across the lines east of Lille.

As early as 9 June, Fred's 19 Squadron had taken on charge a new Spad XIII, with a 200-hp engine, for evaluation. This aircraft (B3479) was the first of the new model to be received by the RFC. On 14 June Lieutenant Geoffrey Buck used it to shoot down an enemy aircraft, several months before the type achieved any success with the French air service. This lead was confirmed on 13 July by Fred who, while escorting some Martinsydes on a bombing mission, saw and attacked a hostile two-seater and drove it down out of control over Houthulst forest.

During the moonless periods when John was not operating at night, he would meet Fred frequently to have dinner in each other's messes, often taking their respective COs and colleagues. Fred's great friend and fellow Zeppelin destroyer Wulstan Tempest, was one of John's pilots and the three met regularly.

July 1917 saw heavy air activity in the run up to the imminent battles and the RFC scout squadrons were in constant action. On the 20th Fred shared in the destruction of a hostile two-seater and the next day he forced an Albatros DIII to land and drove a hostile scout down out of control. He had now achieved 'ace' status having accounted for five aircraft.

An indication of the intensity of operations during the month is illustrated by the resumé in the RFC Communiqué No. 99:

> 'For the month of July we have claimed, officially, 122 EA brought down and 120 driven down out of control by aeroplanes. The number actually reported to us far exceeds this. Nearly sixty-seven tons of bombs have been dropped and over 13,000 photographs have been taken. 1940 hostile batteries have been successfully engaged for destruction by artillery from aeroplane observation…'

The Third Battle of Ypres opened up on 31 July but a period of poor weather curtailed operations in the first ten days. Bombing operations were not possible and, after a dinner with Fred and Tempest, John left on 7 August for two weeks leave in England.

A feature of the battle was the assistance given to the infantry by aircraft attacking enemy positions with machine guns and bombs. Some fighters were modified to carry 25-lb Cooper bombs and 19 Squadron's technical sergeant devised a box arrangement behind the pilot allowing the Spad to carry two bombs. However, the aircraft's centre of gravity was disturbed and the pilots had some misgivings about the arrangement.

With the armies advancing slowly eastwards, 19 Squadron moved on 14 August to the aerodrome at Poperinghe, eight miles west of Ypres, which Fred described on arrival as 'a bloody place, nothing ready'. With the passing of the bad weather, there was intense activity over the next period and the German air service was particularly aggressive against Allied troops and trenches.

Fred took off at dawn on the 17th to lead a patrol. They joined a fight between SE5s and several enemy aircraft and Fred drove down an Albatros DIII, which a member of his patrol saw crash near Roulers. Later in the day two more aircraft were driven down by 19 Squadron pilots.

With the new aerodrome situated closer to the front line, it was subjected to German bombing, and, apart from a lack of sleep, little damage was done and squadron operations were not affected. Another dawn take-off on the 20th resulted in more success for Fred. With Lieutenants Pentland and Ainger, the former gaining a reputation as a very aggressive pilot who ended the war with twenty-three victories, Fred intercepted a two-seater over the Menin-Roulers road. He drove it down from 10,000 feet before his gun jammed. His two colleagues opened fire and the Albatros crashed.

After two more days patrolling, but without adding to his score, Fred left for two weeks of leave in England just as John returned from his two-week break. During his absence, 100 Squadron had been heavily engaged in supporting the major ground offensive attacking the rail network in the Lys valley and aerodromes. By this time the main armament carried by the FEs was the 230-lb bomb and considerable damage was inflicted. The bomb was designed to be dropped from above 400 feet but, fitted with a fifteen-second delay fuse, it could be unloaded from 150 feet.

Trenchard had always taken a very close interest in the operations and activities of 100 Squadron. On 14 August he wrote to the Air Board outlining the qualities and abilities pilots and observers needed for the night-bombing role. His view on the selection and training of aircrew was far sighted. He wrote:

'I would therefore recommend the following:-

'That both pilots and observers of night-flying squadrons are carefully selected from among those showing [sic] keenness and aptitude for the work, and that those proving themselves unsuitable be eliminated at home.

'That pilots and observers should do considerably more night reconnaissance work before proceeding overseas, flying for distances up to at least 100 miles on clear nights without flares to guide them, reconnoitring unlit aerodromes, railway stations, camps, towns etc., and learning to utilise water, wood, roads and railways as landmarks. A feature should be made of memorizing the map and photographs by previous study. Pilots should also carry out practice in using their compass by night and flying through clouds.

'Pilots and observers to be given practice in bombing by daylight, moonlight and darkness, and made to pass a test. It is suggested that the moonlight test might be carried out from these heights, 500, 1,000 and 2,000 feet, and that the target should be a circle thirty yards in diameter, seventy-five per cent of bombs to fall on the target from 500 feet, fifty per cent from 1,000 feet and thirty-five per cent from 2,000 feet. Bombing a lighted target on a dark night is more difficult and a somewhat easier test should be fixed.

'Observers to go through a gunnery course as now.

HT
Major General

Commanding, Royal Flying Corps
In the Field'

This is a remarkable document and the demands Trenchard believed were achievable by the aircrew are equally remarkable bearing in mind the infancy of flying operations.

On John's return from leave, Major Christie, the squadron commander, left for leave and a series of meetings in London when Trenchard's paper was discussed. On his return he reported to the chief of staff at HQ, Royal Flying Corps. He wrote:

'During my leave I discussed the training of night-flying pilots with Colonel Higgins, OC Home Defence pretty thoroughly, and in addition I was present at a conference with General Brancker and Colonel Higgins, the trend of which was as follows:

1. 'That night-flying pilots would be chosen mainly, if not entirely, from RFC observers sent home from France for instruction in aviation. This arrangement would ensure the securing of pilots thoroughly experienced in finding their way, and acquainted with the area of operations behind enemy lines.

2. 'That the training of a night pilot will first be carried out at one of the three home defence depot squadrons on the ordinary lines, and after graduating a pilot would be trained in night flying at a home defence squadron for some weeks, after which if he appeared promising he would be posted to an advanced depot squadron where his training in night bombing would take place and where he would gain experience in long night reconnaissance work and at the advanced depot squadron the tests as described in the enclosed syllabus would have to be passed by the pilot.

3. 'Observers selected for night bombing will, on completion of their gunnery course at Hythe undergo training at an advanced depot squadron and pass both night and day bombing and reconnaissance test before being posted overseas.

'With regard to the advanced depot squadron, it is suggested that Captain Sowrey – senior flight commander of 100 Squadron – might be given charge.

'May I be allowed, please, to support this suggestion? Captain Sowrey has been with this squadron from the start and has done a large amount of extremely good work in night bombing, as well as in suggesting and assisting in technical improvements of all kinds. It was proposed at the conference that the advanced depot squadron should also act as an experimental squadron for night work, keeping in touch with our requirements over here. For this I venture to think that no better man could be found than Captain Sowrey, who has a BSc degree, and combines theory with a sound practical inventive turn of mind.

'Though still doing good work in the squadron, night bombing, Captain Sowrey is obviously becoming tired and I should like to recommend him for a home position such as the proposed advanced depot would appear to offer.

'I have the honour to be
Sir
Your obedient servant

M.G. Christie, Major
OC 100 Squadron, RFC
3/9/17'

An FE2b returns at dawn after a bombing raid.

This important letter, allied with the proposals made by Trenchard, put night training on a formal and professional footing and would almost immediately affect the remainder of John Sowrey's war service.

During this period of debate, John flew on a maximum effort on the night of 31 Aug/1 Sep when twenty-one 230-lb bombs were dropped, the majority on the aerodromes at Heule and Lezennes. The latter came in for special attention and nine 230-lb bombs were dropped and several direct hits on hangars were claimed. 100 Squadron mounted twenty-two sorties on this night and it proved to be one of the squadron's most successful. This followed another earlier excellent raid and the success of the squadron was noted by General Trenchard who wrote to Major Christie:

> 'Please congratulate all pilots and observers on their splendid work last night, [21/22 August] when the night was particularly dark. This bombing by 100 Squadron is, according to a prisoner's statement, the greatest use to our operations.'

On the night of 2/3 September John flew his final operation when he attacked the aerodrome at Ramegnies. Several direct hits were recorded.

One of John Sowrey's fellow flight commanders, Captain W.E. Collinson, wrote an interesting paper on night operations for the benefit of those training in England and new arrivals on the squadron. It is comprehensive and full of detail on all aspects of a night operation from briefing to the final landing on return. Some of his comments indicate the difficulties and potential dangers the pilots faced in addition to enemy searchlights and anti-aircraft fire. Under the heading 'Engines' he comments:

> 'Another point to be remembered is that in cold weather the radiator runs the risk of freezing on a glide with the engine ticking over. This can be avoided by the pilot putting his arm outside the nacelle and preventing the cold air passing into the louvers.'

During his time as a flight commander with 100 Squadron, John had flown at least twenty-seven night bombing operations, all but three without an observer. At this stage of the war, when enemy fighters were not encountered at night, the bomber's opponents were the lonely, implacable night, the perplexities of night navigation and a highly-sophisticated German anti-aircraft system – all of which was hard enough to manage and wage war against with a crew of two but even more difficult flying alone. One historian has commented:

> 'I am inclined to take my hat off to John Sowrey who, apparently by choice, headed off on his own in a BE2e. It would have taken a very special man to do this in a force, which seems to me to have been composed of 'special' men. Night flying was just so perilous. Those who undertook it on their own were, in my opinion, very stout fellows.'

This eloquent summary of John Sowrey's achievements with 100 Squadron needs no amplification. After driving over to have lunch with Fred on the 14th, he left France and returned to England.

Having returned from leave, Fred rejoined his squadron on 9 September and was soon in action. During the afternoon of the 11th, his friend Pentland had destroyed a two-seater before his gun jammed and he was set upon by a second aircraft. Fred saw the combat and dived to give assistance. He closed to within a few feet of the enemy, a Rumpler two-seater, and shot it down.

Patrols were flown every day but on the 16th it was a different type of operation. With Pentland and Lieutenant Graham they crossed the lines flying east at 200 feet and started attacking the enemy ground troops. East of Armentières he fired at troops and near Lille found a road convoy, which he attacked before scattering some teams dragging artillery into place. Graham failed to return from this sortie, almost certainly the victim of ground fire. During the afternoon he and Pentland were on patrol when 'we were attacked by four Albatri, Pent got one'.

After driving down a two-seater and a balloon during this hectic phase of fighting, the weather interfered with scouting operations but many of the scout squadrons went out on ground-strafing sorties. On the morning patrol on the 20th, his formation was split up due to low cloud. Fred descended and fired at a large group of infantrymen but he came under heavy anti-aircraft fire and climbed back into cloud. When he descended again near Oosthoek, he found a battery of three guns and he expended all his ammunition during which there was an explosion on the ground causing the gun crew to scatter. He next found a long-range gun and dropped a bomb on it and aimed his second on a group of sheds.

Later in the day he was leading a patrol at 8,000 feet when twelve enemy aircraft were seen above. Two dived down as if to attack Fred's formation but he closed in on one and fired at close range. The Albatros DV rolled and other pilots in his formation saw it go down out of control.

The squadron was heavily engaged over the next few days and four pilots were lost in some fierce combat. Fred reports these losses in a very matter-of-fact and simple way but when Lieutenant Powers was lost, he commented, 'Powers missing, damn shame'; a rare display of emotion.

During the last week of September Fred attacked a number of enemy aircraft and drove some down but he made no claims that they were out of control. Ground-attack operations continued to be a regular feature when attacks with machine guns and with the Cooper bombs were conducted east of the lines. On the 26th he had a narrow escape. On the Ypres-Menin road he and Lieutenant Jones attacked, from 200 feet, a large force of troops but they were immediately set upon by eight enemy aircraft. He descended to a few feet and came under very heavy fire from the ground, before managing to get away in the clouds. Jones was wounded but was able to despatch one of the enemy before getting back to the aerodrome. On the return flight Fred dropped a message at the army HQ to alert them to the build up of enemy forces. That afternoon he led another patrol but was not engaged.

After driving down another Albatros two-seater on the 30th, bad weather set in and low-flying operations were all that could be achieved in the build up to the Battle of Passchendaele. The weather was described as 'very bad' with strong winds, but 19 Squadron sent out a number of Spads on ground-strafing sorties. Following the Menin road, Fred chased a two-seater and fired a few rounds but it escaped into the clouds. He then attacked troops and scattered them. It was sorties such as this, in poor conditions and forced to fly very low where his aircraft was under constant fire, that marked Fred out as one of the most aggressive and effective pilots on the squadron. The following day, his CO Major Sanday wrote to him:

'The colonel has just telephoned and says that he has sent in a general appreciation of your work yesterday to General Trenchard, in which he has said it was "a very good show" to even fly on such a day and the work you did was magnificent. You know what I think about it. You were simply splendid and I am ever so proud of you.

W.D.S. Sanday'

The next day Trenchard sent a signal of congratulation to Sanday 'tell your pilots what splendid work they did yesterday under impossible weather conditions'.

A fierce fight on 7 October resulted in Fred destroying a Fokker DV and two days later he was on a patrol looking for German wireless aircraft. His patrol was driven off by enemy scouts but Fred returned to the area when he attacked two enemy aircraft engaging an RE8 and he destroyed one of them.

Fred was in action throughout the following week, often in contact with the enemy. On the 15th, on his last patrol, he saw a formation of five enemy aircraft emerge through a gap in the clouds. He dived on them and got behind the rear one and fired 120 rounds into it before it disappeared. It was seen diving away in flames by another patrol. It was Fred's twelfth and final success and his time on 19 Squadron came to an end. It had been a very hectic period with the German air service proving a very aggressive opponent. The loss of twenty squadron pilots during the four months that Fred was on the unit is a sad reminder of the intensity of the fighting and the sacrifices made. His CO was sad to see him go and wrote;

'Good bye old Sowrey. You have been a brick and I am awfully grateful to you and I only hope that we shall soon hear that they've given you a reward that you have so very well earned.

'I shall miss you awfully, but you have done splendidly and thank God you're going safely home.

Yours
W.D.S. Sandy'

Fred left for London and it brought to an end for the time being the service with the British Expeditionary Force of the three Sowrey brothers who, between them, had been involved in some of the First World's War major battles at Arras, the Somme, Messines, Ypres and Passchendaele. On 27 October, the *London Gazette* announced that Second Lieutenant (Temporary Captain) F. Sowrey DSO had been awarded the MC 'For conspicuous gallantry and devotion to duty'.

Chapter Six

THE GOTHA MENACE

Although the German Imperial Navy continued to operate Zeppelins until 1918, the virtual end of the threat was signalled by the loss of two airships on 28 November 1916. In the months that followed, the home defence system to counter them, developed at considerable cost and with the diversion of aircraft from the theatres overseas, was allowed to run down to a dangerous level.

In the meantime, the German High Command had recognised the limitations of its Zeppelins as a bombing force and steps were taken to form a special squadron of aeroplanes to continue and expand the air attacks against Great Britain. In March 1917 the first twin-engine Gotha G IV bombers, which could carry at least six hundredweight of bombs, began to arrive in Belgium to equip a newly reconstituted Kampfgeschwader der Obersten Heeresleitung Nr 3 (Battle Squadron 3 of the High Command of the army, usually abbreviated to Kagohl 3). Initially established to have four flights of six aircraft, two more flights would be added in July.

The inter-service rivalry over the responsibilities for the home defence of Great Britain festered on, and the intransigence of the Admiralty over service aviation, and the supply issues that occurred, held back the development of an effective air defence organisation. The emergence of the new and much greater menace of the heavy bomber created an urgent need to completely restructure the air defence organisation and one that would lead to the amalgamation of the RNAS and the RFC to form the Royal Air Force.

The few home defence squadrons were still equipped with aircraft that were obsolescent, most struggling to reach 12,000 feet. The anti-Zeppelin force of night fighters simply could not cope with well-led formations of the enemy's new and advanced bomber aircraft.

The German army had built up the capability of Kagohl 3 in great secrecy and British intelligence had failed to identify its full capability. Hence, the arrival over the Essex coast near the Blackwater estuary of twenty-one Gothas late in the afternoon of 25 May

Gothas of the England squadron at Gontrode, near Ghent, in Belgium (Mike O'Connor).

1917 came as a great surprise and sent shock waves through the government and the population of London. Seventy-seven defence sorties were flown but no interceptions were made and the inadequacies of the reporting system, lack of co-ordination and inability of many aircraft to reach the bomber's height were stark reminders of the urgent need to overhaul the air defence organisation.

High-level meetings were called and these inadequacies were addressed. Some aircraft with a better performance were allocated to squadrons, and the Air Board ordered the training squadrons to make aircraft available to the squadrons. Wireless communications were improved, despite the resistance of the Admiralty, and the need to improve night defence was also recognised. However, progress was slow and Field Marshal Lord French, the commander-in-chief home forces, wrote to the War Office on 5 June and concluded:

> 'I cannot too strongly impress on the Army Council my opinion that the means placed at my disposal for aeroplane defence are now inadequate and that a continuance of the present policy may have disastrous results.'

It was against this gloomy forecast that Bill commanded his flight equipped with its obsolete BE12s.

On the day that French wrote these comments, a major raid developed with twenty-two Gothas heading for Sheerness in the late afternoon. They were spotted as they crossed the Channel and a RNAS pilot managed to engage one of the bombers without success but the anti-aircraft defences at Shoeburyness shot one of them down into the sea.

Six of Bill's flight at Goldhanger took off in an assortment of aircraft, which included two Sopwith 1½ Strutters, an RE7 and Bill flying a BE12. Unfortunately, the Gothas did not penetrate 37 Squadron's patrol area and no sightings were made.

The Germans mounted another large daylight raid on 13 June. This time the target was London when fourteen bombers penetrated to the capital's East End. Casualties were heavy with 162 killed and nearly 500 injured, the greatest inflicted in any one raid. Ninety-four defence sorties were flown and this involved no less than nineteen different types of aircraft. Perhaps the most improbable was an RE7 flown by Bill.

The use of this 1915-vintage unwieldy day bomber indicates the desperate shortage of appropriate fighters capable of climbing to 17-18,000 feet. Bill managed to crawl up to 12,000 feet between Rochford and Stow Maries where he saw seven Gothas a few thousand feet above him. He opened fire with his upward-firing Lewis gun but the departing bombers were never under threat. His report highlights the problems faced by the obsolete fighters against the high-flying and faster bombers:

> 'Opened fire with the Lewis gun at one machine which appeared to be lower than the remainder. That machine appeared to me to be at 13,500 feet. The drum was nearly empty when it flew off, and I immediately replaced it with another, and emptied that into the formation. By this time the formation of seven had drawn away from me, but I noticed two more hostile aircraft coming behind which I followed for about one mile out to sea. The difficulty I experienced was in keeping height and level with the hostile aircraft at the same time.'

The Gothas next appeared on 4 July when eighteen attacked Harwich and Felixstowe. Flying a BE12, Bill and his fellow pilots were alerted too late to be effective and the enemy bombers got away without being intercepted. Two days later, French once again wrote to express his deep concern about the lack of appropriate fighters. He concluded his letter:

> 'The aeroplanes which I can dispose of are not sufficient for effective action against raids in force. Such raids may certainly be expected, and if London is again subjected to attack the results may be disastrous.'

The timing of this letter could hardly have been more telling as the Gothas mounted their second heavy attack against London the following day. Twenty-two bombers reached London and the home defence squadrons made a better response with a number making contact but just a few getting close and only one bomber was shot down. Bill was airborne in a BE12a at 9.35 am, the bombers having been sighted twenty minutes earlier by a lightship off the Kent coast. At least 108 defensive sorties were flown and the aircraft came from naval stations, home defence squadrons, training units and some from acceptance parks. It was an emergency force of very varied elements but the unit lacked cohesion.

The 37 Squadron pilots were well placed to intercept and two, flying recently-acquired Sopwith Pups, engaged them. Bill caught them near Romford but was unable to climb the final 1,000 feet to get to close quarters. He remained in contact with the large formation until they bombed but they pulled away from him as they climbed for the return flight. He described his frustration in a letter to Fred:

A BE12a, an aircraft frequently flown by Bill.

'When those fellows came over town I was up about 1,000 feet below them and got four drums at them and they put some holes in my machine but I couldn't see that I did them any damage.'

There was great public indignation following this second attack on London and within a few days, the Cabinet formed a committee to examine the air defence organisation with the South African Lieutenant General J.C. Smuts as the chairman. His interim report was finished on 19 July and the main recommendation was the establishment of a senior RFC officer to be placed in command of the London Air Defence Area (LADA). This brought the RFC squadrons, anti-aircraft guns and the observation posts under the command of one man. Major General E.B. Ashmore, a RFC pilot, was appointed to take on this command but it was not until 8 August that he took up his post. When Smuts presented the final report on 17 August it made the far-reaching recommendation for the creation of a separate Air Ministry and this led to the formation of the Royal Air Force on 1 April 1918.

New orders were issued to the squadrons and their aircraft had to be maintained at a higher state of readiness. When ordered on patrol they headed for individual areas already allotted. The next attack came at 8 am on 22 July when twenty-one bombers raided towns on the Suffolk coast. Bill was airborne for ninety minutes but, as with the other 121 sorties, the warning came too late and he was unable to make contact.

At the beginning of August, two of 37 Squadron's BE12s were equipped with pilot-operated continuous-wave wireless (W/T) transmitters to report by Morse signals enemy bomber movements to a ground station. The squadron patrolled north of the Thames and two aircraft of 50 Squadron had a similar role over Kent. This was further evidence of the development of a more sophisticated air defence organisation.

Two raids were mounted during August and Bill was airborne in his BE12 on both. On 12 August, eleven Gothas attacked Southend and 139 defensive sorties were flown, an indication of the increasing capability of the defences of the home defence group.

The next raid on 22 August attracted 138 defensive sorties. From a German perspective it was a major failure with five aircraft turning back and three shot down by RNAS fighters and anti-aircraft guns. Bill was again airborne in a BE12 but the raid was against targets on the Kent coast and he and his fellow pilots on patrol north of the Thames were unable to engage.

In the event, the raid of the 22nd proved to be the last made by the Gothas in daylight. Mounting losses, added to a number of landing accidents, and the clear evidence of a more organised air defence organisation with a larger number of aircraft and anti-aircraft guns, persuaded the German Army High Command to switch to night attacks.

In the course of eight daylight raids, all of which Bill flew against, over twenty tons of bombs were dropped, and the casualties inflicted were 401 killed and 878 injured.

Just as the measures for dealing with the day raids had been improved, the Germans launched the first significant night attack on 3/4 September when five of the new Gotha G V bombers attacked Chatham. This night offensive, similar in concept to the Zeppelin raids, presented new problems for the night-fighter pilots. Locating and attacking a relatively fast aircraft was a very different proposition to engaging a huge Zeppelin lumbering along in the beams of a searchlight. By the end of the year, fifteen of these night raids had been carried out, nine against London.

The raid on Chatham resulted in the death of 130 naval recruits. Bill was airborne from Goldhanger at 9.12 pm in a BE2d to patrol north of the Thames but the bombers were too far south and turned for home after bombing Chatham. This raid, however, had considerable significance for the night defenders. More or less on his own initiative, the OC 44 Squadron, Captain G. Murlis-Green, launched three of his Sopwith Camels. Although they failed to make an interception, the three pilots proved conclusively that one of the RFC's latest day fighters could be flown safely at night and, from that time, fighting at night by high performance single-seaters was steadily developed.

The lack of opposition on the Chatham raid prompted Hauptmann Rudolph Kleine, the commanding officer of *Kaghol 3*, to send eleven of his Gothas to attack London on the following night. Bill took off in a BE12a at 1.00 am by which time the five bombers that had reached London were already heading home. Only two fighter attacks were made and one was by Second Lieutenant S. Armstrong of Bill's flight. However, the anti-aircraft guns managed to shoot down one of the Gothas.

During September there were further developments to improve the air defence system. Separate zones for aeroplanes and guns were established and an outer gun barrage was set up for the defence of London. Other measures to combat the night raiders were the installation of a 'Balloon Apron' round the perimeter of London. This consisted of steel cables suspended from lines held in the air by a series of captive balloons at a height of some 8,000 feet. The aim was to force the incoming bombers to climb above this curtain and fly at the patrol heights of the fighters.

In conjunction with these night patrols a large number of searchlights were introduced into the aeroplane zones. The barrage system of anti-aircraft fire, originally devised as a result of the day raids, was also put in place but this proved very costly in ammunition.

Bill was airborne again in a BE12a when the Gothas next visited London on the night of 24/25 September. The Germans intended to co-ordinate this attack with a Zeppelin raid on the Midlands but both forces became widely dispersed. Thirteen Gothas crossed the coast, three having turned back, between Orford Ness and Dover but bombing was scattered. Four of the BEs were tasked to be 'wireless trackers' and whilst there is no evidence that Bill was used in this role, he was airborne for two hours, longer than the majority of the thirty sorties launched that night. In the event, due to the scattered force flying on random routes, no bombers were sighted.

During September, aerial photographs, supported by other intelligence, identified the Germans' new four-engine 'giant' bomber capable of carrying 2,200 lb of bombs. They made their first appearance

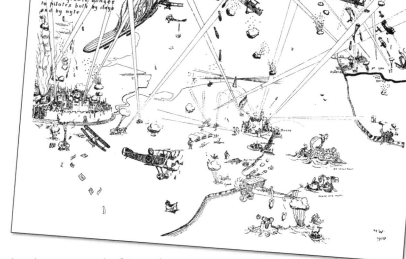

Bill's 1917 Christmas card to brother John depicts the many facets of VI Brigade's operations.

on the night of 25/26 September when two joined a force of fifteen Gothas to attack London. At the end of the month, there were three consecutive nights of attacks against London but Bill was not involved and his Goldhanger flight mounted few sorties.

In October the Home Defence Brigade was up-graded under the command of Brigadier-General T.C.R. Higgins and renamed VI Brigade. The month saw a great deal of development work being carried out to enhance the home defence organisation. Experiments and trials were carried out with various combinations of gun armament for the aeroplanes, sound locator systems were developed and night-fighting tactics were reviewed regularly.

The Gothas returned during the next moon period at the end of October. Poor weather thwarted the three bombers on the night of 29/30 October and Bill was one of only seven RFC pilots to take off in the very windy conditions to intercept them. Because of the weather, the Gothas limited their attack to the southeast coastal towns but damage was negligible. There was a large raid the following night but Bill was not involved.

It was the middle of December before the Germans launched another bombing raid. In the meantime, the steady build up of night-fighting squadrons was being hindered by a lack of experienced pilots to fill the key posts. Fred had finished his home leave having returned from France and he was sent to 39 Squadron for two weeks to complete some refresher night flying. On 26 November he joined brother Bill on 37 Squadron when he took command of B Flight at Stow Maries on the River Crouch in Essex, just a few miles south of Bill's landing ground at Goldhanger where he commanded C Flight.

Bad weather prevented any attacks for five weeks and it was not until mid-December that the German bombers returned. On the night of 18/19 December fourteen bombers, including a Giant, attacked London. Bill took off in one of the new BE12bs, which was fitted with the 200-hp Hispano Suiza engine giving the aircraft a ceiling of 18,000 feet. It was the type's first operational sortie but Bill's efforts were thwarted when he had to return to his landing ground after an hour when the radiator developed a leak.

The night, however, was a noteworthy one as it provided the first positive success by a night fighter against a bomber when Captain Murlis-Green flying his Camel used his upward-firing Lewis guns to shoot down a Gotha, which was forced to ditch off Folkestone. Murlis-Green was awarded a second Bar to his MC.

Four nights later, Bill was airborne on the Gothas' next visit, but this last bombing attack of 1917 achieved little and the night fighters made no contact and so ended the night bombing offensive of 1917. The defending aircraft could do little at first against the raiders, but by the end of the year they had gained valuable experience which was to bear fruit in the New Year.

Chapter Seven

THE FINAL YEAR

As the final year of the war dawned, the expansion of VI Brigade's night-fighting force, the success of the night-bomber squadrons deployed in France and the plans to create a much larger force of longer-range bombing squadrons in France (later called the Independent Force) all added to an increasing need for pilots and observers for night-flying duties. Whereas the training of night-fighting crews when the Sowrey brothers trained was in the earliest stage of development, the RFC had started to form specialist night-flying training squadrons during 1917 and the brothers would all spend the rest of the war in these units.

Having returned from France as one of the RFC's most experienced night-bomber pilots, John was, following the recommendation of OC 100 Sqn, gazetted as a squadron commander with effect from 20 September 1917. There was further good news for John when his wife gave birth to their first daughter, Julie. Now a major, John was posted to East Retford where he took command of 192 Depot Squadron on 24 October. Within a few weeks the squadron moved to Newmarket race course, which the Jockey Club had placed at the disposal of the War Office free of charge. Not long afterwards Bill followed suit when, on 1 January 1918, he too was gazetted as a squadron commander, taking command of 190 Night Training Squadron at Rochford a fortnight later. In March he took his unit to Newmarket where it was to operate in tandem with John's squadron.

Soon after settling at Newmarket, John received a letter from Malcolm Christie, still in command of 100 Squadron, which indicates the hopes the front-line squadron commanders had for the new night-training initiatives:

> Headquarters
> 100 Squadron, R.F.C.
>
> 'My dear Sowrey
> 'Officer Commanding School of Military Aeronautics has been asking for information concerning the training of bomber pilots and observers. I told him to write to you unofficially, and you would be able to send him the necessary memo.
> 'I am very keen on hearing how far you have progressed with your squadron and how soon the new standard of training will make itself felt out here. At the present we are still being supplied observers direct from Hythe, and pilots direct from home defence squadrons, who have not passed the standard tests recommended from here. I sincerely hope you will not relinquish one inch from the conditions of the test and only pass forward those who have satisfied the conditions in every way.

'When you have time do please write and tell me whether the training is still more or less a farce, or whether it is now being carried out on sound lines.

Sincerely yours,
M.J. Christie. Major'

Christie was referring to the state of night training as it stood in the autumn of 1917. At this stage the six depot squadrons (three of which, including both of those to be commanded by Sowreys, had only recently been formed) had evidently yet to have much impact downstream at squadron level. It was already the case, however, that the RFC was adopting a far more realistic approach to all aspects of flying training, as was indicated in the case of night flying, by the re-designation of the depot squadrons as night training squadrons (NTS) in December 1917. Thereafter, each NTS had a specific task. In the case of Newmarket, Bill's 190 NTS acted as an elementary night-flying school, using BEs, DH 6s and some Avros. Having completed the necessary practical exercises and passed the associated examinations, most pupils were posted on to John's 192 NTS to be trained as night-bomber crews on FEs, although some of the pilots may have been sent instead to HD squadrons to complete their training on night fighters.

The specific details changed with time, but in the summer of 1918, by which time the training sequence had been considerably refined, pilots would be earmarked for night operations at an early stage. After completing three ground-based preliminary courses, those destined for light night bombers (the FE2 remained in service in this role until the Armistice) were sent to an elementary NTS where they did a course that covered navigation and gunnery and included twenty hours of solo flying time with six night landings on DH 6s or Avros.

They were then posted to an advanced NTS where, apart from having to pass a series of written examinations, practical exercises included bomb dropping by day and by night, flying in searchlight beams and completing a 100-mile night reconnaissance. The whole sequence took seven or eight months at the end of which a pilot might have logged sixty or more hours of flight time, at least fourteen of them by night. Observers underwent a broadly similar five to six month sequence of which only eight weeks was spent with VI Brigade during which they should have flown at least five hours at night.

Meanwhile, Malcolm Christie had written to John in a somewhat light-hearted manner to update him on the latest situation on a night-bombing squadron.

'My dear Sowrey
'Many thanks for your numerous letters, all of which I read with great interest. You know however, what a rotten correspondent I am, and now that we have moved to a larger scope of work you can imagine the terrific theories, plans and vast eddies of hot air that are being manufactured by the officer commanding 100 Squadron.

'Bombing has now been reduced to the highest art in bombing boilers and steel works; pilots refrain from attacking the gauge glasses, and only place their 20-lbrs on steam mains! However, as you can imagine, the working out of schemes affords me much pleasure and does no one else any harm, except perhaps the Hun.

'I see W's name in the *Gazette*, but mighty brains always get through to the top......by the way, many congratulations on your majority; you never treated me with much respect, and now the last remnants have disappeared, in fact, I suppose having a depot squadron with a higher number makes you senior to me.

'The squadron is still going strong, but the weather has been impossible – only two flying days and nights during the last four weeks – that is about a record. You have no idea what a treacherous spell we have been having, thick fogs form everywhere in two minutes. Bearings are lost rather easily, lighting has to be quickly improved.

Fred (centre front row) as CO of 143 Squadron with his officers in their wide selection of uniforms following the establishment of the RAF.

'The surrounding country is not easy to decipher at night and a great deal has to be done to ensure pilots' safe return.

'Best of luck old man with your squadron. I shall come over to learn some tips shortly. I expect Newmarket will be stiff with gadgets and filled with corpses of would-be night pilots who died trying to drop 120 per cent of their dummy bombs into a 30-inch wide circle from 15,000 feet!

Con amore
M.G. Christie. Major'

100 Squadron had recently moved to Ochey, where the local terrain was more difficult for navigation, and a bombing campaign to include industrial plants and steel works had started. However, in the latter two months of 1917 the weather had curtailed operations severely. It needs to be remembered that these pioneer night-bomber crews were still flying old single-engine aircraft and were relying on the moon for navigation and beacons to guide the bombers back to their ill-lit landing grounds. With a plan to increase significantly the size of the bomber force, the need and value of dedicated night-training squadrons (in effect operational conversion units of the modern era) is evident.

In the meantime, Fred, who had been appointed as a squadron commander on the same date as Bill, remained with 37 Squadron until 4 February. From there he was given command of a new night-fighting squadron, 143 Squadron based at Detling near Maidstone, close to the route taken by the German bomber force. The squadron was equipped with the SE5A powered by a 200-hp Wolsey Viper engine. After some initial troubles with earlier engines, this single-seat fighting scout was considered to be one of the best British fighters of the day.

The steady improvements to the air defence organisation which began in the autumn of 1917 continued. In mid-March 1918 the searchlights in the aeroplane zones were reorganised into companies and placed under the appropriate squadron commander for operations and tactical training. This further advance ensured closer co-operation between aeroplanes and searchlights and enabled the tactical training to be accelerated resulting in greater efficiency. The searchlights were gradually provided with sound locators, and as further experience was gained in their use, excellent results were obtained.

Early in May, with the introduction of the wireless telephone and the provision of further telephone land lines, a scheme was instituted for the mutual exchange of information between various authorities, such as GHQ Home Forces, the London Air Defence Area, anti-aircraft defence commanders and the squadron commanders. This allowed a reasonably accurate plot of attacking aeroplanes, which enabled squadron commanders to concentrate their machines on the anticipated approach of enemy bombers. Here was an embryo organisation that, with the addition of early-warning radar, would become the air defence system that would save Great Britain when German bombers next attacked the country during the Battle of Britain.

During the first few months of 1918, there were eight significant raids by the Giants and Gothas. There had been a few fleeting sightings and one or two indecisive combats but on the night of 29/29 January the first German bomber to be shot down over mainland Britain fell to the guns of two 44 Squadron Camels. The Gotha came down at Wickford in Essex.

Following the recommendations of the 1917 Smuts Report the RNAS and the RFC were amalgamated and, on 1 April 1918, the RAF was formed following an Order in Council made by His Majesty King George V. The three Sowrey brothers were transferred to the new service and retained their ranks until the new RAF rank structure was established.

With the German 1918 spring offensive in France, their heavy bombers were committed to targets behind Allied lines and London suffered no raids for almost three months. When they resumed their attacks on London on the night of 19/20 May, they faced a much more effective night-fighter force and this time the enemy was made to pay dearly. Forty-three Gothas and Giants were sent to attack London, making this the biggest bombing raid of the war, with thirty-one aircraft dropping

Fred's Sopwith SE5a.

bombs. They were met by nine squadrons based around the capital, including Fred's 143 Squadron, which launched a total of eighty-four night fighters.

The first enemy aircraft, which proved to be a reconnaissance Rumpler, was reported over east Kent at 10.17 pm. Fighters were put on readiness and a procession of bombers appeared over the next forty-five minutes. Four aeroplanes of 143 Squadron were airborne in five minutes and Fred took off at 11.30 pm, a few minutes after the OC of 112 Squadron, Major C.J.Q. Brand, (later Air Vice-Marshal Sir Christopher Brand, AOC 10 Group in the Battle of Britain) had shot down a Gotha near Faversham.

Fifteen minutes after taking off, Fred saw an inbound bomber near Maidstone. He closed under the aircraft and fired a full drum of ammunition from his elevated Lewis gun but observed no results. In removing the empty drum, which fell into the cockpit, he lost sight of the bomber.

Some thirty minutes later, Fred found another Gotha and positioned underneath it before firing two double drums from his Lewis. The bomber evaded but Fred maintained contact and pulled up to fire his Vickers guns, eventually stalling and falling away. Conscious of the trouble he had encountered with the empty drum from his earlier engagement, he threw the next empty drum over the side. It landed on the roof of a house in Maidstone and was returned to the squadron the following day.

Five minutes after his attack, the Gotha was picked up by a Bristol Fighter of 61 Squadron and the observer fired into the bomber's port engine. The Gotha lost height and the Bristol crew did not engage it again and soon lost sight of it. The bomber came down near Frinsted and there was one survivor. The Bristol Fighter crew, lost and short of petrol, landed at Detling.

There was considerable confusion and debate as to who had destroyed the Gotha. Initially, Brigadier-General T.C.R. Higgins, GOC VI Brigade credited the destruction of the bomber to Fred but it was later changed and the credit was given to the Bristol crew. Fred contested this, not so much for personal acclaim but on behalf of his squadron, which had only recently been formed. He wrote on 25 May to the OC 53 Wing and explained his case:

'I wish to dispute the statement that Lt's Turner and Barwise brought down the Gotha which crashed at Frinsted at 12.35 am on 20 May. I do not contend that no other machine attacked after I left it going down at about 9,000 feet but if any such attack did take place it must have been between 12.30 am (the time I lost the Gotha) and 12.35 am (the time it landed at Frinsted).

'That I was attacking the machine at this time is almost conclusively proved by the fact that an empty Lewis gun drum dropped through the roof of a house in Maidstone at 12.30 am and that my machine gun fire was heard between Maidstone and Frinsted at that time. This drum has been returned and is identified as belonging to this squadron...A statement from Mr White is attached.

'Further I wish to make the following report concerning Lt's Turner and Barwise:

'These officers landed at Detling at 1.25 am, 20 May on Bristol Fighter C851 and this was the only strange machine to land here that night. I was on the aerodrome at the time and immediately the engine stopped I questioned the observer as to why he had landed and whether they had seen anything. The reply was that they were lost and they had had a 'bit of a scrap' over South Ash but that his gun had jammed. They stayed here until 2.30 pm in the afternoon and during conversation with officers made various statements, evidence of which is attached. They were in this squadron office while reports were being made out and carried on the conversation freely with officers in the mess, until after lunch when they

The wreckage of the Gotha engaged by Fred Sowrey on the night of 19/20 May 1918.

left. They made no written report until they returned to their squadron. (See Capt. Earnshaw's report attached.)

'During this time that they were here they did not once suggest that they thought they had brought down a machine or had a decisive combat.'

It is very clear what Fred is suggesting and this is supported by seven separate statements, most by officers on 143 Squadron who met and spoke with the pilot and observer of the Bristol. One officer in the squadron office when the Bristol crew arrived stated: 'they made no definite claim to having shot any H.A. down and were very vague in what they had done.' Another stated that the observer had told him that his gun had jammed and a third stated: 'they did not see it come down nor did they seem to think that they had brought it down...they were very vague with regard to heights and times.' The observer told the armament officer that he had used three drums before the fourth jammed yet, on inspecting the aircraft, there was only one empty drum and four full ones.

The crew, who had listened to Fred's debrief, declined to file a report until they returned to Biggin Hill the following afternoon.

Fred was clearly upset when it was decided to credit the Bristol crew with the destruction of the Gotha. He wrote to the commander of 53 Wing;

'I wish it to be clearly understood that I do not claim to have definitely brought down the Gotha but I do wish to emphatically point out the questionable conduct of these two officers who are credited with having brought the machine down...before making out their report at their squadron both the pilot and observer had become acquainted with the details connected with the landing of the Gotha. I respectfully beg to request, quite apart from any personal interest that an independent enquiry be made into the accuracy of their statements.'

The most sensible outcome would have been to officially share the credit but Fred's request for an enquiry was to no avail and both the crew members of the Bristol were eventually awarded the Distinguished Flying Cross (DFC).

The anti-aircraft defence, which fired 30,000 shells, and the eighty-four night-flying aircraft which went up, destroyed between them six bombers, while a seventh crashed with engine trouble in Clacton, and an eighth in Belgium. The Germans never attacked this country again. Their big attack on the night of 19/20 May 1918 saw the first Battle of Britain peter out and the people of London were spared more sleepless nights and the possibility of more loss of life. A grateful Lord Mayor wrote to the GOC VI Brigade RFC:

'The citizens of London are filled with admiration and gratitude for the splendid defensive measures taken by the air force against the enemy attack on Sunday and will be glad if their thanks and appreciation may be conveyed to those who so gallantly and successfully protected the capital on that occasion.'

This was the last air attack on this country for twenty-one years. Altogether the German bombing aircraft had dropped seventy-three tons in fifty-two raids, killed 857 persons and injured 2,058. However, the raids, by throwing into sharp relief the inadequacy of our air defences, helped in no small measure to bring into being the RAF.

Understandably, there were no indications that these attacks would be the last to be mounted against Great Britain and the build up of the night-fighting defences continued. Fred's squadron replaced its SE5s with Camels and training continued. As part of the steady improvement of the air defence organisation, a greater use was made of wireless and the fighter squadrons took a varying degree of interest

John Sowrey (centre front) as CO of 192(NT) Squadron with his officers in the summer of 1918.

in the trials. One squadron commander that took the trial seriously was Fred.

During July, his aircraft flew a series of 'wireless telephony tests' with Aperfield Court Wireless Station. One test involved a formation of six aircraft, led by Fred, each equipped with receiving equipment. The tests were successful and the aircraft received messages up to a distance of forty miles. 143 Squadron mounted twenty-five separate flights, sometimes with formations of four or five aircraft, and there were no wireless failures. The 53 Wing report concluded, 'I should like to point out that wireless telephony is regarded with a great deal of confidence amongst the pilots of this squadron [143]'. After receiving this report, the GOC of VI Brigade wrote to OC 53 Wing:

> 'With reference to your letter, the standard of efficiency attained by 143 Squadron in wireless telephony is excellent, which is due to the fact that the squadron commander has given the matter great attention.'

The GOC went on to offer some stern words to other squadron commanders and made it clear that he expected an 'early improvement' and, within two weeks, the failure to receive wireless messages 'should be practically nil'. Fred remained in command of 143 Squadron until the end of the war but, with the cessation of the German bomber offensive, he was to see no more action.

Throughout the spring and early summer of 1918, John and Bill continued to command their night-training squadrons. Both left their units in August to return to front-line squadrons. Bill was given command of 50 Squadron, a night-fighter squadron equipped with the Camel and based at Bekesbourne near Canterbury but, like Fred based fifteen miles to the west, he and his squadron would see no further action. With John's departure to France imminent, there was one last opportunity for the brothers and their family to get together and this was on the occasion of Bill's marriage at Rochford in Essex to Maud Standish on 8 August, Bill's twenty-fourth birthday. (Maud was always known as Daisy.)

John returned to the night-bombing role in August and left for France to take command of 101 Squadron at Famechon near Abbeville on the 26th. The squadron was still flying the FE2b with its 160-hp Beardmore engine but it also had a number of FE2ds, with the more powerful 250-hp Rolls-Royce (Eagle) Mk 1 engine. 101 Squadron was the only night-bomber squadron of the RAF's V

Brigade, which flew in support of General Sir Henry Rawlinson's Fourth Army, engaged in the area north of the Somme. The bomber squadrons of the Independent Force, which were based in eastern France, were ranging deeper into Germany to attack industrial targets but 101 Squadron bombed targets at shorter range and, just as with 100 Squadron in 1917, John attacked trains, transport on the move and German assembly areas close to the front.

On the eve of the battle to capture the Hindenburg Line on 29 September, 101 Squadron attacked enemy villages opposite the Fourth Army front, before the battle opened. Explosions and fires were

started at Busigny station and in the villages of Outreaux and Fresnoy-le-Grand. They were also tasked to 'keep flying about the front-line area in order to drown the noise of the assembling tanks'. The following night rainstorms made night bombing impossible but the ground advance continued. Bad weather again limited the night bombers' opportunities, but the squadron was able to resume attacks on 4 October and bombed enemy communications, a notable success being the destruction of the Lichtervelde railway sidings. These attacks behind enemy lines provided crucial indirect support to the advancing army by limiting the flow of enemy reinforcements and supplies.

Despite continuing bad weather, John and his crews supported the next phase of the advance, which commenced early on 8

112-lb bombs being prepared for a night attack.

October south of Cambrai. Railways were again a priority target and, until the Armistice a month later, 101 Squadron attacked whenever the weather allowed.

Back in Kent, Fred managed to get himself into some hot water by celebrating the end of the war a month early. After reports of rowdiness and bad behaviour by his officers, Fred was asked to explain the activities of the evening to his wing commander. His response casts an amusing light on the events:

'On Saturday, 12 October, at about 9.45 pm I first heard that Germany had accepted President Wilson's terms and that hostilities had ceased. I obtained a number of reports that confirmed this.

'I announced it in the officers' mess and told the sergeant major to announce it to the men. He asked for special permission to open the canteen in honour of the occasion. The statement that the canteen was wrecked is absolutely untrue and without foundation.

'The only transport that left the squadron were two Crossley tenders and a Ford tender all containing officers; myself being among them…We had intended to go into Maidstone, but I thought it was inadvisable, so we stopped at the Cock Inn, Detling instead. We stayed there talking and being generally cheerful for about an hour…

'We left the Cock Inn at about 11.30 pm and returned to the aerodrome. Before doing so I got in the driver's seat of one of the Crossleys, and drove it down the hill with the intention of turning it round at the bottom. When I got about a quarter of a mile down the hill the lights went down so I left the car in charge of the driver and went back to the aerodrome in the Ford. It is absolutely untrue to say that the car was in the ditch and that it was left unattended.

'As far as I know nobody was up after 1 am with the exception of the officers with Captain Potter [who had gone to another inn] who did not get back until 3 am. No rockets or lights of any kind were fired later than 10.30 or 11 pm, and the suggestion that the camp was a 'blaze of light' after 3 am is without a shadow of truth. No transport of vehicles were wrecked or even damaged, and there was no disorderly or noisy behaviour other than that I have stated. The only irregularities of any nature that occurred, and which I admit, were the driving of the cars by Captain Potter and myself, and the firing of the rockets and Very lights…

'I very much regret the occurrence. However, I was very much misled by the various messages that were received…

Major
Commanding 143 Squadron
Detling. 22.10.18'

One wonders how long it took Fred to write this letter with its thinly-veiled account of an enjoyable, and almost certainly boisterous, evening. It would be even more interesting to know how it was received by the HQ and the scale of the celebrations when the war was officially ended.

The year ended in a unique and memorable way. On 30 October, John learnt that his wife Audrey had given birth to a daughter, Edith Margaret. Then, on 2 November it was announced that Major John Sowrey had been awarded the Air Force Cross (AFC). This was in recognition of his services in command of 192 (N) Training Squadron. The family had little time to digest this long overdue honour for John before the *London Gazette* of 1 January 1919 carried the announcement that Major Frederick Sowrey DSO, MC and Major William Sowrey had also both been awarded the AFC.

These awards stem from the three brothers' outstanding contribution to the development of night flying, both operationally and in the training role. The advances in the night capability of the RFC and the RAF had been dramatic. The final word should rest with the compiler of VI Brigade's 'Report on Night Flying':

'During the present war it has been discovered that night-flying aeroplanes can be put to a variety of uses including reconnaissance, bombing, 'low strafing', offensive and defensive patrols and artillery co-operation. In the next war the night pilot will play a part equal to, if not more important than, that of the day pilot.'

Chapter Eight

SETTLING DOWN

The period immediately after the war's end was one of great turmoil, disbandment of squadrons and demobilisation of many thousands of men all anxious to put the war behind them. There was, however, a need to retain a large force on the continent with some squadrons moving into the western part of Germany.

John remained in command of 101 Squadron, which moved into Belgium but on 12 January 1919 he returned to England and was given command of 37 Squadron based at Biggin Hill, equipped with the Sopwith Snipe. Fred remained in command of 143 Squadron and Bill had just left for France to take command of the Camel-equipped 152 Squadron based at Carvin between Lens and Lille in northern France.

In April 1919 the three brothers attended an investiture at Buckingham Palace with their mother and John and Bill's wives. Each brother was invested with the AFC, almost certainly a unique, and probably never to be repeated, event.

For short periods throughout 1919, the brothers were given command of other squadrons as the rapid drawdown of RAF units was implemented. John was a very innovative and technical thinker, and throughout his service he had shown a keen interest in invention and modifications. On 15 April 1919 he wrote to the OC, 49 Wing and outlined his proposal for the establishment of squadron warrant officers:

'May I draw your attention, please, to the urgent necessity now that the RAF is about to settle down to peace conditions of a reform that is badly needed as regards the establishment of a squadron, RAF. I refer to the existence in one squadron of two warrant officers class 1, one technical and the other disciplinary.

'In over eighteen months experience

The three brothers: John (left), Fred (centre) and Bill (right) leave Buckingham Palace with John and Bill's wives and mother (behind Fred) after receiving their AFCs.

as a squadron commander both at home and overseas, I have come to the conclusion that the existence in one squadron of two warrant officers whose duties are so diametrically opposed and whose relations with the men are so utterly different is detrimental to efficiency.

'In the first place, the TSM, being better paid and having a more pleasant duty to perform is naturally looked up to more by flight sergeants. In turn, the DSM is generally regarded in the squadron as a relic of the old pre-war army and as a man whose duty it is to make himself thoroughly disliked.

'I venture to suggest that in the reconstruction of the RAF which is about to take place, that each squadron should have one and only one SM who is the most important man in the squadron as far as the NCO's, and men are concerned. And one who is analogous to the RSM of the infantry battalion. Squadron SM's should be selected from those existing technical and disciplinary warrant officers who, as far as possible, combine the qualities at present in those two classes.'

He went on to discuss how the attitude of the NCOs towards a single sergeant major would improve and, since the majority aspired to the technical aspects of their work, it would also act as an incentive to their own attitude to promotion. John went on to draw the comparison if a squadron had two commanders, one regimental and the other technical and the confusion this would create. Hence, he argued, there was no need for two sergeant majors. He also highlighted the value of having a 'technical officer' on the squadron establishment. He concluded his letter:

'Finally, I would make a plea for the air force SM as against the army SM. I submit that a man who has had technical training has had discipline knocked into him and can impart it so on others, is a far more suitable man to lead a squadron RAF than an ex-army SM who views the squadron solely from the old army standpoint.

J Sowrey. Major, Commanding 37 Squadron
Biggin Hill
Kent'

This is a most interesting letter. It is not known what effect it had on higher authorities but it indicates a great deal of foresight since, in the future, an RAF squadron was established along the lines proposed by John Sowrey (although, sadly, his suggestion that dedicated technical officers should be provided was not implanted until the Second World War). The letter also gives an indication of the future direction of John's long RAF career.

With the RAF starting to reorganise and look to the future structure of the force, all three brothers decided to apply for continued service in the peacetime RAF. The first postwar permanent commissions to be granted in the service were announced in the *London Gazette* of 1 August 1919. The list comprised 1,065 officers of all ranks, including six major-generals, and the names of John and Fred appeared. The introduction of distinc-

Rita White, Fred's future wife, and her brother Hugh, later an air vice-marshal.

tive titles for personnel of the RAF also came into effect in August 1919 and John and Fred were gazetted with the new rank of squadron leader, equivalent to the rank of major. Bill was appointed to a short-service commission as a squadron leader, which in 1922 he extended by seven years, until he too was awarded a permanent commission.

The latter part of 1919 was to be a momentous period in the history of the RAF. There was great pressure, particularly from the Royal Navy and the army, for the RAF to be abandoned with the appropriate elements transferring back to the two senior services but Chief of the Air Staff Air Marshal Sir Hugh Trenchard, was determined to fight for the future of the service he had nurtured.

At the invitation of Secretary of State for War and Air Winston Churchill, Trenchard prepared his 'Memorandum on the Permanent Organisation of the Royal Air Force', which he issued on 25 November 1919. This was presented to parliament on 11 December in a White Paper, which provided a scheme to establish the peacetime basis of the service. Trenchard's Memorandum, as it became known, stressed the importance of planning for the future and highlighted, *inter alia*, the foundation of a sound and appropriate manpower structure and the extreme importance of training to create a cadre for the future. Trenchard also made the important point, 'to make an air force worthy of the name, we must create an air force spirit, or rather foster this spirit that undoubtedly existed in a high degree during the war, by every means in our power'.

One of the key results of the memorandum was the establishment of the RAF's three great centres for training and education, the RAF College at Cranwell, the RAF Staff College at Andover and the RAF Apprentice School at Halton. Added to these was the already-established Central Flying School at RAF Upavon. Over the next few years, the three Sowrey brothers would be closely involved in the development of these key organisations.

Trenchard had made it a condition of service that practically all of his officers should learn to fly but he did not see that flying should be their primary job. Above all, they were to be officers able to organise and operate a military service. There was no Technical or Engineering Branch envisaged and engineering posts were to be filled by pilots. In an increasingly technical service this need for suitably-qualified officers to command and manage the ground crew, who would be (under Trenchard's scheme) apprentices trained at the RAF's apprentice schools, was crucial.

With their futures in the peacetime RAF secure, John and Fred decided to complete their university studies. John, with his science background and qualifications, together with his increasing interest in the technical issues, decided to specialise in aeronautical engineering.

At this stage in the development of the RAF, there had still been insufficient time to establish a formal pattern for training technical officers. In September 1919 he commenced a series of courses that would last three years, initially attending a course of instruction at Queen's College, Cambridge, which his RAF service record described as 'special engineering'.

During his time at Queens, there was an early indication of his interest in the wider aspects of aeronautical engineering. On 21 January 1920 he called a meeting in the Engineering Laboratories, which resulted in the formation of Cambridge University Aeronautical Society. It was formed with the object of promoting interest and knowledge of aeronautical science. This was to be achieved by a series of lectures and demonstrations in addition to visits to works and places of practical interest. Professor B.M. Jones was elected as president and Sowrey was one of the five members of the committee. The first meeting was held on 4 February when Mr Hamshaw Thomas, who had served in the RAF, gave the inaugural lecture titled 'The Use of Aircraft in Exploration and Survey'.

John's time at Cambridge was also marked by a very happy occasion when his wife Audrey gave birth to their first son, John Adam, on 5 January. Throughout his life, John junior was Johnnie to the family.

On completion of his course at Cambridge, where he enjoyed being a member of the rowing eight, John attended the recently-introduced course in practical engineering for RAF officers, initially completing the first term at the Central Flying School before moving to the Royal Aircraft Establishment at Farnborough. On 26 July 1921 Audrey gave birth to their second son, James Alan Frederick, and a month later he completed the second term in August 1921. This was just in time to start a one-year course in the Aviation Department of the Imperial College of Science and Technology, London where he took the fourth year of the aeronautical engineering course and gained a certificate for post-graduate work. On completion he was awarded the specialist symbol E*, which appeared against his name in the Air Force List.

By the time John had completed his engineering studies in April 1922, the RAF had started to implement Trenchard's policy that pilots on the General List should fill specialist appointments in engineering, signals, armament, photography or navigation between their flying duties. This policy was to stand the RAF in good stead for the next ten years when a series of 'expansion periods' was implemented and this gave rise to a need for the establishment of a Technical Branch manned by specialist officers with the appropriate qualifications and training.

Just as John had taken advantage of the opportunity to return to university for a year, Fred entered Caius College, Cambridge in September 1919 and was in residence for three terms. After the rigours of the recent war, and the loss of so many friends, this interlude not only had academic value but was also an opportunity to relax and enjoy some of the youth that his generation had missed. Fred took advantage of this and enjoyed sporting activities which included rowing with the college eight and participating in the 'May Bumps' on the River Cam.

Soon after finishing his time at Caius, Fred enjoyed a period of leave before reporting to the HQ 11 (Irish) Wing to start his next appointment.

During the time that his two brothers were at university, Bill filled a number of short-term appointments in preparation for his departure to Mesopotamia.

John (left rear) with the Queen's College, Cambridge University Rowing Eight.

Chapter Nine

AIR POLICING

A key feature of the Trenchard Memorandum was the disposition of the limited number of the RAF's squadrons to be retained in the austere financial climate that followed the end of the First World War. Eighteen squadrons and three seaplane flights were to be deployed overseas. Eight squadrons and one depot were to be established in India, seven squadrons and a depot in Egypt and three squadrons and a depot in Mesopotamia. In one significant passage, the value of air force squadrons as a substitute for expensive overseas garrisons was mentioned. The paper stated:

> '...it is perhaps not too much to hope that before long it will prove possible to regard the Royal Air Force units not as an addition to the military garrison [in India] but as a substitute for it.'

In presenting the White Paper that stemmed from Trenchard's Memorandum, to parliament, Winston Churchill had said, 'The first duty of the RAF is to garrison the British Empire'.

Within weeks this sentiment became reality with the RAF developing an operational theory and practice which became known as 'air control'.

Military operations against the Mahsud and Waziri tribes of the North-West Frontier of India were launched in November 1919 and the small RAF force was immediately in action in support of ground forces. A few months later, RAF aircraft were used against tribesmen in British Somaliland against the 'Mad Mullah'. Nine aircraft successfully conducted a series of independent strikes against insurgent strongholds at Jid Ali and the Mullah's main camp at Medishi allowing a small ground force to follow up. Operations were completed in three weeks and Colonial Secretary Leopold Amery would later describe the event as, 'the cheapest war in history'. The political effects for the RAF were out of all proportion to the local impact in Somaliland.

To some degree this brief campaign vindicated Trenchard's views that the RAF could play a major role in colonial policing and avoid the great expense of maintaining very large garrisons. Within months further opportunities developed for this new RAF role. Armed opposition to the British presence soon broke out in Mesopotamia, initially in the Middle Euphrates area but later in the remote northern areas, a region inhabited by warlike Kurdish tribes.

With the successful example of Somaliland still fresh in his mind, Churchill, by now the colonial secretary, was encouraged to adopt a similar approach to the much larger and more politically-charged situation in Mesopotamia. It was to this area, in February 1920, that Bill headed.

On the 13th he arrived at Tilbury and boarded HM Transport *Macedonia*, an elderly P & O liner

DH9As of 30 Squadron in 1920.

which had seen service as an armed merchantman during the war. The passengers included officers and men of the Manchester Regiment and a number of RAF personnel travelling to India, with some going on to Mesopotamia. In the cabin next to Bill's was one of his old friends, D'Arcy Greig, who commented:

> 'When I first made his acquaintance two years previously, he was the CO of the night-training squadron. I remembered having a great admiration for his prowess as a pilot and for his exuberance in the mess. He now seemed somewhat subdued and spent a great part of his time practicing the ukulele, an instrument on which he was obviously a novice.'

The ship headed for Bombay where the Mesopotamia-bound officers spent some time before embarking for Basra. Bill finally arrived at Baghdad West, the home of 30 Squadron, on 31 March when he assumed command of the squadron.

30 Squadron had fought in Mesopotamia since 1915 but it had been reduced to cadre strength at the end of the war. Early in 1920 it started to build up to full strength again equipped initially with the RE8 but soon to start receiving the DH9A. Known affectionately as the 'Ninak', the aircraft served for many years and gave great service to the RAF in overseas theatres.

With just one other squadron based in Mesopotamia at the time (6 Squadron), and with an increasing number of disturbances there and in Persia, Bill's new command was widely dispersed with the squadron HQ and C Flight at Baghdad West, while A Flight was at Mosul in the north and B Flight at Kasvin in Persia.

Churchill's intervention, and Trenchard's determination to enforce the case for a greater role for the RAF in policing the area, resulted in the formation of more squadrons in Mesopotamia. A plan was drawn up by the air staff to station ten of the RAF's thirty-three squadrons in the area. They would be supported by only small forces on the ground, a proposal that inevitably attracted considerable opposition from the many critics of the now independent RAF.

When Bill arrived in the region, sporadic disturbances were occurring, particularly in the north of the country where the Kurds, covertly encouraged by Turkey, were an increasing concern. Almost every week Bill and his pilots dropped a few bombs on villages in the valleys of the Greater and Lesser Zab Rivers in Kurdistan. Before the few 20-lb Cooper bombs were dropped, leaflets were scattered to give the villagers time to stop making trouble or to clear the area. However, there was more to air control than proscription bombing and reconnaissance, re-supply and a mere presence in troublesome areas were equally important.

Disorder in the region increased in June 1920 and Bill flew to visit his dispersed flights. In addition to bombing raids, the Ninaks were also used to drop supplies to the army columns in the area. Pilots had to be careful as hostile tribesmen were remarkably good marksman and it was not uncommon for low-flying aircraft to be damaged.

In July the situation in Mosul deteriorated and Bill was a regular visitor to his A Flight. Consideration was given to evacuating the area but this was discounted and the crews of 30 Squadron had plenty of opportunity to practise their supply-dropping skills when food, ammunition and medical supplies were dropped over a period of a few weeks. The siege lasted ninety-eight days.

During this summer of considerable unrest, the burden of activity fell on the two Mesopotamia-based flights of 30 Squadron and 6 Squadron resulting in a very busy period of operations flown in difficult conditions. During the summer of 1920 temperatures in the shade in Baghdad were almost 120 degrees Fahrenheit, a particularly demanding climate for the hard-working ground crew who also had to accept very basic living conditions and few leisure facilities.

Churchill had become the colonial secretary in November 1920 and soon instigated a review of the policy in the Middle East including the establishment of a new Middle East Department. In March 1921 he left to confer with local authorities in Palestine and Mesopotamia and it was as a result of this visit that he favoured the idea of the RAF taking control. Following his visit, Churchill called a conference in Cairo, which Trenchard attended, when it was decided to pass the responsibility for both internal and external security in the two regions to the RAF, although this was not completely finalised until October 1922.

B Flight of 30 Squadron based at Kasvan was commanded by the Canadian 'ace' Flight Lieutenant Raymond Collishaw DSO*, OBE, DSC, AFC and Bill made regular visits and took part in some of the actions. In October a Russian aircraft was reported as flying over Persia and the flight was reinforced with a DH9A. Conditions at Kasvan were very different from those in Baghdad. The winter of 1920-21 was particularly severe and, for much of the time, flying had to be conducted from a snow-covered airfield.

In February 1921, A Flight left Mosul for Baghdad to join the squadron headquarters. On 16 March, just three days before Bill handed over command of 30 Squadron to Collishaw, a historic event for the RAF in Mesopotamia took place. A special demonstration flight was staged with every serviceable aircraft in Baghdad taking part. The recently-received RAF Ensign was flown for the first time and was attached to one of the squadron's DH9As. As the aircraft passed the high commissioner and the GOC-in-C the ensign was streamed but tore in half. There is no evidence to suggest that Bill's departure three days later to take command of 84 Squadron was connected with this unfortunate incident!

Some months later it was announced that Bill had been mentioned in despatches for his service with 30 Squadron.

A serious insurrection along the lower reaches of the Euphrates had given added impetus to Churchill's proposal to expand the role of the RAF in the region. Additional squadrons were required and it was to the recently-reformed 84 Squadron that Bill headed. The squadron was the RAF's only unit based at Shaibah near Basra. Its isolated position at the head of the Persian Gulf, its climate and its complete lack of amenities made it the most inhospitable and least popular of the RAF stations in Iraq (Mesopotamia was officially designated Iraq in September 1921). Many regarded it as the RAF's 'punishment station'; hence it was

Bill with his polo pony during the spring of 1921.

John Glubb with Sheikh Laglan.

a difficult command appointment that Bill inherited.

The squadron was equipped with the Ninak and as the army withdrew from the area, patrols by 84 Squadron's aircraft increasingly became the method of exercising control over the troublesome sheikhs and their followers. The deserts of Southern Iraq are huge and featureless, especially from the air. Maps were inadequate, if they existed at all, and identifying friendly tribes and locating them precisely when there were so few landmarks was extremely difficult. A young army officer, Captain John Glubb (later Lieutenant General Sir John Glubb, but better known as 'Glubb Pasha') was on special service in Iraq and had formed close links with the local tribes in the area, part of which was known as the Nejed, and he recognised the value of close co-operation with the RAF, and with 84 Squadron in particular.

Bill came to the area in the early days of this development in the Southern Desert. He found that operations in the vast, virtually unexplored area were very different from the regions around Baghdad, the rugged Kurdistan and in north-west Persia where ground features were prominent and maps more accurate. However, the method of air control was similar. Reconnaissance patrols were regular tasks and, when required, leaflets were dropped on the camps of troublesome sheikhs and if they failed to concur with instructions then the next raid would result in the dropping of a few 20-lb bombs.

By the middle of 1921, with the RAF tasked with an increasing role of 'air policing' it was clear that some ground forces were required to follow up the sighting and reports of aircrew. The army was unable to deploy further troops so the RAF created its own ground force. In the years immediately following the First World War, an irregular force had been raised and in 1919 they were reconstituted as the Iraq Levies and by 1921 they had come under the control of the RAF.

Meanwhile, plans were being finalised for the RAF to take over the army's armoured car companies and to expand that capability with additional vehicles and personnel, many of whom were about to start their training at Manston. The transition should have been completed by October 1922, but, due to unforeseen circumstances, the new RAF armoured car companies didn't become fully operational until early-November 1922.

A feature of air control operations over Iraq was the regular use of 'demonstration flights', a form of deterrence with aircraft overflying villages and concentrations of tribesmen. A typical action was carried out on 6 June 1921, when 84 Squadron was tasked to send four aircraft over the village of Khamisiyah, some twenty-five miles south east of Nasiriyah. The village was suspected of being a centre for gun running and the political authorities requested a demonstration flight. A combined operation was set up between the Iraq Levies and the aircraft, and it was carried out in the early morning, the Levies searching the village whilst the aircraft flew overhead. The post-operation report concluded, 'The flight is reported to have had a quietening effect on the district'.

Bill's squadron was soon in action again. Early in July the rebel faction of the Albu Khalifah tribe, who for some time had been giving considerable trouble in the marsh area of south-eastern Iraq, attacked a friendly tribe causing many casualties. In addition to these disturbances, inter-tribal fighting was taking place in an adjacent area and on 5 July, the political adviser in Nasiriyah sent the following cable:

> 'In addition to disturbances in Albu Khalifah, sections of Jawabar and Amairah tribes are fighting amongst themselves north of Lake. In other parts, Suq tribes are restless due chiefly to sowing and transplanting rice which is signal for re-opening ancient land and tribal boundary disputes. In order therefore to prevent disorders spreading I suggest no time is lost in attacking Albu Khalifah outlaws. Twofold object in my view (a) morale effect on re-mainder of district (b) punish outlaws for their numerous misdeeds.'

Due to the state of the surrounding marshland the Levies could not be used against the positions taken up by the outlaws. However, the fort in which they were established was within gun range of defence vessels and it was decided that a combined operation between these vessels and aircraft of 84 Squadron should be mounted.

The first attack took place on 7 July. Eight Ninaks co-operated with the defence vessels and the fort was badly damaged by a combination of gunfire and bombs causing twenty casualties. On completion of the operation, what was left of the fort was occupied by friendly groups of neighbouring tribes who completely destroyed it. The survivors of the attack took refuge in a nearby village of the Albu Jassin tribe. They were given until sunset on the 10th to report to Suq but they failed to do so and a similar operation was planned for the following day.

On the 11th the visibility was very poor, and as the villagers had anticipated an attack, they had fled but the village was badly damaged. The result of these operations is best summed up by an extract from a memorandum sent by the local political authorities to the general HQ dated 19 July 1921:

> 'Effect of recent operations against the outlaws of the Albu Khalifah: The attack on the fort of the outlaws on July 7th completely disillusioned the people of the Suq district of any opinion which they may previously have held that aeroplanes and gun-boats would not be used, and if they were they would not cause serious damage. The destruction of the fort and the high percentage of casualties was the sole topic of conversation in Suq-Ash-Shuyukh for some days, and doubtless the account of this attack grew in importance as it spread to the other tribes in the district.'

This operation is an excellent example of how Trenchard's policy of providing control from the air could be executed successfully. Without the aid of any ground forces, a few aircraft had completed a difficult task in a matter of a few sorties. It is mere conjecture but without the use of air power, this local difficulty could have taken ground forces a great deal of time and effort to resolve. Bill had every reason to be pleased with the role played by his squadron.

Over the next few weeks, the squadron continued with its patrolling and co-operation with local police forces in the Southern Desert. More serious trouble started to brew in September. On the 8th, Bill sent two aircraft to Nasiriyah, a regular forward operating airstrip for the squadron. From there they carried out a reconnaissance some thirty-five miles to the west of the town where they found large numbers of camps and abnormal movements of armed tribesmen. They also discovered a large fort

A DH9A of 84 Squadron over Shaibah.

being built and took photographs. Later in the day, these two aircraft provided support for a police force that searched the village.

Matters remained quiet for a few days before inter-tribal fighting over boundaries started in the Lake Hammar district in the Nasiriyah area. Owing to the low state of the river, new land had appeared for the first time, an event that invariably led to dispute. The immediate result was the failure of the tribes to submit to repeated government orders and a refusal to come to an agreement. The tribal leaders were then given an ultimatum to report to government authorities by sunset on the 14th. This they failed to do and Bill was ordered to be ready for action on the 16th.

Attacks were carried out by nine aircraft operating out of Shaibah and the tribe promptly evacuated and burned their village but still maintained a defiant attitude. On the 24th ten aircraft mounted more attacks against other villages in the area. The tribal leaders, in spite of being deserted by the majority of their followers, then concentrated at Albu Nusf. To avoid misidentifying potential targets, the squadron sent an officer, with an escort, into the area to positively identify the leader's position. On the morning of the 30th, nine aircraft of 84 Squadron took off and bombed the village. On completion, friendly Arabs advanced and took possession of the village. The rebel leaders fled and their forts were taken over by the government authorities.

Later that day, a second raid was planned for another target but tragedy struck when a bomb on one aircraft exploded as it took off. The pilot and airman gunner were killed and the crew of a second aircraft taking off alongside were injured. This unfortunate, and unforeseen, accident was a sad end to a particularly successful period of operations by Bill and his pilots and gunners.

September had been the busiest month in 84 Squadron's time in Iraq. Almost 200 hours had been flown, eight tons of bombs had been dropped and over 6,500 rounds of ammunition had been fired. Sustaining this during the hottest period of the year was a sterling effort by air and ground crews. It particularly reflects great credit on the latter who had to work in the open with limited facilities available and just as few for their off-duty time.

After a quiet few weeks, Bill and his pilots were back in action again in mid-January. Leaders of the Alwan and Badran sections of the Madinah tribe had long been guilty of ignoring government officials and had refused to visit the king in Baghdad. They had declined to pay rent and revenue and openly defied the government who then issued an ultimatum. This was ignored and on 16 January 1922 eleven aircraft of 84 Squadron took off to bomb the Alwan villages, which were badly damaged. The police followed up on the ground without opposition and burnt the remaining houses. The following morning, the insurgents surrendered unconditionally.

In the last few weeks of his time in command of 84 Squadron, Bill was in action again in March. On 6 March eleven aircraft carried out a successful bombing attack on Dabit and, five days later, the troublesome Akhwan tribesmen were attacked. A patrol of the Police Camel Corps had been attacked whilst visiting the peaceful Budir tribe, thirty miles south of the main railway line. In a fierce fight many villagers were killed and 100 of the Camel Corps were reported missing.

An air reconnaissance pinpointed the tribe on the 12th and their movements were monitored for two days. A number of aircraft located them and came under heavy fire, some sustaining damage. In the afternoon, four aircraft found the Akhwan in a large circular camp with a number of sheep and camels, stolen during the raid a few days earlier. The aircraft attacked from low level and all the bombs were seen to burst in the centre of the camp causing a great deal of confusion and activity. Three of the aircraft were heavily fired at during the operations but were able to return to Shaibah. The following morning, four more aircraft attacked with bombs and machine guns and the Akhwan were seen scattering to the south.

This was the final significant skirmish before Bill handed over command to Squadron Leader S.V. Brown in May. Having spent a year on operations in the north of Iraq, his final year was in the inhospitable south where he had led his squadron in a number of significant operations in the troubled southern desert of Iraq.

He sailed for home after being away for over two years. Shortly after his return, the *London Gazette* announced that he had been awarded the DFC, the citation recording:

> 'For continuous devotion to duty and gallantry when flying. This officer was in command of 30 Squadron in 1920 and of 84 Squadron in 1921. He has continually led his officers on bomb raids and on demonstrations, and as a leader and as a pilot he sets an excellent example to all serving under his command.'

During the time that Bill was in Iraq, Fred was involved in a different type of air policing. On completion of his time at Cambridge University, he left in September 1920 for Baldonnel Airfield in County Dublin to join the air staff of HQ 11 (Ireland) Wing. The wing was formed in May 1920 taking over the responsibility of 11 Group which had been in Ireland since August 1918.

The Irish War of Independence had begun in January 1919, a guerrilla war mounted by the Irish Republican Army (IRA) against the British Government and its forces in Ireland. The IRA's main target was the Royal Irish Constabulary (RIC) which was the British Government's eyes and ears in Ireland. Its members and barracks (especially the more isolated ones) were vulnerable, and they were a source of much-needed arms. The British responded to the escalating violence with increasing use of force. Reluctant to deploy the regular British Army into the country in greater numbers, they set up two paramilitary police units to aid the RIC.

Fred's arrival at Baldonnel coincided with a dramatic increase in violence and a difficult time for the RAF. Trenchard was fighting for the very survival of the new service; resources and finance were very limited and the large army garrisons in Ireland were being re-organised following the 1920 Restoration of Order in Ireland Act. This partitioned the island into two separate jurisdictions, Southern Ireland and Northern Ireland, both devolved regions of the United Kingdom.

With just thirty-six aircraft in Ireland, the RAF had a limited capability to provide support. 100 Squadron was equipped with the outstanding First World War Bristol Fighter, known throughout the RAF as the 'Brisfit', but the squadron suffered from a serious lack of spares so aircraft serviceability was poor. Trenchard resisted a suggestion to send more aircraft and dictated that greater efforts should

Bristol Fighters of 100 Squadron prepare to start up at Baldonnel.

be made to improve the serviceability problem. An independent flight in the north of the island, later to be reinforced by 2 Squadron, suffered with the same problems.

With the escalation of guerrilla activities by the IRA the limited capability of the RAF was stretched to provide a range of support for the army. Small detachments of aircraft were deployed to minor airfields at Fermoy in County Cork and Castlebar. In October 1920 there was an important debate about the wider use of aircraft in support of the army who wanted to have the aircraft available, armed with bombs and machine guns, for operations against guerrilla parties, but this met with firm resistance.

Fred was pitched straight into this very difficult political and military situation and, despite being on a staff appointment, he flew occasionally and carried out patrols. In this way he was able to gain valuable experience of the tasks in hand. He was airborne in a Bristol Fighter on 21 November 1920 when he flew a patrol over Croke Park in Dublin, an infamous day that is still remembered as 'Bloody Sunday'. In the early morning an IRA squad attempted to wipe out some British intelligence operatives in the capital. They shot nineteen people, killing fourteen and wounding five. The victims included British Army officers, police officers and civilians. This action resulted in widespread action across Ireland, particularly in the south and over the next six months the violence reached a peak.

Travel between military posts became virtually impossible. Roads were blocked with felled trees and ambushes were a constant danger. There was also an increasing frequency of raids on mail trains and the cutting of telephone and telegraph wires was a common occurrence. All these difficulties, and dangers, resulted in aircraft being used extensively to convey military correspondence and to ferry senior officers. With no authority to fire weapons from the air in support of the army, these were the RAF's main tasks together with the provision of an escort for military road convoys and scouting for military patrols engaged in policing and search operations.

Fred flew some of these tasks and on Christmas Eve 1920 he took Group Captain I.M. Bonham-Carter, the commander of 11 Wing, to Fermoy, the most remote of the airfields. On the return flight he encountered bad weather and commented 'clouds fifty feet over mountains'.

Early in 1921 Bonham-Carter had become increasingly concerned about the morale and efficiency of 100 Squadron and decided to act. The squadron had been brought up to full strength in February 1920 by absorbing the cadres of 117 and 141 Squadrons and this had caused some friction. Bonham-Carter wrote to Air Ministry:

'There is a matter I want your advice on; the officers of 100 Squadron are very "cliquey", the main clique being the remnants of 141 Home Defence Squadron whose former commander is now a flight commander with his following from that squadron. Most of them have, as it were, grown up together and cannot appreciate the old difference of "on parade" and "off parade", and the senior officers cannot bring themselves, or are not strong enough, to give "orders" to their subordinates who have been their friends and equals and yet retain their positions as such "off parade".

'I wanted to keep the squadron intact and get the officers to settle down and look upon the squadron as their home. In fact I had asked Newall [group captain, deputy director of personnel] not to post away officers who have commanded squadrons but are now flight commanders in order to try to attain a squadron feeling but I feel now, after giving it a trial and some thought, that it would be better to shift round some of those who have been in Ireland some time, not because they are inefficient but because they have got into a groove out of which it is hard to move them and they are inclined to drag others into that groove.

'I hope I have made myself clear and that you can advise.'

Undoubtedly, this was not a unique problem in the months following the great reduction in the number of RAF squadrons in the immediate postwar years and this letter resulted in Fred being appointed to command 100 Squadron on 19 February 1921.

In addition to the mail and passenger carrying tasks, squadron aircraft were used increasingly for reconnaissance and photography and they also became adept at message dropping to troops in the field. Patrols were flown in support of infantry and cavalry units and escort was provided for troop trains. A selection of entries from Fred's logbook gives an indication of the diverse nature of the work:

22 April	To 5 Div at Curragh with Bonham-Carter as passenger.
25 April	Recon for captured vehicle. Message dropped at Ennisberry.
7 May	Co-op with RIC Raid.
12 May	Squadron formation over Dublin.
21 May	Test of Holt Flares.
23 May	To 3 Cav HQ with staff officer.
25 May	Squadron formation Dublin. Customs House on fire.
2 June	Inspection of landing ground at Dundalk.
21 June	To Curragh. Could not land owing to sheep.
24 June	Recon for landing ground. To Dundalk with Bonham-Carter.
13 August	Patrol Dublin District.

This brief selection serves to indicate the variety of tasks and it is likely that the squadron pilots, who flew a great deal more than their CO, were engaged in many other activities.

Not all mail could be carried to airfields and 'mail drops' were a regular feature. Some had a watery grave and other bags were dropped occasionally by mistake to the Sinn Féin who had set up 'spoof' dropping zones near to those of the army. The entry for 25 April is interesting. On the 21st, Fred had attended a meeting and when he returned to his staff car, he found that it had disappeared and a short, hastily written note had been left:

'Car taken by order
IRA 4 ASU
Taken on Crumlin Road 1115 and everything connected with her
OC 4 Sec'

As the conflict escalated, IRA losses in men and material started to increase but their biggest single loss came in Dublin on 25 May 1921. Several hundred IRA men from the Dublin Brigade occupied and burned the Customs House (the centre of local government in Ireland) in Dublin city centre, an event that Fred witnessed from his aircraft flying above the city. Symbolically, this was intended to show that British rule in Ireland was untenable. However, from a military point of view, it was a catastrophe in which five IRA men were killed and over eighty were captured. This showed the IRA was not well enough equipped or trained to take on British forces in a conventional manner. However, it did not, as is sometimes claimed, cripple the IRA in Dublin. The Dublin Brigade carried out 107 attacks in the city in May and ninety-three in June, showing a fall off in activity, but not a dramatic one. However, by July 1921, most IRA units were chronically short of both weapons and ammunition.

Many military historians have concluded that the IRA fought a largely successful and lethal guerrilla war, which forced the British Government to conclude that the IRA could not be defeated militarily. The failure of the British efforts to put down the guerrillas was illustrated by the events of 'Black Whitsun' in May 1921. A general election for the parliament of Southern Ireland was held on 13 May and the Sinn Féin won virtually every seat but its elected members refused to take their seats. The southern parliament was dissolved, and Southern Ireland was to be ruled as a crown colony.

Over the next two days (14-15 May), the IRA killed fifteen policemen. These events marked the complete failure of the British Coalition Government's Irish policy – both the failure to enforce a settlement without negotiating with Sinn Féin and a failure to defeat the IRA.

On 24 June 1921, the British Coalition Government's Cabinet decided to propose talks with the leader of Sinn Féin. The Irish responded in agreement. De Valera and Lloyd George ultimately agreed to a truce that was intended to end the fighting and lay the ground for detailed negotiations. Its terms were signed on 9 July and came into effect two days later. Negotiations on a settlement, however, were delayed for some months as the British Government insisted that the IRA first decommission its weapons, but this demand was eventually dropped. It was agreed that British troops would remain confined to their barracks. The war of independence in Ireland ended with a truce on 11 July 1921. The conflict had reached a stalemate.

With the situation becoming less active, Fred headed home for a period of leave and on 18 October 1921 he married Margarita Beatrice White at Bexhill-on-Sea. Always known as Rita, her brother had

served as a pilot during the war and she had served with the RFC as a driver. Within a few days, the newly-married couple headed back for Baldonnel where they established their first home.

The peace talks led to the negotiation of the Anglo-Irish Treaty signed on 6 December 1921. The treaty allowed the six counties in the north to opt out of the Irish Free State which they did two days later.

Throughout these protracted political developments, 100 Squadron remained busy but there was a significant reduction in armed conflict. With the likelihood of the withdrawal of British forces, the GOC-in-C, Ireland, General Sir Neville Macready, inspected the squadron on 6 December when Fred led a flypast in his honour. After his visit the GOC commented:

'I was very struck with the turnout of the three flights of 100 Squadron in formation flying, the general

Fred and his bride Rita.

smartness of their appearance, and the fact that they were back in the hangars within an hour. In addition, without being in a position to criticise, it struck me that the performance was an extremely good one in view of the fact that a 30 mph wind was blowing with rain and heavy gusts.'

By the end of 1921 it was clear that 100 Squadron's days in Ireland were coming to an end and Fred and his men prepared to return to England. Early in January 1922, the last Lord Lieutenant of Ireland, The Viscount FitzAlan of Derwent, made a formal visit to the squadron when Fred again led a formation of Bristol Fighters in a salute. A few days earlier a letter had arrived from the Air Ministry directing 100 Squadron to prepare to evacuate Ireland and on 17 January 1922 the executive order to leave was received. Six wireless operators were detached from RAF Inland Area, only three had flown before, and the aircraft were prepared and stores packed.

A series of wireless tests was carried out on each aircraft and on 29 January 1922, Fred climbed into his Bristol Fighter, with Sergeant Williams in the rear cockpit, said goodbye to his wife, who was to leave a few days later, and took off at the head of his thirteen aircraft. They departed in formation for RAF Shotwick (later called Sealand). To aid navigation, and act as a safety boat, a destroyer was positioned in the Irish Sea at the mid-point on the aircraft's route and was in wireless contact with the formation. Twelve aircraft arrived at Shotwick after a two-hour flight, one having turned back with a wireless failure. Two days later the formation headed for their new home at RAF Spittlegate (later renamed Spitalgate) near Grantham where an advance party of 11 (Irish) Wing had been sent from Baldonnel to open a new wing headquarters.

Soon after arriving in Lincolnshire the situation in Ireland deteriorated towards civil war. The squadron, which had re-equipped with DH9As, also added a fourth flight, D Flight, comprising four Vickers Vimy heavy bombers. Within days, Fred received instructions to prepare one for possible service as a bomber in Ireland but the call for its services never came.

Towards the end of seven quiet months at Spittlegate, Fred's wife gave birth to a son, Frederick Beresford, on 14 September. After just six weeks enjoying the early days of fatherhood, Fred sailed from Tilbury Docks on the SS *Mulbera* for Iraq and arrived at the group HQ in Basra on 7 November to take up duties as an air staff officer. It was only a few months after Bill had left the area and so Fred was soon immersed in the same issues. His arrival also coincided with major developments in the conduct of military operations in Iraq.

Young Freddie with his grandmother a few months after his father left for Iraq.

Despite the agreements reached at the Cairo Conference in March 1921, it was not until 1 October 1922 that the RAF assumed responsibility for the defence and security of Iraq. The strength of the RAF had been built up to eight squadrons and these were supported by three armoured-car companies and two regiments of the locally-recruited Iraq Levies. There was also a build up of the service organisations to support the operational units and these included a large maintenance and supply depot, hospital and signals unit at the RAF's main base at Hinaidi. An air headquarters was established and the first AOC was Air Vice-Marshal Sir John Salmond. However, the implementation of the Cairo agreements meant that Salmond had the wider responsibilities of 'military commander' with overall command of British forces in Iraq. He was described as 'a born leader' and was greatly admired by officers of all ranks and by the airmen.

In the months leading up to the arrival of Salmond, and Fred, the situation in Iraq had worsened. With Turkey's growing ambitions in the Middle East, Turkish forces had grouped on the northern border to pose a major threat to the garrison at Mosul, which at one time, could only be supplied by air. Kurdish irregulars had also occupied a number of villages in the north where the troublesome Sheikh Mahmud was establishing himself. He would be a thorn in the side of the British authorities for a number of years and the RAF was engaged against him on so many occasions in the years that followed that he was dubbed 'Director of RAF Training'.

Whilst these operations in the north did not affect Fred and his colleagues in Basra, there was continued unrest in Southern Iraq and he was faced with similar issues that had occupied so much of brother Bill's time when he was in command of the resident 84 Squadron.

In July 1923 Fred moved to Hinaidi to join the AOC's air staff. He lost no time in visiting Mosul to assess the situation and flew to the town in a DH9A of 8 Squadron. Over the next few months Fred kept in practice flying with 8 and 30 Squadrons and on 20 October, he took Sir John Salmond flying in a DH9A to observe the bombing and shooting of the Snipes of 1 Squadron who were based at Hinaidi.

Another important initiative that stemmed from the Cairo Conference in March 1921 was the decision to establish an air route between Baghdad and Amman (later extended to Cairo). The objects of the route were set out as:

• A link in an aerial chain of Imperial communications between Europe and India and possibly further afield.
• A line of rapid reinforcement from Egypt or Palestine to Iraq, both for machines and personnel.
• A means of rapid communication for service purposes by means of a regular service air mail.
• A form of training in long-distance flying.

This perceptive and innovative idea had a far-reaching impact on the administration and control in Iraq and paved the way for civilian air routes that provided an essential link with Great Britain and the colonies east of Suez. The responsibility for administering, servicing and co-ordinating the use of the route fell to the air staff at HQ Iraq.

The route had been initiated in June 1921 and over the next two years the en-route facilities were improved significantly. The track was constructed by survey parties sent out from Cairo on the one side and Baghdad on the other, and, to make the track conspicuous from the air, the wheel markers of heavy tenders were used. Auxiliary markings in the form of ploughed furrows made the track more conspicuous. By April 1922, a series of landing grounds had been prepared along the track at average intervals of twenty miles. All these grounds were conspicuously marked and fuel and emergency supplies were provided. A very detailed 'Pilot's Handbook of the Cairo-Baghdad Route' was produced and carried by all pilots.

The handbook provided detailed maps, with distance markers, and chapters dealing with specialist

A fuel dump under construction on the mail route.

topics such as wireless procedures, actions in event of a forced landing, of deviating for bad weather, signals and other important issues. Crews were required to keep a detailed log of observations and experiences so that the handbook could be continually updated. In his preface of January 1923, Air Vice-Marshal Sir Edward Ellington, the AOC Middle East, wrote:

'In consequence of the great length of the track, the severity of the climatic conditions, the lack of water, the enormous extent and uniform appearance of the desert and the uncertainty of the weather in this area, a very detailed organisation has been found necessary to ensure the safety of machines and pilots undertaking the desert crossing. It is only by strict adherence to set procedures that difficulties can be overcome and the security of pilots assured.

'This book has been compiled, therefore, with the object of assisting pilots in every way, without harassing them with endless special orders. Every effort has been made to foresee the more probable misadventures which may arise, but it is realised that it is not possible, or even desirable, to try to provide against every possible contingency.

'In cases where such contingencies are encountered, pilots may rest assured that if they act in accordance with the spirit of these instructions, and if they display initiative and resolution, then their action will always be supported.

'The success of the route rests more in the hands of the captains of aircraft than in the hands of those who are responsible for its inauguration and maintenance.'

Force landings were very common on the mail route. Overheating or leaking engines required a quick dive into one of the string of landing grounds marked out along the route, and a quick brew-up was prepared whilst the fitter fixed the fault. If that was achieved before late-afternoon, the crew would set off again; if not, it meant camping out around a cheerful camp-fire and a departure at first light.

Fred decided he should be familiar with the route and on 1 November he set off as the co-pilot of a 45 Squadron Vickers Vernon and headed for Cairo. His logbook records a 'force landing' on his trip to Cairo but gave no details. No doubt the flight was a useful practical exercise that helped to give Fred a clearer insight into the problems that were frequently encountered by the crews flying the route.

On the return flight, another force landing had to be carried out, this time the Vernon landed at Fallujah, just thirty miles before reaching Hinaidi. Again, Fred gave no details of the trouble.

Two weeks after his return from Cairo, Fred was appointed to command 8 Squadron based at Hinaidi and flying the ubiquitous Ninak. At the time he assumed command, the squadron was mainly engaged in carrying out communications flights, which included transporting senior officers to the numerous airfields and landing grounds. One of Fred's first flights was to visit one of the landing grounds on the mail route where an aircraft had made a force landing. In the rear cockpit was the First World War fighter ace, Flying Officer Ira Jones DSO, MC, DFC & Bar, MM, who was the wireless officer at Hinaidi. He had little opportunity to fly as a pilot but amassed over 200 hours as a wireless operator/air gunner.

Jones captured the atmosphere of RAF life and flying in Iraq when he wrote:

'I shall always remember my feelings when I arrived in Iraq for the spirit of comradeship exuded in this strange land, just as it did in the good old war days.

'There were no wives in the country and there was a distinct active service and offensive spirit atmosphere prevailing wherever I went. It was a wonderful tonic after the spirit which I had left in England, where jealousy was beginning to paralyse comradeship due to a system of promotion which had come into operation since the peace.

'The cream of air force fighting-men were here at the same time. What names come to memory! Kinkead, 'Mary' Coningham, …Fred Sowrey…What a fighting "Circus" these officers would have formed!'

The guy with the gun is "Taffy" Jones

To Bill from your Freddy 19

Fred, in his personal DH9A, with Ira Jones in the gunner's position.

Jones listed no less than forty-eight names of fighter 'aces' and others, many of whom rose to the highest ranks. He also gave special mention to the staff officers, an equally distinguished group who worked 'in their various branches under the popular Sir John Salmond'.

Flying in a single-engine aircraft was always hazardous. Due to the nature of the operations, flown at low level, and often in the face of ground fire, it was extremely dangerous to make force landings in hostile territory. To assist the crews, DH9As carried spare wheels, bedding, emergency rations and a water supply.

On 6 April 1924, Sir John Salmond left Iraq having established that air power could exercise air control effectively. On his departure he left in a Vernon and was escorted along the route through the Middle East by aircraft of the various squadrons. Five aircraft of 8 Squadron, led by Fred, flew to Dair-es-Zor, a French air force outpost close to the largest city in eastern Syria, on 7 April to position ready to escort Salmond's aircraft the following day to Aleppo in the north west of Syria and some seventy-five miles from the Mediterranean. He recorded in his logbook, 'weather bad from Dair to Aleppo'. Over Aleppo, messages were exchanged between the wireless aircraft and the W/T station at Baghdad.

Having fulfilled their task the five aircraft returned to Hinaidi two days later, the non-stop flight of 520 miles taking four hours and twenty minutes.

During the spring of 1924 Sheikh Mahmud, after declaring himself King of Kurdistan, used a clash between British-led Assyrian Levies and Moslems in Kirkuk to declare a *Jihad* (Holy War) against the British. He gathered a large force but failed to respond to an ultimatum air dropped by the RAF indicating that Sulaimaniyah would be bombed should he fail to comply. Forty-two aircraft from 6, 8, 30, 45, 55 and 70 Squadrons gathered at Kingerban and Kirkuk on 26 May prior to commencement of operations the following day.

Fred and his squadron flew into Kirkuk and the following day the RAF aircraft dropped twenty-

In the clouds above Baghdad! June 1924

Yours ever Freddy

Fred sent this photograph to brother Bill. (Note the spare wheel under the fuselage.)

eight tons of bombs on the town over the next two days. The population had been forewarned and there were no civilian casualties, but extensive damage was caused. Fred and his 8 Squadron crews returned for a second attack on the 28th and during the two days, the squadron dropped 13,232 lbs of bombs and almost 5,000 of the 6½ oz 'baby incendiary bombs'. Sheikh Mahmud fled to nearby caves returning on 1 June. Sulaimaniyah was reoccupied by Iraqi troops, supported by RAF armoured cars and aircraft, on 19 July. This effectively marked the end of the *Jihad*.

During the summer of 1924 an inter-squadron bombing competition was held for the Iraq-based squadrons. This event was sparked by the appointment of a new squadron commander of 45 Squadron, Squadron Leader Arthur Harris (later the wartime commander-in-chief of Bomber Command). Flying the Vickers Vernon, his squadron was tasked in the transport role but Harris believed it could carry a useful bomb load and he set out to prove his point. When he was ready, he suggested to Air HQ that his squadron should compete against the DH9A and Bristol Fighter squadrons.

Practice started early in June and Fred was flying most days. The DH9As used a bomb sight on the side

Twenty-five DH9As in position at Kirkuk for operations on 27 May 1924 (8 Squadron records).

The later stages of an 8 Squadron officers' mess dinner in the summer of 1924.

of the forward fuselage with the pilot dropping the bombs. The competition was flown at Hinaidi on 16 June and the DH9A squadrons were well beaten by the two Vernon squadrons. This prompted Fred to abandon the front-seat method and fit the sight in the floor of the rear cockpit. He decided to take on the role of bomb aimer himself. Perhaps he had heard that Harris of 45 Squadron had elected to be the bomb aimer with one of his experienced pilots flying the aircraft.

On 20 June, Fred took off with Flying Officer Nevill Vintcent as his pilot. Vintcent had recently distinguished himself and been awarded the DFC, the first ex-Cranwell cadet to receive the award. Over the next two weeks they flew fifteen practice sorties before a squadron competition on 9 July when the squadron's average error from the centre of the target improved by sixty-three yards. As a result of this significant improvement, the squadron adopted the 'back-seat method' as standard practice and a programme to train the air gunners as bomb aimers commenced.

In July 1924, four Nieuport Nighthawks were sent to Iraq for service trials under tropical conditions. Two were attached to 8 Squadron and Fred appears to have undertaken most of the test flights.

The Nighthawk was the RAF's first fighter powered by a stationary radial engine, instead of the wartime rotary, and a number of its features appeared in later Gloster-designed fighters. Over a four-week period in August and September, Fred flew twenty-three sorties testing the Nighthawk including climbs to height, stopping and restarting the engine in flight, dive tests and other flights to evaluate the engine and aircraft performance. In the event, the aircraft did not enter RAF service.

During his time in Iraq, Fred developed a keen interest in the ancient civilization of the area and he also took up polo and became very proficient. He played as the No. 2 in the 8 Squadron team and in the annual Baghdad American Tournament, with ten teams entering the September 1924 matches, the squadron team were victorious.

A few days later, Secretary of State for Air Lord Thompson, took advantage of the coolest part of

The victorious 8 Squadron polo team of Cook, Fred, Jones-Williams and Vintcent.

the year to visit RAF units in Iraq. After meetings and visits in Baghdad he toured units in the north of the country. 8 Squadron was tasked to transport Lord Thompson and Fred prepared five aircraft for the tour. The formation was led by the flight commander, Flight Lieutenant J. Cottle, who carried the AOC, Air Vice-Marshal J. Higgins, with the S of S travelling in Fred's aircraft. The other three aircraft carried staff officers with the irrepressible Ira Jones flying in the fifth aircraft to act as the wireless operator.

The formation left Hinaidi on 27 September at 6.30 am and headed for Mosul. The following day the party left for Kirkuk after inspecting the northern frontier and making brief visits to Zakho and Erbil. On the 29th they returned to Hinaidi after stopping en-route at Sulaimaniyah.

The return flight to Hinaidi in his personal aircraft (E9939) turned out to be Fred's final flight as the OC 8 Squadron and in October he handed over command and headed for England on the overland route through Cairo after spending two years in Iraq.

Fred's return to England in November marked the end of the Sowrey family's activities in Iraq until Bill returned in the mid 1930s. The two brothers had served in the troublesome region for some five years when the policy of air control and its effectiveness was amply demonstrated by the squadrons of the RAF. Unfortunately, the operations were not widely reported at the time because Iraq was difficult to reach and uncomfortable for press correspondents.

With Great Britain having such extensive commitments around the world, it was inevitable that those who served in the RAF would spend a considerable amount of time overseas and in April 1927 Bill headed for China.

Chapter Ten

CHINA

For many years small parts of China, particularly some of the ports and commercial areas, had been occupied by foreign powers but the vast republic had been troubled by internal fighting and revolution for decades. In January 1927 Chinese communist revolutionaries had sacked Hankow, 400 miles from Shanghai, and had started to advance towards the city. A Shanghai Defence Force (SDF) had been hurriedly dispatched to China, and by April, the situation around the international settlement at Shanghai had become very tense with local war lords fighting amongst each other and harassing the 'white devils' in many ways. The British Government decided to act with a show of strength and build up the defence force. On 8 April 1927, Bill was tasked to prepare his 2 Squadron to be ready to move to China with a date of departure set for the 20th.

The object of the SDF was to protect British lives and property in Shanghai against Chinese forces and to prevent their entry into the settlement. The broad principle governing the disposition of troops was that they should be confined to the settlement unless the tactical situation rendered their movement outside imperative. It was also the policy that a completely neutral attitude was to be adopted towards the contending Chinese forces.

During March, the aircraft carrier *Argus* had sailed into Chinese waters and, in anticipation that aircraft would be deployed ashore, a survey had been carried out to identify a suitable aerodrome near Shanghai. The survey party of two flight lieutenants reported on 31 March:

'We have the honour to submit our report on the suitability of the Shanghai Race Course for an aerodrome.

'Subject to the alterations set out below, the ground is considered to be suitable for flying under the conditions prevailing. There is sufficient space for landing and take-off for practically every direction of wind. The surface generally is good and, from the nature of the soil, appears to dry off quickly.

The surrounding buildings are far enough back to be cleared easily by machines.

It is considered that the following alterations should be made before flying takes place:

    a.   The bank up from the road (of about one foot) on the west side of the recreation ground should be graded off.

    b.   The following obstructions should be removed:

1. Two steeple chase jumps on west side
2. One golf bunker in S.W. corner
3. Fence round recreation ground on three sides
4. Rugby posts and track distance posts
5. Chinese graves and garden

c. 'The Chinese graves at south should be marked with whitewash, or with white flags, if this is not possible.

d. 'The live electric wires round the ground should be buried, or, if this is not practicable, they should be distinctly marked with flags.

'Grass mat sheds could be quickly erected for hangars, and could be placed in a position that would not interfere with flying.

'It is also thought that the Race Club could provide space in which to billet the personnel.'

The report failed to mention the potential difficulties of operating from the racecourse. The only safe landing run was a mere 400 yards and parallel to the racetrack grandstand. The landing approach was over the crowded city and between two large ten-storey buildings. However, on the strength of this report, it was decided that the racecourse would be used as an aerodrome and, predictably, this decision would cause problems to both Bill and his pilots and also to the local community.

Headquarters' staff at the Shanghai Defence Force wrote on 7 April to the chairman of the Shanghai Municipal Recreation Ground Committee that it would be necessary to use the recreation ground as a landing ground for aeroplanes and the necessary preparations would be put in hand immediately. A day later, the first of five bamboo and mat hangars arrived.

Once the decision had been announced, objections by the local European population

Bill (left) hosts a local army officer and his daughter on the racecourse airfield.

started to arrive. These protests were always presented politely but they indicate a lack of awareness, or *laissez faire* attitude to the deteriorating situation and a determination that their long-established routine and social activities would carry on uninterrupted. The chairman of the Shanghai Race Club wrote on the 14th expressing concern that training would be interrupted and he was informed by the general staff of the SDF that no flying would take place until after 8 am on each day.

Three days later a notice was posted:

'Public Recreation Ground
'To facilitate flying exercises and in the public interest, the PRG within the mud riding track will be closed on weekdays between the hours of 8 am and 12 noon until further notice.
'Golfers etc. making use of the ground before 8 am are requested to be clear of the RG by the hour.
'The police have instructions to carry out the above arrangements.

'BY ORDER

A notification is being sent to the press for publication.'

In the meantime, there was feverish activity at Manston with all squadron personnel involved in packing. The aircraft were flown to Ascot where they were crated and four Crossley Tenders and three trailers arrived to transport the stores to Birkenhead where the flight stores were loaded on to the SS *Sarpedon* and the ammunition on the SS *City of Poona*. Finally, during the early hours of 20 April, the men marched to Birchington, Kent to board a train for Southampton. They boarded the SS *Neuralia* after a final inspection of the eighteen officers and 197 men by Air Vice-Marshal Longcroft, the AOC Inland Area. Also on board the *Neuralia* were men of 38 Company RASC and other army reinforcements for the SDF. Sailing via Malta, Port Said, Colombo and Singapore, the ship finally arrived at Hong Kong on 21 May after almost a month at sea.

As the men of 2 Squadron sailed eastwards, work continued in Shanghai to prepare the racecourse. The Shanghai Waterworks Fitting Company dug a trench in order to install a fire main. Unfortunately, one of the recently-erected larger bamboo hangars collapsed when one of the struts fell into the trench. At this point, the Shanghai Fire Brigade offered to put in a fire engine permanently on the racecourse if the SDF would build a garage for it. This was approved.

More requests were also received from the various sporting authorities that used the public recreation ground. The horse-racing fraternity were particularly concerned and on 4 May they wrote once again to seek some dispensations, this time to Group Captain E.D.M. Robertson DFC, the RAF commander at the Defence Force HQ:

> 'I am directed by the stewards to ask if it can be arranged that no flying be done during Saturday next, the 7th inst. This day is the fourth day of the Spring Meeting and the Grand National Steeplechase will be run in the afternoon. It is proposed to, immediately after you finish flying on Friday 6th inst., replace the three jumps, remove a section of the fence by the east entrance and put the steeplechase course in proper order. Jumps will be removed and fence replaced on Saturday night, so that the ground will be available for taking off and landing for Sunday, 8th inst. should you wish to send up planes.
>
> 'The stewards will appreciate an early reply.'

At the time, there was a limited amount of flying by the Fairey IIID aircraft of 441 Flight of the Fleet Air Arm disembarked from the aircraft carrier *Hermes*. This request for the major annual event was made just three days before the big day!

After arriving in Hong Kong, Bill's men spent the next four days transferring stores to the P & O steamship *Karmala*, which sailed for Shanghai on the 26th. Four days later, the squadron finally arrived at Shanghai. The men disembarked and the following day the first four of the crated Bristol Fighters were unloaded and taken to the racecourse where the men of B Flight started to erect them.

This flurry of activity generated another letter, this time from the secretary of the Shanghai Football Association:

> 'Sir,
>
> 'In view of the great shortage of playing fields in Shanghai, I am directed by my committee respectfully to approach you with a view to ascertaining whether something can be done before the beginning of the next football season in regard to making the Shanghai Football Club ground available for association football. This is the ground which is partly occupied by the aeroplane hangars.
>
> 'My committee realises fully the fact that the hangars were undoubtedly placed in their present position only after the most careful consideration; and appreciates the necessity of military exigencies taking precedence over outdoor sports. It is with diffidence, therefore, that the suggestion is made that it might possibly be convenient to re-arrange the situation of two of the four hangars in such a manner as to permit the marking out of a full-sized playing field.
>
> 'In this connection, my committee, while admitting ignorance of the technical reasons that

necessitated the erection of the hangars in their present position, consider that possibly the removal of two of them a short distance eastward might not present insuperable difficulties.'

The letter went on to explain how the football season would suffer and also anticipated a greater use
for the new season by the 'new military arrivals'. It went on to offer to pay for any costs that might be
incurred should the request be agreed. There is no evidence that it was!

This fascinating, and gentlemanly letter once again clearly illustrates that the local British community
had not fully appreciated the significance of the arrival of a squadron of aircraft from Britain.

An officers' mess was established at the race club and the men were billeted in a shop. Local labour
was employed for the cleaning requirements and a working routine was established, which made some
allowances for the numerous requests for continued use of some parts of the recreation ground.

By 7 June the first four Bristol Fighters had been re-erected and were ready for air testing. Bill took
off in J7665 and the flight commander, Flying Officer Moreton, tested the other three. From the
outset, Bill was very unhappy about the suitability of the racecourse as an airfield. On the 13th he
wrote to the RAF HQ to express his concerns:

> 'I have to report on the extreme unsuitability of above aerodrome for Bristol Fighter aero-
> planes except in cases of urgency for operations.
>   'This unit has at present one flight of four aeroplanes erected and serviceable, but of the
> personnel I do not consider that more than four of the total strength of pilots are capable
> of using this aerodrome within any degree of safety. The aerodrome can only be used in
> two directions of wind, i.e. either N. or S. and even in the most favourable circumstances
> with a most skilful pilot I do not consider a Bristol Fighter could be taken off with more
> than half of its normal complement of bombs i.e. four 20 lb Cooper. For training purposes
> this aerodrome is out of the question.
>   'The above report is rendered after a personal test.'

Clearly, the receipt of such a damning letter from a pilot of Bill's standing and experience had to be
considered very carefully. The headquarters' staff accepted Bill's views and an alternative landing ground
was identified on land reclaimed from a river and now owned by the Shanghai Soap Company. However, Bill's letter had arrived at the headquarters whilst the RAF air staff officer, Wing Commander
Barratt, was away at Tienstan looking for a landing ground to support forces in that area. On his return,
Barratt did not agree with Bill's assessment and wrote;

> 'I did not concur with this report and after satisfying myself after personal tests and from
> tests by Flt Lt Hollinghurst (staff officer) I informed the OC that, with the exception of
> those officers who had come out from England in January 1927, as observers for army co-
> op to the FAA and consequently had done no flying for six months, I considered that the
> aerodrome was fit to use and that all officers had to fly and keep themselves in practice.'

It must be unusual for a staff officer, not in flying practice, to overrule such an experienced squadron
commander so Barratt's motive is unclear. Perhaps he felt that Bill was trying to take advantage of his
absence. However, Barratt did accept that an alternative should be considered and recommended that
the squadron HQ and two flights should be dispatched to Tienstan. The GOC decided against this
recommendation so Barratt re-visited the possibility of using the reclaimed land but, since it was outside
the commission, it too was rejected.

On 17 June the squadron flew its first sortie when vertical photographs were taken of the Shanghai
detachment. There followed a number of similar photographic sorties to provide more accurate mapping
and to monitor Nationalist Chinese activities. The local Chinese administrations made loud protests regarding territorial rights but there were no incidents until 15 August when an aircraft made a force

landing after an engine failure and landed near a Nationalist camp. The aircraft was dismantled and after a serious of threats and protests, the crew and the engine and instruments were returned. After much haggling, and the threat of a bombing raid, the Nationalists finally returned the wings of the aircraft.

Just five weeks after the establishment of the Shanghai detachment, the Air Ministry announced that the Cabinet had decided to withdraw 2 Squadron from China. The signal indicated that preparations for withdrawal were to be made and all outstanding demands for air photographs were to be completed as soon as possible. There was some concern over this sudden decision and, after the senior RAF commanders had conferred, Wing Commander Barratt signalled the Air Ministry expressing concern about the situation in North China and offering the view that 'the squadron would be invaluable in controlling routes and places inaccessible owing to terrain and distances to ground forces'. This, of course, is very much in line with the doctrine of air control and no doubt Bill's experiences in Iraq were voiced at the various meetings. However, despite Barratt's recommendation that the withdrawal should be held in abeyance, the Air Ministry's view held.

By the end of August the packing of stores and equipment had commenced and some men were transferred to 440 Flight which was to remain in the area. The squadron thought it appropriate to alert the headquarters staff to some of its requirements for storage space and forwarded a letter which included:

> 'There will be approximately two-and-a-half shipping tons of spirits and tobacco (mess stores) included in the estimate of twenty tons of stores.'

Since there were only eighteen officers on the strength of the squadron, it is surprising that there is no record of the reaction of the staff to this extravagant need. Perhaps there was and it was unprintable!

On 6 September a parade was held at the racecourse prior to embarkation. Bill and seven officers, together with 122 men, embarked on SS *Novara*. The officers travelled in first-class cabins and Bill was appointed OC Troops. The bulk of the officers returned on the SS *Devanha*, which sailed a week later. After six weeks at sea the two parties returned to Manston. Judging by the report submitted after their return, the men on *Devanha* appear to have had some difficulties:

> 'Ran out of beer and cigarettes. The "Beer in Casks" placed on board at Shanghai being found to be quite unfit for human consumption. Shortage of cigarettes was due to the abnormal quantity smoked, 200,000 being consumed between Shanghai and London.'

Soon after arriving home, Bill was invited to meet Trenchard to give him a first-hand account of the RAF's latest demonstration of air control.

A few days before Bill arrived back in England, John had set sail for Egypt where he was to take up the chief technical staff appointment at HQ Middle East, which was lodged in the Villa Victoria in Cairo. The command had control of Egyptian Group and the Aden Flight and, for supply and equipment purposes only, HQ RAF Palestine and Trans-Jordan based in Amman.

Egypt, owing to its central position, its comparative proximity to Britain, its equitable climate and its situation in the highways of the world's commerce, was regarded as the natural keystone in the RAF's overseas organisation. It was the most suitable location for the headquarters of the RAF throughout the Near and Middle East, was an excellent training ground and, of growing importance, a vital link and junction of the Imperial Air Route.

On John's arrival at HQ Middle East on 14 October 1927, there were two bomber squadrons, an army co-operations squadron and a transport squadron. There was also a bomber squadron based at Khartoum in the Sudan. The RAF's only flying training school based abroad, 4 FTS, was at Abu Sueir near Port Said and there was a large depot at Aboukir near Alexandria, which also accommodated a large maintenance unit. In Jordan, 14 Squadron flew the DH9A and there was an armoured car unit and a large wireless transmitting station. This very large parish, with its diverse equipment and technical support requirements, provided John and his small staff with a heavy work load over the next eighteen months.

Chapter Eleven

HOME SERVICE

Following Trenchard's visionary paper 'Permanent Organisation of the Royal Air Force', the RAF Cadet College had been established in 1920 to be the main channel of entry for permanently-commissioned officers. On leaving the college after a two-year course it was intended that the newly-commissioned officer would:

> 'Have a general although somewhat elementary knowledge of the navy, army and air force – will be a first-class pilot of the Avro – will have an elementary knowledge of the work carried out from flying machines and will have a solid grounding in the duties of the mechanics of an aeroplane squadron.'

The first course of fifty-two cadets entered the college in February 1920. The syllabus for the first year was a mix of academic studies, military history, practical work in the metal and wood workshops and instruction on aeronautical subjects. The second year was geared much more towards flying training and aeronautical engineering. Needless to say drill and sport played a very important role in the daily life of the cadets.

Cadets were organised in squadrons and in August 1922, John arrived to take command of B Squadron of the Cadet Wing. Arriving three weeks later to join the September 1922 entry were two cadets who would achieve great fame, Richard 'Batchy' Atcherley, one of the RAF's most charismatic officers who retired as an air marshal, and Dick Waghorn. Both gained international fame for their ac-

tivities with the winning Schneider Trophy team and with the RAF High Speed Flight in 1929.

John's time at Cranwell was short and in the following January 1923 he left for Upavon and the Central Flying School (CFS) where he was appointed as the assistant commandant, deputy to

2 Course Central Flying School. John seated third from right in front row (CFS records).

the hugely popular commandant Group Captain F.V. Holt. CFS, which had been formed in 1912, making it the oldest military flying school in the world, was the sole training centre for RAF flying instructors and attracted the service's best pilots. Using the revolutionary techniques devised by Robert Smith-Barry, CFS attracted pilots from the world's air forces. It also pioneered blind flying.

In the early 1920s the mainstay of the CFS fleet was the rotary-engined Avro 504K aircraft. Advanced flying was done on the Sopwith Snipe and the Bristol Fighter.

At the end of October 1922, Bill had joined the instructing staff at 1 Flying Training School (FTS) based at Netheravon and in the following April he joined 10 Flying Instructor's Course at CFS where he spent the next four months seeing plenty of his brother John who, as assistant commandant, was responsible for the day-to-day running of the courses. At the end of the course, Bill was awarded the coveted, and rarely awarded, 'A' category identifying him as one of the finest instructors. His course report concluded: 'exceptionally good instructor and excellent officer'.

Bill returned to 1 FTS where he spent the next three years as one of two squadron commanders before he was appointed as the chief flying instructor (CFI). In August 1924 he was joined by Gilbert Insall who had been awarded the Victoria Cross in November 1915 in France.

About this time, Fred took up an appointment in the training arena. After returning from Iraq in October 1924, he spent a year at 1 School of Technical Training, the home of the RAF's Apprentice School, at Halton near Wendover. The apprentice scheme was one of Trenchard's three crucial pillars for the training of personnel for the peacetime RAF – the others were the RAF College at Cranwell and the RAF Staff College – and the first entry commenced training at Halton in February 1922.

Situated on the old Roman road, the Icknield Way, the large estate in the lee of the Chiltern Hills was acquired by Lord Rothschild in 1879. The parklands had first been used by the military in 1913 and it served as a training camp throughout the First World War. After the death of Lord Rothschild in 1918, the estate was bought by the government on Trenchard's recommendation and soon became the home of the RAF's Apprentice School and a major hospital.

Boys aged fifteen and sixteen attended Halton where they spent three years learning an aircraft engineering trade before beginning main service in the regular RAF. Throughout the long history of the RAF apprentice scheme, the schools (others were located at Cranwell, Flowerdown and Ruislip) provided the core of specialist ground tradesmen and, for decades, these ex-apprentices formed the bedrock on which the RAF functioned. Over twenty per cent were commissioned, with 120 attaining air rank and several serving on the Air Force Board. Over 800 decorations were awarded to ex-Halton aircrew for gallantry.

In 1927, the great aviation pioneer and industrialist Sir Alan Cobham wrote:

'To my mind the future of this great service, the Royal Air Force, depends largely on Halton, for the boy at Halton today is the fellow who will man the RAF tomorrow. It is to-morrow we must prepare for, and so the success of Halton as the birthplace of the RAF mind and spirit is of the most vital importance.'

Fred spent a year at Halton

Halton apprentices on parade during Fred's period as a squadron commander (Halton Aircraft Apprentice's Association).

in command of the boy's squadron and he and his family lived in Canal Bank Cottage, one of the Rothschild village homes that had been converted to be an officer's married quarter. In his spare time, he was able to indulge in his love of polo. He created an indoor simulator for training. In the centre of a hut he placed a wooden horse and around it he had a wire-netting arrangement shaped in such a way that once the ball had been struck by the player on the horse, it would be gathered by the netting and roll back to the rider.

At the end of January 1926 Fred left Halton for Northolt to join 41 (F) Squadron, irreverently called 'The Spit and Polish Squadron', and six weeks later he assumed command there.

Fred wasted no time becoming familiar with the Siskin and during his two-and-a-half years in command he amassed almost 400 hours with few sorties exceeding one hour. There were a number of airfields situated close to London, including Northolt, and they attracted many dignitaries. In October, the Dominion prime ministers made a visit to Croydon and Fred and his pilots flew down to give a demonstration of formation flying and aerobatics. Their efforts attracted a letter of thanks from the CAS:

> 'Dear Sowrey
>
> 'I send you this note, which I meant to have sent three or four days ago, congratulating you and your pilots on the wonderful show they put up at the Croydon Display. I would have done so before but I have not had time.
>
> 'I would like you to let your people know what a good show it was, and the maintenance of the machines by your men is really splendid. Keep it going!
>
> Yours Sincerely
> H Trenchard'

Aerobatics and formation flying featured heavily in fighter squadrons at the time and 41 Squadron was no exception. Most squadrons participated in the annual RAF Air Display at Hendon, usually held early in July, and a great deal of flying time was devoted to practicing for the most important event in the RAF's calendar. The importance to the RAF of the Hendon Display was recognised at every level. It was realised that this was the service's showpiece and that it must portray a blend of showmanship, colour, spectacle and high professionalism. For the 1926 event, Fred led a formation of nine of his squadron aircraft in an event which proved to be the most popular of the day. A reporter wrote:

> 'At 2.30 the first of the afternoon's events started, and this was, perhaps, also the event of the day. It was an exhibition of group evolutions by two wings of three fighter squadrons of nine machines – fifty-four in all…41 Squadron based at Northolt was led by Squadron Leader F. Sowrey.'

A feature of a fighter squadron's annual training programme was a visit during the summer to one of three armament practice camps (APC) located on the east coast. The 'season' was eight months long and a squadron spent two weeks detached to one of the sites. An experienced, senior pilot was appointed to command the camp and he had a small permanent staff. The squadrons attending the camp provided one or two personnel for the minor duties.

In September, 41 Squadron headed for Sutton Bridge near Holbeach, which had opened earlier in the year for use by fighter squadrons for bombing and gunnery training. Squadrons lived under canvas and flew daily practices on the nearby Wash weapon ranges. Even in summer, life was spartan at Sutton Bridge, tucked away in the backwaters of the Fen country with few off-duty outlets.

The Siskin IIIA was fitted with two Vickers .303 in. air-cooled guns mounted forward and either side of the cockpit and with 600 rounds per gun. Four 20-lb bombs could be carried under the lower wing. Targets on the coastal strip and others moored just off the coast were used and accurate scoring of the fall of shot was available from quadrant huts. The whole training period was devoted to weapon delivery culminating in a competition amongst all the pilots.

The 1926 armament camp appears to have been something of an ad hoc affair since Fred spent much of his time flying between Northolt and Sutton Bridge in addition to flying weapons sorties.

In January 1927, Fred hosted a visit to 41 Squadron by Prime Minister Stanley Baldwin, who was accompanied by Trenchard and Sir John Salmond. According to the station report they 'witnessed some excellent formation flying'.

In March the squadron was re-equipped with the more powerful Mk IIIA, which was the first all-metal aircraft (fabric covered) to enter RAF service. Powered by a 450-hp Jaguar IV engine, over 450 of this variant were produced and equipped 11 fighter squadrons. For the 1927 Air Display, Fred devised a new routine and for two months leading up to the event he put his nine pilots through a rigorous training programme. The event was called 'Air Manoeuvres to Music' and, in addition to providing a new spectacle, was designed to demonstrate the efficiency of radio telephony for communication between the ground and air. During 1927, a regular feature of flying was wireless and radio telephony (R/T) tests.

Fred shows young Freddie over a 41 Squadron Siskin at Northolt, 1927.

For the event on 2 July, Fred acted as the 'conductor' and flew alone in a position where he could correct any irregularities in the station keeping of the nine Siskins. All the pilots were in R/T communication with ground control and with their airborne CO, who the *Flight* magazine reporter called 'Dancing Master Sowrey'. Music to the aircraft was transmitted by means of a microphone placed on the bandstand and relayed to each aircraft by an R/T transmitter. The music from the band and Fred's orders were broadcast to the spectators by means of Marconiphone loudspeakers.

The official programme for the Air Display described the procedure:

'The squadron will taxi out to a position ready for take off into wind. The band will, at a given signal, strike up with the tune "I'm an Airman", which will be the signal to the squadron commander to take off.

The choruses of several well-known tunes will be played by the band; immediately the tune changes, so will the formation change to conform as nearly as possible to the ideas expressed by the music.

Finally, the squadron will fly past to the music of the "Royal Air Force March".'

Seven tunes were played and the novel idea, superbly executed, was a great hit with the spectators, which included members of the royal family. Three of the pilots went on to have distinguished careers as air marshals (C.A. Bouchier, T.N. McEvoy and C.B.S. Spackman) and another (C.S. Staniland) became the chief test pilot for the Fairey Aviation Company. The reporter of *Flight* magazine wrote:

'A new and highly original event, "Air Movements to Music", was carried out by 41 (Fighter) Squadron and one that was much appreciated by all present.'

Two weeks after the Hendon Display, Fred took his squadron to Castle Bromwich to position for a similar display over Birmingham.

The summer months of 1927 were busy ones for the RAF. A five-day major exercise commenced on 25 July with the aim of testing the efficiency of the plans for defending London with the combined use of ground observers, anti-aircraft guns, searchlights and fighter squadrons. It was the first time that operations on such a scale had been carried out in such detail.

The 'enemy' was four day- and four night-bomber squadrons, two of the latter commanded by Peter Portal, the wartime CAS, and Arthur Harris recently returned from Iraq. Defending London were twelve fighter squadrons including 41 Squadron operating from Northolt.

Success for the defending force depended on the efficient co-operation of all the units and a good reporting system. Observers and

A Siskin IIIA of 41 Squadron at Northolt (RAF Northolt records).

special constables were positioned on the coast to sight the incoming bomber forces and report their position and strength. Next was the belt of anti-aircraft batteries manned by volunteers of the Territorial Force and sited nearer to London were the searchlights working in conjunction with the fighters. With the bombers having a performance similar to the fighters, it was essential for accurate and speedy reporting if the bombers were to be intercepted before they had travelled the relatively short distance from the coast to London.

The difficulties were soon apparent. On the first morning, there was a lot of cloud making visual observation difficult, so many bombers got through the defences. Fred and his pilots were launched to intercept a force of Horsley bombers that had crossed the coast near Havant. The cloud cover defeated them and they failed to intercept. This was to set a pattern for the rest of the day and, of the eight bombing raids, only two were intercepted and one of these was the result of a fortunate sighting.

Over the course of the exercise, Fred flew seven sorties when 41 Squadron enjoyed the same mixed results as all the other fighter squadrons. In the post-exercise analysis it was recognised that there had been some success but, inevitably, there were many lessons. The principle of the reporting system and the communications was satisfactory but relied on the observers being able to see the approaching enemy.

The aeronautical correspondent of *The Times* concluded that more single-seat fighters were needed with a higher speed combined with a rapid rate of climb. He went on to make the interesting observation:

'Between these zones [around London] and the coast there is an area for which a special type of intercepting fighter might well be developed with a very rapid rate of climb to take the first bite, as it were, at an enemy formation long before it could reach the heavily-armed and highly-organised zones. So far there are only about three squadrons designated more or less experimentally for this duty, but in any complete scheme no enemy aircraft could be allowed to approach the main protective zones without previous interference.'

The next APC for Fred and his squadron was in May 1928. Judging by the entries in Fred's logbook the camp appears to have been on a more organised basis. Perhaps this was the influence of his brother Bill who had arrived to command Sutton Bridge for the 1928 season in early April. Fred recorded a sortie 'firing on range' on each day throughout the two-week detachment.

When Bill arrived, he had a staff of four officers and fifty-two airmen. Both aircraft and airmen were accommodated in tents but the training facilities were more organised and formal and the two-week detachments for each squadron had been established as a significant part of a squadron's annual training programme. If the number of senior officers visiting the camp is an indication of the importance placed on this concentrated period of weapon's training, then it is clear that the RAF was recognising the need for a professional approach by its pilots in addition to the showmanship and publicity of pageants and record-breaking exploits.

In May 1928, an Avro 504N aircraft was allotted to the camp and this gave Bill and his small staff the opportunity to remain in flying practice. Two days after a visit by Trenchard, air firing ceased on 29 September and a few days later Bill closed the camp. During the 1928 season, twelve fighter and four army co-operation squadrons had completed air gunnery and bombing training camps. Bill left in October and a month later arrived at Uxbridge to join the personnel staff at HQ Air Defence Great Britain (ADGB).

Fred was promoted to wing commander on 1 July 1928 and there was further celebration on 6 September when his wife gave birth to Margarita Elizabeth. A week later he assumed command of RAF Northolt. During his time at Northolt, he and his family lived in the 'Red House' where he was able to keep his horses in the field behind the house.

A regular visitor to Northolt during Fred's time as the station commander was the Prince of Wales. He was a very keen flyer and in 1928 he established a personal flying unit at the airfield, which subsequently became the King's Flight. Two Wapitis arrived at Northolt in June 1928 and were soon in demand for a variety of VIPs. Fred established a close association with the prince, who sometimes flew in a Fairey IIIF. The Sowrey family today have a painting of the aircraft in 41 Squadron markings and

Students of the 1927 Staff College course at Andover. John seated second right with Sir Hugh Trenchard seated in the centre.

Johnnie and Jimmy with their sisters Margaret and Julie.

there is a cryptic note in Fred's writing on the back outlining the procedure when the Prince of Wales visited Northolt.

The prince is reputed to have told Fred, 'if they ring from the palace, say I am not here'. Fred's time in command of Northolt came to an end in January 1929 when he left to attend the Army Staff College.

By the middle of 1926, John's long period at CFS came to an end. He had been selected to attend the Staff College course at Andover. Trenchard saw attendance at Staff College as a key aspect of an officer's training and a place on a course was much sought after and considered to be essential for those with the potential to reach senior rank.

The course commenced on 10 May with twenty-nine students. To provide a valuable element of 'jointery', the Royal Navy and the army were each represented by two students in addition to two each from the RAAF and the RCAF. Some of the students on John's course went on to have distinguished careers including Lloyd Breadner who became chief of the RCAF Overseas during the Second World War. Others commanded operational groups during the war.

The course lasted a year, during which time students had to maintain flying practice on the station's Avro 504Ks. The wide-ranging syllabus provided the students with the opportunity to study the principles of war, imperial strategy, national and international politics, and joint military operations. Basic staff duties had to be mastered including report writing. Senior military figures gave presentations and there were numerous visits to military installations and formations of all three services. With none of the responsibilities that came with command and staff appointments, the course also offered the opportunity for personal study on topics of interest.

Another important aspect was the opportunity for a relaxed social life and making friendships, many of which lasted for years and helped pave the way for close and valuable co-operation in future appointments. At the end of the course, John was promoted to wing commander and he spent three months at the RAF depot at Uxbridge before heading for the Middle East just a few days before Bill returned from China.

Chapter Twelve

SETTLED YEARS

Bill at the time he commanded Sutton Bridge.

Bill's arrival at Uxbridge at the end of November 1929 was the beginning of a period of unprecedented stability for the three brothers. In the following January, Fred moved to the Army Staff College at nearby Camberley. With John's return from Egypt in February 1929, and his posting on to the staff of HQ Fighting Area at Uxbridge, the three were all stationed within a few miles of each other and a short distance from the family home near Staines, where their parents and sisters were still living. Although their appointments changed during the next five years, they remained in the same area and were able to enjoy the most settled period of their service giving them the opportunity to see each other regularly. This period also presented a rare chance for cousins to spend time together.

Bill was appointed to the HQ ADGB and for a few months worked with the judge advocate general before taking up a post on personnel staff duties. He and his wife and daughter Heather lived near the base. On promotion to wing commander in January 1932 he remained in post and was finally posted away in February the following year after spending four years at Uxbridge.

Fred joined the course at the Army Staff College on 21 January 1929 as one of the two RAF students. Attendance at Staff College was a must for any army officer with ambitions for senior rank and so he was amongst some high flyers. The course always included representatives from the other two services and the senior Commonwealth countries. Joining Fred as the second RAF student was Robert Willock, a pilot who had fought in Palestine and who would eventually retire as an air vice-marshal.

Amongst the army student body were some who rose to high rank in the Second World War including Captain N.M. Ritchie of the Black Watch who took over the command of the 8th Army in North Africa in November 1941 and was the commander-in-chief of British Land Forces in the Far East in the postwar years. Other army students rose to senior ranks including Captain H. Lumsden of the 12th Lancers, who commanded an armoured division at the Battle of El Alamein, and Captain G.W.E.J. Erskine of the King's Royal Rifle Corps who commanded the 7th Armoured Division in North Africa and Normandy.

During Fred's time at Camberley, the RAF was also well represented. In addition to Willock, Wing Commander Arthur Harris was in the senior term during 1929. Not surprisingly Harris was outspoken on numerous issues and was so critical of some of the army's ideas that he was almost asked to leave during his first year. He became disillusioned as he realised that the army was still thinking in terms of trench warfare and cavalry charges and seemed determined to ignore the development and effectiveness of modern weapons, in particular the tank and the aeroplane. He was, however, full of admiration for the type of young army officer on the course. He described them as 'first class men whose problem was that of being heavily sat upon by top brass which was still apparently fighting the last war'. He had little time for the instructors but was full of admiration for one in particular, Bernard Montgomery.

John had returned unwell from Egypt at the end of February 1929 but after a period of sick leave he took up the appointment of senior equipment officer at HQ Fighting Area, which was accommodated in Hillingdon House. Two months before he took up his appointment at the end of May, Wing Commander Keith Park had arrived to fill the second wing commander post in the headquarters.

Soon after his arrival at Uxbridge, there was an urgent requirement for a wing commander to take temporary command of the nearby fighter station at RAF Northolt and John spent the next ten months in command. During this period, the Prince of Wales' interest in flying was such that he decided to qualify as a pilot and he bought a de Havilland Gipsy Moth, finished in the red and blue colours of the Brigade of Guards. These colours subsequently became the standard colours of the royal aircraft. In November, the prince flew a short solo flight.

Throughout John's time in command, the prince and other members of the royal family were regular visitors to Northolt. There were numerous flights in RAF aircraft for official visits but the Prince of Wales took every opportunity to fly his own aircraft. The Wapitis taken on charge during Fred's time as station commander were still in use and John was one of three pilots authorised to fly the aircraft with members of the royal family.

On his return to Uxbridge in July 1930 John joined brother Bill on the headquarters' staff at ADGB, where the AOC-in-C was Air Chief Marshal Sir Edward Ellington. Initially he was on the engineering staff but, with the expansion of the command staff, the headquarters was re-organised and John became the senior technical officer, which included the engineer and stores sections.

After completing the Army Staff College course, Fred returned for a second period at RAF Halton in April 1930, this time to command 2 Aircraft Apprentice Wing, which consisted of four squadrons of apprentices. He and his family moved into 'Treetops', a large house with a lake reserved for senior officers and across the road from the grass airfield.

Fred was a tough disciplinarian but he took great pride in the smartness and bearing of the apprentices who made a big impression on him. He enjoyed the large parades and the marching of the apprentices. On one occasion a twelve-mile march to a camp at Shardeloes Estate near Amersham was arranged and one former apprentice recorded:

'We marched on the Friday of the weekend. It was a beautiful sunny day when we departed, led by the wing CO, Wing Commander Sowrey, DSO, MC, AFC, superbly mounted on a chestnut. Marching distance to Amersham was about twelve miles. Soon everyone was in good humour, including those who had had expressed gloom. We marched at attention passing through villages, but at frequent intervals we marched "easy", which permitted songs and talking.'

On Fred's arrival at Halton, there were almost 3,000 apprentices under training but the bleak economic years of the early 1930s saw a steep decline in the number of new apprentices and the school was re-organised around two wings. Fred continued to command No. 2 Wing where he was responsible for the training of 1,100 apprentices.

Halton apprentices march behind their band (Halton Aircraft Apprentice's Association).

Just to the north of the main camp was the grass airfield where hangars housed obsolete aircraft used to provide practical aero-engines and airframe training for the apprentices. There were also a number of airworthy aircraft, mostly the de Havilland DH 60 Moth and Fred flew regularly, often flying to Northolt on visits to see his brothers and, later, to Sutton Bridge where Bill was having a second period as the camp commandant. On 9 June 1933, he recorded a flight to Charterhouse School in his logbook. His son Freddie started his studies at the school a year later.

The three years at Halton were happy ones for Fred and his family. In addition to enjoying the professional side of his appointment and the flying, he still played polo, kept ponies for the children, organised field shoots and had regular parties with his brothers and their families when the three men 'put the world to rights'. Young Freddie described this period of his life:

Fred and his family with the Bentley three-litre in May 1929.

'These were halcyon boyhood days of adventure and country pursuits when father played his polo and we went on game shoots on the airfield, which included shooting snipe near the sewage farm on the edge of the airfield.'

Fred and his brothers had always had a passion for cars and their infectious enthusiasm was passed on to his son Freddie who, in later years, would achieve some success as a racing and rally driver. At various times Fred owned magnificent Bentleys, Lagondas, Sunbeams and Rolls-Royce cars. He was once heard to say, 'If I flew behind excellent aero-engines, then I will rely on the same makes in my cars'.

Sadness struck the close-knit Sowrey family on 3 September 1931 when John and Audrey's eldest daughter, Julie, died aged fourteen of peritonitis.

Bill's long period at HQ ADGB came to an end in February 1932 and in early March he left for

Sutton Bridge to command the annual armament camp. In the years since Bill's last tenure as camp commandant, the unit, (which came under the command of the Air Armament School based at Eastchurch in Kent), had been developed to cater for more activity and renamed 3 Armament Training Camp. As the unit's title suggests, there were other camps, No. 1 at Catfoss near the east coast of Yorkshire and No. 2 at North Coates near Cleethorpes.

The CO of the Air Armament School was Group Captain Arthur Tedder, the architect of the Desert Air Force in the Second World War and later CAS. He saw a great need for more realistic and practical training and throughout 1932 he made regular visits to Sutton Bridge to assess the weapons-training facilities and the standards achieved by the visiting squadrons. The pattern of rotating each fighter and army co-operation squadrons for fourteen-day training periods had changed little since Bill's previous time in command but the weapons range facilities had improved significantly. In August, experiments were carried out on a new ground target and in October, Tedder visited to see experiments with a target towed behind an aircraft and used for air-to-air gunnery training.

The 1932 season came to an end in October and on 14 November Bill closed the camp down for the winter. He spent the next few weeks at RAF Worthy Down in Hampshire with 58 Squadron flying the twin-engine Virginia bomber and he qualified as a first pilot in December. Within eighteen months he would be flying the aircraft regularly in Iraq.

During the early 1930s there had been virtually no expansion of the RAF and there were times when there were insufficient appointments for all senior officers. For short periods between appointments, officers could be placed on the half-pay list. For three months Bill found himself with time on his hands

The Armament Practice Camp at Sutton Bridge (Eric Absolon).

before he was posted to the staff of the Air Armament School, only to find himself almost immediately heading for Sutton Bridge for his third season as the camp commandant.

Bill took command of the camp for the 1933 season on 28 February. Three weeks later, three aircraft arrived for the station flight. Tedder made his first visit in April and the next entry in the station record book for the following day notes that Bill drove into Boston to 'see about fishing rights'.

By 1933, the pattern of activities at Sutton Bridge was well established with squadrons arriving and departing every twelve days. Fleet Air Arm squadrons also joined the training programme. The stream of visiting senior officers was almost relentless but the most welcome was brother John who flew up from Northolt in a Moth to have lunch with Bill on a number of occasions. Another welcome visitor was Tedder who attended all the various trials conducted on the weapon ranges. On 7 October, he arrived to see 23 Squadron carry out night firing with tracer and, two days later, was present when air firing night trials, with the support of two searchlights provided by the Royal Engineers, were carried out. After the annual competition for the Brooke-Popham Cup, won by Flying Officer Teddy Donaldson of 3 Squadron, the camp was closed in November.

After just over three years at Halton, Fred left on 13 July 1933 to take command of the RAF depot at Uxbridge, one of the biggest RAF station commander's appointments at the time. In addition to housing the HQ of ADGB, the largest RAF Command based in the United Kingdom, and HQ Fighting Area with its old operations room, the depot housed many other main RAF units including the re-

John's two boys, Johnnie and Jimmy.

cruit depot, the RAF School of Music and a large RAF hospital. It was also an ideal location for many of the RAF's representative sports fixtures. With its close proximity to London and to the ministries of state in Whitehall, Uxbridge also provided ceremonial facilities and an officers' mess frequently used by the senior officers stationed in the Air Ministry.

Fred and the family lived in 'The Orchards' in the nearby village of Iver. John was still on the ADGB staff at Uxbridge and his two boys, Johnnie and Jimmy, attended Gayhurst School at Gerrards Cross. In 1932 they were joined by their young cousin Freddie, who cycled each way, attending as a weekly boarder. To identify the three boys, the masters simply called them Sowrey 1, Sowrey 2 and Sowrey 3.

This was a happy time for all the Sowrey cousins. Not only did they see plenty of each other but they lived close to their doting grandmother and two aunts at Staines. The Governor had long retired from the Inland Revenue and joined a firm of financial advisers as a consultant. This proved to be an astute move and he was able to buy two farms, one at the family home at Staines and the other at Chobham in Surrey. Over the years, Queenie took an increasing responsibility for running the two farms.

In the ideal settings of a large house and a nearby farm, there were many family gatherings and the children helped their grandmother to collect and grade eggs and to pick fruit. On one occasion, the three uncles decided to settle an argument with a £1 stake with the three boys as stakeholders. Some days elapsed and it wasn't claimed so the boys showed initiative using the money to buy Diana air rifles. In July 1933, John's eldest son Johnnie left his preparatory school and in September headed for Tonbridge School where he was to spend the next five years with Jimmy joining him in January 1935.

John was promoted to group captain on 1 January 1934 but a few weeks later the Sowrey family's happiness was tragically interrupted. On 13 February, Fred's wife Rita gave birth to a daughter, Celia Joan, but the infant died two days later. Fred had just relinquished command of Uxbridge after eighteen months and was preparing to go to Sutton Bridge to command the Armament Training Camp but his departure was delayed until the beginning of March. His family remained at Iver and Fred made regular use of the Moth aircraft at Sutton Bridge to fly to Northolt for weekends with his family.

Fred's time at Sutton Bridge followed a similar pattern to the three periods during Bill's tenure at the camp. Tedder continued to make numerous visits and there was a period during April when it appeared that all of the most senior RAF commanders paid a visit. Air Marshal Sir Robert Brooke-Popham, the AOC-in-C of ADGB was followed by Air Vice-Marshals A. M. Longmore (AOC Inland Area) and P. B. Joubert de la Ferté (AOC Fighting Area). Even the chaplain-in-chief found time to visit. The CAS, Air Chief Marshal Sir Edward Ellington, visited in August and he was followed by Under Secretary of State for Air Sir Philip Sassoon. Fred had a close friendship with Philip Sassoon who was godfather to Fred's only daughter Elizabeth.

It can only be a matter of conjecture why so many senior officers descended on Sutton Bridge. Without doubt, Tedder's determination and drive to improve the operational efficiency of the fighter squadrons, and the importance he placed on this, was being understood by the senior operational commanders who were, in turn, taking an increased interest. Fred closed the camp on 5 November and returned to his family to prepare for their departure to Egypt.

Chapter Thirteen

OVERSEAS SERVICE

After the five years of stability, with all three brothers based around London, the year 1934 saw each of them leave for service overseas.

The first to go was John who departed at the end of March to take command of RAF Base Malta located at the Kalafrana seaplane base on the western shore of Marsa Scirocco Bay in the south east of the island.

The resident squadron at Kalafrana was 202 Squadron equipped with the Fairey IIIF floatplane. Soon after John's arrival they were due to be replaced by Supermarine Scapas, a twin-engine flying boat designed by R.J. Mitchell. John had no seaplane experience so before departing he was attached to the Seaplane training flight at RAF Calshot for six weeks where he flew the Saro Cloud and the Fairey IIIF floatplane before qualifying as a second pilot on the Scapa.

John assumed command of the seaplane base on 16 April and, the following day, found himself hosting the CAS, Air Chief Marshal Sir Edward Ellington, who arrived by flying boat from a visit to Athens before inspecting the station.

John's arrival coincided with news that the delivery of the Scapas had been delayed and it would be necessary for the Fairey IIIFs, with their relatively short range, to remain in service for another few months.

Fairey IIIFs of 202 Squadron lined up at Kalafrana (202 Squadron records).

The base also provided facilities for Fleet Air Arm flights that disembarked when their parent aircraft carrier moored in Malta's Grand Harbour. With its strategic location in the Mediterranean, Kalafrana also played host to numerous civil flying boats and, for a period, Imperial Airways flying boats on the Brindisi to Alexandria route used the facilities. It was also a favourite destination for government ministers and senior military officers to visit, many transiting to and from Egypt, usually arriving by flying boat. Amongst these dignitaries was Under Secretary of State for Air Sir Philip Sassoon, who arrived in a Singapore III on 23 September and stayed with John for the next two days.

Life on Malta followed a serene passage with plenty of opportunities for sport and social activities. It was a close-knit military community and John, who was one of the most senior officers on the island, had numerous official and social duties. He was also ideally placed to pursue his great interest in sailing. His boys developed into excellent swimmers, which enabled them to shine at school. However, there were frustrations and the frequent delays in re-equipping 202 Squadron with the Scapa generated considerable correspondence with the Air Ministry. In the meantime, John flew the station's Moth aircraft 'round the island' a few times thus able to fulfil the annual requirement to fly twenty hours.

At the end of the year, younger brother Fred, who had been promoted to group captain in July, arrived in the Mediterranean region to take command of the large RAF base at Aboukir, just outside Alexandria. He and his family sailed from England on the RMS *Otranto*. His young daughter was so worried about her dolls suffocating in the suitcases that they were carried up the gangplank in a large bundle with a strap around them!

Aboukir was one of the earliest British flying bases overseas. Opened in 1916 as the Royal Flying Corps Base Depot, it had been developed steadily over the next few years. In 1918 separate depots were established for aircraft and for stores and a cadet wing of two flying training squadrons was established. In the postwar years, the depots expanded as the RAF presence in the Middle East increased and by the time of Fred's arrival in January 1935, it was one of the largest RAF overseas stations.

Fred and his young family lived in the palatial Aboukir House, the station commander's residence. He had also transported his Rolls-Royce open tourer to Egypt and occasionally used it as a staff car in preference to the one provided by the RAF, particularly on formal occasions. With an RAF driver in a white suit and flying the station commander's pennant, the car caused quite a stir and drew comments from the British High Commissioner whose official car was rather more modest. Young Freddie attended the local British-run Victoria College (the 'Eton of the East') in Alexandria whilst his young sister was taught by a governess.

Aboukir House, Fred's residence during his time as station commander.

Egypt was one of the RAF's most important overseas garrisons and Aboukir was central to the operational efficiency of the many units based in the country. In addition to the RAF depot and a large maintenance unit, the airfield was used as a staging post and regularly hosted carrier-borne Fleet Air Arm flights when their parent aircraft carrier was in Alexandria for maintenance. In March 1935, the airfield at nearby Dekheila was being expanded and so the Handley Page HP 42 airliners of Imperial Airways used Aboukir as a staging post for their Far Eastern and African services. There was also a steady steam of civilian aircraft flown by their intrepid pilots attempting various record and long-distance flights and others involved in oil exploration.

On 6 May the Silver Jubilee of King George V was celebrated; beginning with a depot parade at 6.30 am when a number of medals were presented including the King's Jubilee Medal. Fred was one of the recipients. In the afternoon a combined parade was held at the stadium in Alexandria and the depot was represented by 100 men and the station band. There was a large RAF contingent and aircraft of 45 and 208 Squadrons flew over the combined parade in which both army and police units were represented. There was a large gathering of the British community in addition to the military presence and a Thanksgiving Service concluded the day's events.

Throughout his time at Aboukir, Fred was able to keep in flying practice. The availability of aircraft passing through the maintenance unit gave him the opportunity to fly a number of different types including the Gordon, Hart, Atlas and Audax. He even managed a sortie in an Osprey to land on the aircraft carrier *Courageous*. In July 1935 he was flying to the aircraft carrier in an Osprey when he sighted an Italian submarine north of Alexandria.

In Malta, John's frustrations at the frequent delays in the arrival of the Scapa were finally relieved when the first arrived at Kalafrana in May 1935, with deliveries of the remaining aircraft occurring every two or three weeks. The Scapa gave a greatly-increased capability and much more range, with both Gibraltar and Alexandria reachable for direct flights. John wrote to R.J. Mitchell on 21 May, 'we are delighted with the first Scapa'.

The arrival of the aircraft coincided with relations with Italy deteriorating and tension increasing. The July entry in the Kalafrana operations record book described the situation:

> 'At the end of this month it became apparent that Mussolini was determined to have a war with Abyssinia and possible complications in the Mediterranean made it necessary, for the first time apparently since the war, to get down to serious military operations in Malta.'

This statement also appears to indicate that life in Malta until this 'wake up call' was indeed serene.

In August there was considerable activity by the Italian Fleet and the Scapas flew regular anti-submarine patrols and escorted the Mediterranean Fleet that had sailed from Grand Harbour. Men of the Royal Engineers and the Duke of Wellington's Regiment arrived to prepare beach defences with barbed wire and lighting and to site machine-gun and anti-aircraft posts for defence against low-flying aircraft.

Reinforcements for the Middle East started to arrive and the pace quickened in September and October with the aircraft carriers *Glorious* and *Courageous* arriving in Alexandria. Singapore flying boats passed through Malta on their way to Egypt and the Far East.

On 27 September permanent reinforcements for the defence of Malta arrived when an advance party of the 2nd Battalion, Lincolnshire Regiment of three officers and fifty-two other ranks disembarked at Grand Harbour and headed for Kalafrana. The battalion, with sixteen officers and 410 other ranks, marched into Kalafrana the following day to take up residence. The long-established tranquil routine of the RAF base was changed overnight.

On 3 October, the Italian dictator Mussolini ordered his armed forces to invade Abyssinia and further precautions were taken by the British during the month. All the Malta-based Fleet Air Arm reserve aircraft and stores were transferred to Aboukir in Egypt, and more flying boats passed through Kalafrana where a number of 'black out' trials for defensive purposes were carried out.

Mussolini's activities had heightened the tension in the whole Mediterranean area, not least at Aboukir, near the entrance to the Suez Canal. Just as John had needed to increase the defences at Kalafrana, so Fred had to complete similar arrangements at Aboukir. Barbed wire and watchtowers appeared and guarding had to be increased. He had the added difficulty of providing adequate security, whilst keeping open the main road that ran through the base.

In addition to the army reinforcements that had been dispatched to Malta, the British Government

The officers of Kalafrana in December 1935 with John seated in the centre.

authorised a reinforcement of the RAF presence in the region. The troop transport ship *Cameronia* arrived in Alexandria on 13 October with over 700 men including the personnel of two fighter squadrons (29 and 33) and those of a Hawker Hart squadron, 142 Squadron, normally based at Andover. In addition to bringing their aircraft and support, they also brought an outbreak of scarlet fever and all the personnel were immediately placed in isolation. Scapas of 204 Squadron flew from Mountbatten, near Plymouth, and, after transiting through Kalafrana, they too were based at Aboukir where they would remain for almost a year. Short Singapores, from the Pembroke Dock-based 210 Squadron, also arrived at Alexandria.

These rapid reinforcements from England to the various bases in the Middle East, and also to Aden, (eleven squadrons in total), amounted to the biggest such operation carried out by the RAF at the time. This was a busy few months for the two Sowrey brothers each commanding one of the RAF's large bases in the region.

Tension with Italy started to ease in December although the higher state of readiness remained in place. The Lincolnshire Regiment remained at Kalafrana and before he departed the island at the end of April 1936, John wrote:

'Though kept a close secret at the time, it is now common knowledge that the 2nd Bn. The Lincolnshire Regiment (commanded by Lt Col E.P. Lloyd, DSO) arrived in Malta from Catterick on 27 September last year and has been accommodated at RAF Station Kalafrana, since that date.

'The close connection of Lincolnshire in general and the Lincolnshire Regiment in particular with the Royal Air Force needs no emphasis. It is worthy of note – possibly as a unique instance of intimate co-operation between the army and air force – that the officers of the battalion share our mess with us, and the regimental colours hang in the dining room. Moreover, the warrant officers and sergeants share the same sergeants' mess, and the soldiers and airmen, though having separate dining halls, share the same institute.

'As I am about to hand over the command of the RAF at Kalafrana on completion of my tour of two years here, I should like to pay tribute to the splendid way in which Lieutenant Colonel Lloyd and his regiment have adapted themselves to the life of a seaplane base and may I say how very much we in the Royal Air Force have appreciated the protection and comradeship afforded us by their stay.'

John, with his wife, daughter Margaret and young son Robin sailed home from Malta on the SS *Atlantis* of the Royal Mail Lines arriving in Southampton on 2 May before heading for their home in Hythe. A few weeks earlier, Fred and his family had arrived home in England from Egypt on the RMS *Strathmore*.

Six months after John's departure for Malta, Bill headed back to Iraq arriving in September 1934 and on the 13th he assumed command of 70 (BT) Squadron based at Hinaidi just outside Baghdad. The squadron had recently been re-designated a 'Bomber Transport' squadron and was flying the Vickers Victoria.

Bill had only been in post for two weeks when Sir Philip Sassoon, having stayed with John in Malta on his outward journey, arrived at Hinaidi to inspect 70 Squadron, the aircraft depot and 1 Armoured Car Company. A week later, there was much excitement and activity when, on 8 October, it was reported that four Moth aircraft of the Bombay Flying Club returning to India from England had failed to arrive at Shaibah after taking off from Hinaidi.

The four aircraft had become lost and landed in the Southern Desert. The leader of the team refuelled his aircraft from the other three and was successful in reaching Shaibah to raise the alarm. A large-scale search was organised and a flight of 70 Squadron headed there to join 55 and 84 Squadrons in the search.

For the next two days the 'probable' and 'possible' areas were searched without success. Finally, on the morning of the third day, an 84 Squadron aircraft located the party. The occupants were fit and well, but had only one pint of water and little food left. After being refuelled, the aircraft were able to fly to Shaibah escorted by the aircraft that found them.

During the period of the three-day search, an area approximately 23,800 square miles had been scanned with twenty-nine aircraft involved flying 437 hours.

The Victorias of 70 Squadron provided the long-range transport force, an in-theatre communications capability and, when required, was a formidable bombing force. In addition to troop transfers within Iraq, it carried many VIP passengers, mail and a regular passenger service to Egypt and Palestine. It also frequently headed south down the Persian Gulf towards Muscat and even further afield.

Bill shortly after arriving to take command of 70 Squadron.

In December, aircraft of 70 Squadron were called on again to search for a missing aircraft. This time it was a KLM Royal Dutch Airlines Douglas en-route from Cairo to Baghdad that had gone missing. The aircraft had been reported passing over one of the mail route landing grounds but had failed to arrive at Baghdad. Two Victorias took off in poor visibility but found nothing. The following day, 21 December, the weather improved and wreckage was discovered by a 14 Squadron aircraft operating from Palestine. Arrangements for salvage were made by representatives of KLM and the bodies of the victims were conveyed by the Victoria aircraft to Baghdad for burial.

The new AOC, Air Vice-Marshal W.G.S. Mitchell, was collected from Ismailia on 26 December and his predecessor commenced his journey home with a flight to Cairo in a Victoria of 70 Squadron.

In February, the squadron was required to fly to the scene of the crash of one of its own aircraft carrying replacement officers and nursing sisters. It had made a force landing at Suweila en-route from Egypt to Hinaidi. The aircraft was damaged, and eventually recovered, but there were no injuries and squadron aircraft delivered the passengers to their destination.

A long-distance flight down the Persian Gulf resulted in the recovery of another of the squadron's aircraft when the Victoria flying the task sank in soft sand at a landing ground between Bahrain and Sharjah. More squadron aircraft were used to fly spares and personnel to the scene and the aircraft was later able to continue its task to Muscat.

In April 1935, it was time for the squadron to practise its bombing skills and also for night-flying practice to be carried out. Night photography was improved and the regular trooping flights to Egypt continued, as did proving flights to Muscat. Personnel and stores were taken to Mosul, Shaibah and Aboukir. Sick personnel were flown from outlying posts to the hospitals in Baghdad and the squadron had the sad task of recovering the bodies of aircrew killed in aircraft crashes. This diverse range of flying activities, whilst enjoyable and exciting for the aircrew, placed significant demands on Bill, his flight commanders and the ground crew. In May, 517 hours were flown on these various tasks, when twenty-seven landing grounds were visited.

During the summer of 1935, supply dropping, instrument flying, night cross-country training and annual bombing training were added to the flying tasks. Two aircraft took the command cricket team to Egypt and returned with stores.

A major event of the year was the regaining of the Sassoon Trophy for bombing competed for by all the Iraq-based squadrons. Over a four-day period at the beginning of September, the squadron dropped bombs on the Hinaidi ranges and was victorious with an average error of seventy-nine yards.

Bill made a number of trips to Egypt during his time in command of 70 Squadron. His aircraft flew regular passenger and freight-carrying flights each month and Bill was able to combine flying these flights with visits to see Fred. He was able to deliver Persian carpets, which were readily available at beneficial prices in Baghdad, to his brother – some are still in use in Sowrey households. More importantly, a tour of duty in Iraq was unaccompanied for most officers so Bill arranged for his wife and daughter Heather to sail to Egypt, where they stayed with Fred and his family at Aboukir House. Bill's visits to Aboukir provided a welcome break from the rigours of a tour of duty in Iraq, gave his family an opportunity for travel and a holiday and allowed family reunions to take place. Fred's young son, Freddie, remembered the family trips to the beach where large wooden packing cases made excellent beach huts.

In November, 70 Squadron started to re-equip with the Vickers Valentia, an enlarged and more

Bill's wife Daisy and daughter Heather on a visit to see Fred and his family at Aboukir.

Vickers Valentias of 70 Squadron at a forward airstrip.

powerful version of the Victoria. Powered by two 650-hp Bristol Pegasus engines the aircraft could carry twenty-two troops and for bombing duties it could be fitted with racks beneath the wings for up to 2,200 lb of bombs. Bill's squadron was the first to receive the new bomber-transport and they did impressive work in the desert areas and amassed an impressive number of hours on routine transport flying.

In the same month, ten of the squadron pilots started training as instructors in anticipation of the arrival of twenty pilots direct from the flying training schools who were to be attached to the squadron in an experiment for a special training syllabus. With Bill's great experience and outstanding reputation as a flying instructor, the RAF authorities chose wisely.

The recently-qualified pilots were given dual instruction before flying solo in lightly-loaded aircraft before they graduated to wind-finding exercises and cross-country flying. They then moved on to flying with heavier loads and accompanied the long-range flights to Muscat and Egypt during which navigation exercises and airmanship lessons were completed. Night flying was commenced in February and instrument flying practice was started. The course was successfully completed in April when twelve students returned to England qualified to fly twin-engine aircraft and the remaining eight were taken on the permanent strength of 70 Squadron.

Early in 1936 the squadron supported the work on a new landing ground and a fuel store on Masirah Island off the south coast of Oman. The new facility was soon in use and on 24 February 1936, Air Commodore T.L. Leigh-Mallory was flown to the island via Bahrain, Abu Dhabi and Muscat. He continued his journey to Aden with the Aden Flight.

After almost two years in command of 70 Squadron, Bill handed over to his successor at the beginning of June and left for a brief spell at the headquarters, also at Hinaidi, before returning to England at the end of August and a well-deserved period of leave.

Chapter Fourteen

RAF EXPANSION YEARS

On 19 July 1934, Prime Minister Stanley Baldwin announced an expansion of the Home Defence Air Forces from fifty-two to seventy-five squadrons, and for other additions to the RAF to bring its worldwide strength to 128 squadrons within five years. This became known as Expansion Scheme 'A', which provided for the growth of the RAF to a strength of 128 front-line squadrons, including the Fleet Air Arm, by 31 March 1939. This was seen as a 'shop window' to deter Germany, and so little provision was made for reserves.

Over the years leading up to the Second World War this first scheme was revised/replaced numerous times until Scheme 'M' was announced on 10 November 1938. One of the most significant was Scheme 'F', which eliminated the light bombers in favour of sixty-eight squadrons of medium and heavy bombers, and for the first time it provided for adequate reserves.

These schemes generated a number of major initiatives across the whole spectrum of the RAF and the three Sowrey brothers were heavily involved in some elements. An extensive aircraft building programme was implemented, new airfields had to be built to accommodate them, and the training system had to be expanded to meet the increased demand for aircrew and for ground tradesmen.

In October 1934 the director of training in the Air Ministry, Air Commodore Arthur Tedder, recognised the need for a radical review of the flying training system if the objectives of Expansion Scheme 'A' were to be achieved. The review had two main aims: establishing a training system in peacetime which should not require radical alteration in wartime; and re-organising the existing system to relieve squadrons of basic individual training and so allow them to give attention to operational training.

The review recommended that ab initio flying training should be carried out at civilian flying schools and applied flying on service aircraft types at the existing FTSs. Four civil schools were already being used for training reservists and new regular entrants would start their service at one of the schools to complete fifty hours flying, including cross-country and basic instrument flying.

On successful completion of the civil school course the pupils were posted to the RAF depot at Uxbridge, where they were given general service and administrative training. From Uxbridge they proceeded to an FTS for a ten-month course. This was split into two terms, the first dealing with flying training on a service type and the second was directed to applied flying. At this second stage, pupils were taught navigation, instrument flying, night flying and air gunnery and bombing.

There was some resistance to Tedder's proposals, mainly from the Finance Branch, but he prevailed and, on 28 June 1935, the Treasury approved the re-organisation and agreed to the Air Ministry adopting thirteen civil schools for the scheme. This gave an immediate requirement to create nine new civil schools. The re-organisation of flying training was introduced in an Air Ministry Order (A.135/35):

'By accelerating the elementary stage of flying and ground instruction to carry service training to a materially higher standard than can at present be attained, without however increasing the total length of training and consequently reducing the period of service by
short-service officers and airmen pilots in squadrons. The extended syllabus is designed to
eliminate a considerable part of the individual training at present given to a pilot in his first
year in a squadron and thus to render him fit to take his part in flight training immediately
on posting to a squadron.'

Whilst the re-organisation was being discussed, plans were also being made for the expansion of the
RAF and this called for a larger training organisation. Scheme 'A' had identified the need for 1,000 additional pilots over and above the normal flow of replacements to be trained in the years 1935-39 and
involved the formation of two new FTSs. In turn, more aircraft and more instructors would be needed.

The new training scheme started in August 1935 and, to accommodate the increased requirement
for the additional pilots, larger courses were introduced until new schools could be formed. As the new
training programme started, Scheme 'C' was published and this planned for a considerably larger and
more rapid increase in the number of pilots. Its target was a Metropolitan Air Force of 123 squadrons
and a total of 1,512 front-line aircraft by April 1937. This created a need for another 2,000 pilots to
be provided in rather less than two years. To achieve this programme a total of eleven FTSs was required
and five new schools were opened between October 1935 and March 1936.

These expansion schemes had a direct effect on the front line. In order to provide instructors, pilots
had to be withdrawn from squadrons. However, if the sequence and length of training were left un-
changed, forty per cent of the front line would have been needed to act as instructors. This would have
had a serious effect on the squadrons. Not only on their operational efficiency and readiness for war,
but also on the amount of post-FTS training which, at that time, was an essential part of the pilot's
training.

Soon after the new system was introduced, other steps were taken to improve the training of pilots.
Night flying was given a more prominent part, although it amounted to no more than six hours, all
on circuits and landings except for one out-and-back flight of twenty miles. In 1936 twin-engine training was re-introduced into the FTSs.

The next three years saw a rapid expansion of the training machine and to meet the increased demand, courses were reduced in length and capacities at the schools increased. The annual output of an
FTS rose from eighty in 1934 to 140 two years later. Between April 1935 and May 1938, 4,500 pilots
were trained, an annual average of 1,500 compared with 300 per year in 1934.

To increase the number of pilots, more men were recruited for the six-year short-service commission
and the two university air squadrons, at Oxford and Cambridge, were increased in size to accept more
than their establishment for seventy-five students each. A scheme was also started to cater for more
airmen pilots drawn from the ground trades, many of them ex-apprentices.

In 1936, Tedder recognised that recruitment into the regular service had to be vigorously supplemented by direct entry reserves if the Scheme 'C' requirement was to be met. As a result, the RAF Volunteer Reserve was created in July 1936 and it contained men from a wide range of educational and
social backgrounds. The scheme started in the following January. Men flew fifty hours at one of the
thirteen Elementary and Reserve Flying Training Schools (ERFTS), civilian-based organisations run
by aircraft firms such as Bristol at Filton and Blackburn at Brough near Hull. After completing their
basic flying training they were required to attend a town centre, weekly, for ground training. Flying
was available at weekends and there was a compulsory fifteen-day period of continuous training annually. Some pilots took advantage of the unlimited flying and flew many hours solo in aircraft such as
the Hart. Some were commissioned as acting pilot officers and others remained as sergeants.

This then was the complex and rapidly expanding situation that met Fred when he reported to the
HQ of 23 (Training) Group at Grantham to take up his appointment of senior personnel staff officer

Students of Oxford University Air Squadron receive instruction on the aircraft compass....from a group captain!

in May 1936. The group, one in the RAF's Inland Area, but soon to become Training Command, controlled the FTSs, the Central Flying School, and the School of Technical Training (Men) at RAF Manston. Fred's arrival coincided with the successive expansion plans and thus the need for a great increase in the number of pilots and additional flying training schools to teach them to fly. By the end of the year, there were ten FTSs and the School of Air Navigation at Manston had joined the group. Two storage units had also come under their command.

To increase the annual output of pilots the break between courses at the FTSs was reduced from one month to two weeks. Also, from April 1937, a centralised maintenance system was introduced. Under this scheme, the aircraft in each squadron were pooled under the squadron commander and this relieved the flight commanders of the responsibility for overseeing the maintenance task to the benefit of their work as flying instructors.

During 1937, many of the new FTSs moved to their permanent stations and the group HQ transferred to offices at RAF Spittlegate in order to allow 5 (Bomber) Group to take over their old headquarters at St Vincents near Grantham.

The group expanded significantly during 1937, giving Fred and his personnel staff an increasing amount of work as officers, airmen and pupils were posted amongst the increasing number of units. Despite the workload, Fred was able to 'escape' occasionally and remain in current flying practice by taking advantage of the availability of a number of Avro Tutor and Hawker Tomtit training aircraft, which were kept for pilots on ground appointments at Grantham.

The output of the training establishments in 1937 was impressive and indicated the speed of the build-up required by the expansion schemes. Almost 1,250 pilots were trained at the FTSs, 117 pilots completed the flying instructors course at CFS and over 200 pilots graduated from the various navigation specialist courses at Manston.

Finally, there was one other significant element that contributed to the increased requirement for pilots and ground crew needed to meet war establishments and this was the expansion of the Auxiliary Air Force. Three months after Fred arrived at Grantham, brother John was appointed as the senior air staff officer at 6 (Auxiliary) Group with its headquarters at Tavistock Place in London.

Provisions for an Air Force Reserve and Auxiliary Air Force were made in the Air Force (Constitution) Act, 1917 and, in his 1919 Memorandum, Trenchard said that a reserve air force should be organised on a territorial basis. In 1922 a bill was drafted, but it did not become law until 1924 when Sir Samuel Hoare was secretary of state for air. He was a staunch advocate of the Auxiliary Air Force and would later comment:

Fred at HQ 23 Group.

'Trenchard envisaged the auxiliaries as a *corps d'elite* composed of the kind of young men who earlier would have been interested in horses, but who now wished to serve their country in machines. He conceived the new mechanical yeomanry with its aeroplanes based on the great centres of industry. *Esprit de corps* was to be the dominating force in the squadrons and each, therefore, was to have a well-equipped headquarters, mess, and distinctive life of its own. Social meetings were to be encouraged and on no account was any squadron to be regarded as a reserve for filling up regular units. The experiment was successful from the beginning. The forebodings of the doubters and critics were soon proved groundless. So far from the non-regular units damaging the reputation of the regular squadrons they actually added some of the most glorious pages to the history of the Royal Air Force during the Second World War.'

By early 1936 thirteen of the squadrons had been formed and the rapid expansion of the regular RAF was matched by the auxiliaries. Three more squadrons formed during the early months of 1936 and two more followed in 1937 with the final two forming in late 1938.

Following the announcement of Expansion Scheme 'C', the Auxiliary Air Force Committee was invited to review the recruitment, training and conditions of service in the Auxiliary Air Force. The committee examined in some detail the whole structure of the force and the system under which it was administered. They were reassured by the Air Ministry that auxiliary squadrons were to be regarded as first-line units and that they must be ready to operate immediately on the outbreak of hostilities. This policy influenced all the committee's deliberations and made it clear that personnel establishments and the training organisation must, wherever possible, be on parallel lines to those of the regular RAF squadrons. However, it was immediately clear that this standard was beyond the capacity of units having only part-time service of their personnel.

Each squadron had a small nucleus of regular officers, usually the adjutant, a flying instructor and one or two flight commanders. The remainder of the pilots and ground crew were recruited locally.

Flying took place at the weekends and weekly ground training periods took place in town centres with each squadron attending a fifteen-day annual summer camp at an established RAF airfield. The annual flying requirement for each pilot and air gunner was a mere twenty-five hours. The review recognised that this was wholly inadequate:

> 'The performance of the obligatory training set out above is not sufficient for the attainment of a standard which will enable Auxiliary Air Force squadrons to function as designed in war. In addition the training of pilots is laid down in a progressive syllabus, involving, apart from the fifteen days continuous training in camp, certain attendances throughout the year. A minimum standard at which all pilots should aim is seventy-five hours flying training each year and, as regards ground training, eighty hours in each of the first two years.'

A revised syllabus was developed by John and his staff at 6 Group, designed to achieve these requirements. This revision took account of the new policy for the training of regular officers, the requirement to be able to meet full operational commitments on the outbreak of war and the recent policy decision that auxiliary squadrons would be transferred to regular groups where the introduction of more sophisticated aircraft demanded more intensive training.

Most auxiliary squadrons consisted of two flights and new pilot recruits were allocated as vacancies arose and it was then the responsibility of the flight commander to co-ordinate the training of all his pilots across the whole spectrum of experience. John recognised that this was totally impractical and he drafted a letter for his AOC, Air Commodore J.C. Quinnell, to send to Bomber Command, 6 Group's parent command. This far-sighted letter of 12 January 1937 would be instrumental in changing the whole policy of training for the auxiliary squadrons.

The thrust of the letter was to establish a training flight in each squadron so that the qualified pilots could concentrate on operational training, which could proceed on similar lines to that of the regular squadrons without the distraction of providing basic training for new pilots. Such a policy would also allow the introduction of a common policy of ab initio and individual service training throughout the Auxiliary Air Force. The letter concluded:

> 'The commands and regular groups are now engaged in the preparation of operational training schemes, based on the altered conditions resulting from the developments mentioned in paragraph 2 [the Scheme 'C' re-organisation of the RAF]. It is important that these schemes should be made applicable to the Auxiliary Air Force as soon as it is possible to do so.
>
> 'Further it is clearly desirable that early steps should be taken to decide upon a common policy for ab initio training and individual service training in squadrons irrespective of the groups to which they will belong. Until this decision is made it is not possible to make satisfactory progress with the preparation of training schemes suitable to the new conditions. Moreover, a protracted period of uncertainty is to be deprecated, as this is likely to affect adversely the existing enthusiasm and efficiency of Auxiliary Air Force personnel.'

This letter and its well-developed arguments led to a meeting at the Air Ministry on 17 February, chaired by Air Commodore Tedder. The operational commands and groups were represented at group captain level and John led the 6 Group delegation.

After opening comments from Tedder, John explained the rationale behind the 6 Group proposals to establish a training flight in each auxiliary squadron. He also addressed a proposal that ab initio training could be carried out at the RAFVR schools that were opening. He pointed out that using these schools would only meet two-thirds of the requirement since some auxiliary squadrons were located where there were none; hence different arrangements would have to be made for those squadrons.

He concluded his opening remarks:

> 'The success of the auxiliary squadrons was, to a large extent, due to the excellent *"esprit de corps"* which has been built up. In fact, it was this spirit which constituted the essential difference between the auxiliary and the normal reserve. It was the opinion of 6 Group that the withdrawal of individual training from squadron control would have a very adverse effect on the spirit and efficiency of these units.'

This generated a discussion with some opposition expressed, but the 11 (Fighter) Group representative supported this view and after further discussion 'the conference decided to recommend the establishment of a training flight or section for each squadron'.

John then went on to highlight the need for each squadron to be established with aircraft on the same two-flight basis as regular squadrons. The minutes of the meeting recorded, 'the conference decided to recommend the adoption of the two-flight organisation for operational purposes with aircraft establishments appropriate to squadron duties'.

Having secured this agreement, John then explained that squadrons could have thirty pilots in the two flights, therefore there was a need for two flight lieutenants in each. Not only would this ease the burden on the flight commander but also it would have an important bearing on the selection of future commanding officers. The minutes recorded, 'the conference decided to recommend four flight lieutenants per squadron'.

Finally, the conference agreed the aircraft establishment for the training flight and it concluded with the telling comment, 'the conference agreed that the individual training should be planned to bring Auxiliary Air Force pilots to a standard comparable with the service pilot in the regular air force'.

To an outsider, the decisions reached by this conference appear to be a triumph for John's staff work and powers of persuasion. In the event, all the recommendations were implemented and the Auxiliary Air Force would operate alongside their regular RAF comrades with equal distinction. Altogether,

An Avro Tutor of 616 (South Yorkshire) Auxiliary Squadron's Training Flight at Doncaster.

twenty-one squadrons were formed and the auxiliaries were mobilised a few days before the outbreak of war, and aircraft from these squadrons were in the air within a few hours of the declaration of war. To one of those 'weekend flyers' fell the honour of shooting down the first enemy aircraft to fall over British soil. During the Second World War the auxiliaries were credited with some of the RAF's most memorable achievements. The re-organisation and foundations that led to these successes stemmed from the work of John and his staff in 1936 and 1937.

The responsibilities of 6 (Auxiliary) Group extended beyond the control of flying squadrons. In mid-1936 the Committee of Imperial Defence approved a suggestion for a barrage of 450 balloons for the defence of London. This led to a national balloon defence organisation, set up by the Auxiliary Air Force, and which came into existence on 17 March 1937 when 30 Group was formed.

The plans for the huge expansion of the RAF and the great increase in the number of squadrons could not be accommodated on the airfields and stations that existed in 1935. A few established stations could be developed but it was necessary to build a large number of new ones. It was clear that the expansion programme was of such a magnitude that the necessary progress could only be achieved if the layout of the airfields, and the design of the buildings, could be standardised. The marked improvement in the quality of design of stations built under the post-1934 schemes reflected government and Air Ministry reaction to public concerns over the issues of rearmament and the pace of environmental change. It was in this context that Prime Minister Ramsey MacDonald instructed that the Royal Fine Arts Commission was to be involved in airfield design.

In the five years leading up to the outbreak of the Second World War, the distinguished architect Sir Edwin Lutyens was very influential in the design and layout of the new stations. The buildings erected for much of the 1930s expansion period were, as a consequence, more carefully proportioned than their predecessors, a clear distinction being made between neo-Georgian for domestic buildings and more modern styles for technical buildings. In many circles, these expansion period airfields became dubbed 'Lutyens' stations.

The Airfield Board determined where the airfields should be built but it was the Air Ministry's Works Directorate that had the responsibility for investigating the civil engineering aspects. This whole programme was a massive undertaking and it had to be achieved quickly. The brilliant success of the

Heyford bombers on RAF Finningley, built in the same style as Honington during the expansion period.

programme is evident in the continued use of some of these airfields by today's RAF.

Work commenced on eight new stations in 1935 and the alterations and additions to eleven existing stations also started. A further eleven new stations began to appear in 1936, many in the east of England in anticipation of a rapid expansion of Bomber Command. In addition to airfields, aircraft storage units, repair depots and maintenance units were also planned and built. New balloon barrage stations were designed and work started at sixteen sites.

One of the eleven new stations built in 1937 was the 3 (Bomber) Group airfield at Honington, eight miles north of Bury St Edmunds in Suffolk. Bill was appointed to be the first station commander and he arrived at the partially-completed station on 1 May 1937 together with four officers and twenty-seven men. The station was initially a hutted camp with the five large hangars completed. Over the next few weeks the build-up of personnel continued and on 28 June the advance parties of 77 and 102 Squadrons arrived.

A decision had been taken that these new, large operational airfields would be commanded by group captains and, on 1 July, Bill was promoted. This coincided with the opening of the sergeants' mess and four days later the main party of 102 Squadron arrived and five bi-plane Heyford bombers flew in to be the first residents.

One of the first visitors to fly into Honington once the airfield had been declared open was brother Fred. He flew in on 14 July in a Tomtit and spent the day with Bill before flying back to Grantham. It was reminiscent of the days when they served in France and flew across to each other's airfield.

Over the next two years, various bomber squadrons were at Honington as they re-equipped with the twin-engine Wellington bomber. In July 1939, 9 Squadron arrived and it was to remain at Honington for the next three years.

With one brother in charge of a bomber station, a second, Fred, was appointed to command a fighter station. After two years at 23 Group, he landed one of the plum fighter pilot appointments when he assumed command of Tangmere, near Chichester, on 30 May 1938. He took over from Group Captain Keith Park who was posted to HQ Fighter Command and was to become the mastermind behind the RAF's victory in the Battle of Britain two years later.

A well-established RAF station, Tangmere had been home to some of the RAF's most famous fighter squadrons and 1 Squadron and 43 Squadron, the 'Fighting Cocks', were in residence flying the elegant Fury bi-plane fighter. The station was being refurbished and modernised with new workshops, more barrack blocks and quarters. The airfield was also being extended eastwards to increase the maximum take-off and landing run to 4,500 feet. A new asphalt perimeter track was also under construction.

The Munich Crisis of September 1938 saw more activity with the construction of air raid shelters, hangars were camouflaged and aircraft and crews were brought to readiness. Even the elegant, gleaming Furies were also camouflaged. Prime Minister Chamberlain's famously-waved paper and his 'peace in our time' statement did not lessen the RAF's vigilance. Sited on the south coast of England, Tangmere's squadrons were to form part of Britain's first line of defence with their two satellite airfields – one now being the home of the Goodwood Road Racing Club.

On 15 October the first three of 1 Squadron's new Hurricane fighters arrived and the squadron was fully re-equipped by the middle of the following month. 43 Squadron then began to receive their first Hurricanes and both squadrons started their preparations for the conflict that was clearly developing. Fred, the First World War fighter ace pilot, flew the new generation fighter for the first time on 14 February 1939.

On 20 May the majority of RAF stations were opened to the public to celebrate the twenty-first an-niversary of the formation of the RAF. Called the Empire Air Day, record numbers of the public visited Tangmere but it was to be the last peacetime occasion for the British public to survey their RAF. The event lasted four hours and the two Hurricane squadrons and the resident Anson squadron, 217, were kept very busy flying a wide range of displays.

There can be no doubt that Empire Air Day had a double aim. It allowed the general public to view their air force but Secretary of State for Air Sir Kingsley Wood took the opportunity to highlight the build-up to war with some remarks in his 'Message', which was printed in the programme available at the RAF stations opened to the public:

> '…I hope too, that many of those who visit the Royal Air Force to-day will consider carefully the opportunities for service which it affords.
> 'In June last year I appealed for 31,000 officers and men to join the air force during the ensuing nine months. This number equalled the entire strength of the force in personnel when the expansion scheme was launched and was more than fifteen times the average number entered during a normal pre-expansion year. Yet this figure was reached four weeks before the end of the recruiting year and constituted a record in recruiting for the Air Arm.
> 'The need is still great, however, and a further effort is required this year. The recruiting programme for 1939 is very large and, including the reserve and auxiliary services, we require 75,000 officers and men this year…
> 'Empire Air Day, 1939, will, I think, show that we have achieved much both in service and civil aviation. Continued progress in both is vital to the welfare of the nation and I am confident that the nation will ensure that this progress is maintained.'

Not only was this unashamedly a 'call to arms' but it does also highlight very clearly how the scale of recruiting had been increased rapidly.

By May, Hitler had broken every promise made at the Munich Conference and war loomed. The two squadrons increased training and operational capabilities with their new aircraft but Fred was not to see them go into action as he was posted away from Tangmere in August 1939 to take up a new appointment.

The rapid expansion of the RAF during the final years of the 1930s witnessed a major increase in aircraft and air armament production. This huge responsibility was given to Air Marshal Sir Wilfrid Freeman, a man of outstanding vision, drive and determination. He was already responsible for research and development and his appointment was re-designated air member for developmental and production (AMDP). It was an awesome charge making him responsible for the whole process from research to the production of the many finished articles and giving him a critically-important role to play in the build-up to war.

One of the major departments in AMDP's organisation was the Aeronautical Inspection Directorate (AID) at the Air Ministry in London, and in March 1938 John took up the appointment of deputy director. His immediate superior was Ernest Lemon who was brought from LMS railway by Freeman to be director general production (DGP).

The AID had been established during the First World War, initially as a department in the War Office and then in the Air Ministry, and it was responsible only with inspection at the factories. Shortly after the war, four store-holding depots and one repair were formed, the latter at RAF Henlow. The four store depots, which also did some repair work in their respective technical spheres, were civilian-manned whereas Henlow was mainly manned by servicemen.

Inspections were carried out by civilian AID inspectors but this failed at Henlow because of opposition by the RAF staff and so they formed, trained and operated their own 'Henlow Inspection Department'.

These arrangements remained in force until the major expansion of the RAF began in 1935 when six new maintenance units (MU) were proposed, three service-manned and three civilian-manned. To control these MUs, Maintenance Command was formed on 1 April 1938. The rapid expansion necessary

The lapel badge worn by civilian workers in the AID.

to man the new MUs with AID personnel was met by training a number of RAF technical personnel in inspection and loaning them to AID for use in the service-manned depots – civilian inspectors were still retained in civilian-manned depots. AID also assumed the policy direction of inspection in overseas depots, although no civilians were employed as aeronautical inspectors.

At the time that John joined AID, the RAF expansion schemes were gathering momentum and Freeman's plans to increase aircraft production significantly meant AID had also to expand in order to have teams of inspectors in the increasing number of aircraft factories.

Soon after his arrival, Colonel Outram, John's superior, submitted detailed proposals on how his department should be decentralised at the outbreak of war. These involved dividing the country into areas and establishing an organisation to co-ordinate and manage the inspection activities. Outram recommended that the chief inspector for each area should be allocated at once to make detailed arrangements to ensure a smooth transition on the outbreak of war. All these proposals were agreed.

In January 1939, on Outram's retirement, John was appointed director. He had worked closely with his predecessor and prepared very detailed plans for the establishment, accommodation and requirements for each of the six areas envisaged. However, when Hitler seized the rump of Czechoslovakia in March 1939, Freeman saw that war was imminent and he was given authority to expand many of his areas of responsibility. John immediately set out a revised plan for the decentralisation of his department, recommending that it should be implemented before war broke out rather than the current intention to establish the system on the outbreak of war. This involved a significant increase in personnel and, initially, his ideas met with considerable resistance, not least from the Finance Branch. At a meeting chaired by the director general of production (DGP) on 15 May 1939 there was still strong opposition from the chief accountant officer but DGP authorised John to prepare a complete scheme for submission to Freeman showing numbers, costs, locations etc to be based on three areas.

During this busy period it was decided that the post of director aeronautical inspection (DAI) should be a civilian one, as it had been when created in the First World War. John had spent just a few months as the director and was the most conversant with the current major work. He therefore was 'placed on the retired list at his own request' and continued in post with the equivalent civil service grade. Over the next few months, he continued to revise his plans. In August he wrote:

> 'After a thorough examination of the position, both as it now exists and as it will develop in the immediate future in the absence of a major emergency the indications are that such a scheme on the basis of three areas would represent a workable arrangement and one which would lend itself to a rapid development in the event of war, by a process of sub-divisions into (say) six areas…'

As was the case on many issues in the lead-up to war, Freeman was thinking well ahead of most of his colleagues and staff and on 24 August he gave approval for John's original six-area war scheme, which should 'take place forthwith'. On 29 August, Air Ministry departments were informed of the new arrangements:

RE-ORGANISATION OF THE AERONAUTICAL INSPECTION DIRECTORATE

> 'Under AMDP's authority issued on 24/8/39, re-organisation of the Aeronautical Inspection Directorate is being brought into operation with effect from Wednesday 30 August 1939. This re-organisation which consists of decentralisation of the directorate into six areas is detailed in AID Weekly Orders, Part 1, No.182.

> 'This AID Weekly Order has been referred to S.8 so that general promulgation throughout

The Governor, Mother and Queenie head for a wedding in Staines, spring 1939.

the Ministry will be made.

'It is to be noted that any matters arising – other than those of policy – concerning the work at firms etc., within the respective areas, should be addressed to the principal inspection officer of the area concerned, in the first instance.'

The six areas, Scottish, Northern, Midland, Western, Eastern and Southern were established immediately, each with a principal inspection officer reporting directly to John in London. Under his management, the organisation would grow dramatically during the war years.

During the five years since the publication of Expansion Scheme 'A', the RAF had experienced a massive transformation. As a result of the comprehensive expansion schemes, the strength of the RAF at the outbreak of war was 11,753 officers and 163,939 other ranks. Almost 8,000 aircraft had been manufactured and dozens of new airfields and maintenance depots and support stations had been built. Throughout this period the three Sowrey brothers had held key appointments in preparing the country for war. Now it was the turn of the next Sowrey generation.

Chapter Fifteen

FIRST YEARS OF WAR

During the uneasy peace that prevailed after British Prime Minister Neville Chamberlain had visited Munich to meet with German Chancellor Adolf Hitler, Britain geared itself for a possible war.

Johnnie, the eldest of the next Sowrey generation, had completed his education at Tonbridge, one of England's leading public schools, where he had been an active member of the OTC, reaching the rank of corporal in his final year. He was awarded a King's Cadetship to the RAF College Cranwell and entered on 12 January 1939 to be the next Sowrey to join the RAF.

Twenty-five cadets made up the January 1939 intake and they included a future CAS, Marshal of the Royal Air Force Sir Andrew Humphrey, who would die in post as chief of the defence staff in January 1977, and an air chief marshal, Sir Peter Le Cheminant. Sadly, many of Johnnie's colleagues were to die in the first few months of the war that was less than a year away.

The daily life of cadets was built around flying and associated academic subjects. Drill and physical recreation were still considered to be important for discipline, and outdoor pursuits were encouraged with a wide range of sports and activities open to the cadets.

Johnnie was airborne for the first time on 16 January when his instructor, Flight Sergeant Rawlinson, took him on a familiarisation flight in a Tutor training aircraft. After eight hours of dual instruction, he flew his first solo sortie and made rapid progress during the first two terms, graduating to the Hart trainer in July.

A ritual at Cranwell, and one that lasted until 1959, was the first term boxing competition designed to allow a cadet to show his mettle and be judged by his instructors and peers. John was pitted against Tim Vigors, later to gain fame in the Battle of Britain and during the fall of Singapore. The college journal reported on the fights in a light-hearted way:

'Vigors and Sowrey, both big men, fought very hard. Sowrey slipped and Vigors got muddled up in a corner by some ingenious sideslip action. From then on, owing to his advantage in weight, Vigors won the honours.

'Bilderbeck and Hatton fought like tigers with no thought of self-defence. Bilderbeck chased in but was unable to inflict the "*coup de grace*". In the second round both went hell for leather, both bled profusely and both were congratulated for a fine performance.

'Cross charged Chandler and tripped him as a preliminary to greater things. In the second round Cross hooked with open gloves.

'Shuttleworth beat Plumb by a series of viscous uppercuts. Plumb relied on native dancing to evade decapitation.

RAF College Cranwell Swimming Team with Johnnie in the rear (fourth from left) and Flight Cadet Arjan Singh seated second left (RAF College Cranwell).

> 'Both Sowrey and Shuttleworth, of this term, showed great promise and boxed for the college, but, unfortunately, owing to their receiving heavy punishment at Shawbury, they were unable to continue their training.'

In the event, Johnnie was badly concussed during his bout representing the college at RAF Shawbury. As a result his flying training was interrupted to such an extent that he had to drop a term in order to complete his training as a pilot. After giving up his boxing, Johnnie was a member of the college swimming and water polo teams and one of his teammates was Flight Cadet Arjan Singh who would later become CAS of the Indian Air Force (IAF).

Together with his friend Tim Vigors, he became a member of the college rowing club. In the summer term of 1939, a maiden crew was formed with Johnnie as stroke and Vigors at number three. They entered a number of local regattas and achieved some success. After beating the University College, Nottingham crew by four feet to win the Malcolm Cup at the Boston Regatta on 1 July, the four were promoted to junior crew status and rowed at the Chester Regatta before the summer term finished.

With war looming, cadets were recalled from leave on 30 August when the college ceased to function with its traditional syllabus and the standard two-year course was reduced in order to meet a more concentrated flying training programme.

Once he had completed 100 hours of flying, Johnnie flew the important progress check sortie with CFI Squadron Leader D.A. Boyle, (later Marshal of the RAF Sir Dermot Boyle and CAS). He was assessed as above average and progressed to the advanced training squadron to fly the Hind and the Audax. With 145 hours in his logbook, he was awarded his pilot's wings and was commissioned as a pilot officer on 6 March 1940.

When war was declared on 3 September 1939, Johnnie's Uncle Bill was still in command of the bomber airfield at Honington. The Wellingtons of 9 Squadron were dispersed around the airfield and on the 4th, six aircraft set off in daylight to bomb ships at Brunsbüttel. Nine German fighters attacked one section and two Wellingtons were shot down. This first attack was a rude awakening to the difficulties of daylight bombing against a well-equipped, large and experienced fighter force.

Johnnie airborne in a Hawker Hind trainer.

Training accounted for most of the Wellington's flying time during this period but a number of North Sea sweeps were flown in the following months. On 9 November, six crews carried out the first of many searches for hostile shipping, often extending to the Heligoland Bight. On 19 December nine aircraft took off for another sweep. Flying at 18,000 feet in clear weather, the formation came under heavy attack and five of 9 Squadron's Wellingtons were shot down, the squadron's most disastrous single operation during the war with the loss of twenty-five aircrew; a bitter blow for the close community at Honington. Such a high loss in the early days of the war created a very difficult and sad situation that needed all of Bill's experience and sympathetic understanding for the families and comrades of those who failed to return.

At the end of January 1940, Bill's two-and-half years in command of the basic airfield he had opened, and then developed into a fully operational bomber station, came to an end. He handed over to Group Captain Harrison and a week later he headed for the Middle East. By April, he was in command of the RAF's forces based in East Africa with his headquarters on the RAF station at Nairobi.

His brother Fred had relinquished command of Tangmere and moved to HQ Reserve Command before becoming president of 1 Aircrew Selection Board, an appointment that did not appeal to him and he was placed on the retired list at his own request on 26 May 1940.

By this time, the second of the new generation, Johnnie's younger brother Jimmy, was training as a pilot. At Tonbridge School he had been an active member of the rowing club and also part of the very successful shooting eight, which competed at Bisley. His talents extended to art and he won a number of prizes.

He was a member of the school's OTC, almost 400 strong and organised like a county regiment. One of the school's maths masters was J.W. Watts, a former RFC pilot who had seen service in France, and he arranged for a Westland Wapiti to be made available for ground training. For those interested in aircraft, an air platoon was formed and Jimmy and his friend Bill Brown were amongst the twelve founding members of the Air Training Section (ATS) of the OTC. In addition to the traditional activities of the OTC, those in the ATS received instruction on the theory of flight, airframes and aero engines and they were able to gain practical experience servicing the Wapiti. Pilots from the nearby RAF station at Biggin Hill would also visit the school and lecture to the air section.

Jimmy (right) and fellow Tonbridge OTC cadets. His friend Bill Brown is on the left (Bill Brown).

In the summer of 1939 Jimmy and his colleagues attended a camp at Norton Priory near RAF Tangmere, where his Uncle Fred was the station commander. About 250 cadets attended the camp from other public schools and they were inspected by the CAS, Air Chief Marshal Sir Cyril Newall. A fleet of Anson aircraft flew them on visits to other RAF stations. The aeronautical correspondent of *The Times* praised the fantastic opportunities the boys were given but criticised a 'lack of urgent interest' on the part of the cadets he saw. He suggested:

> 'So much flying had taken the edge of their keenness or it may be that obvious enthusiasm is bad form in the senior public school boy…several of the boys fell asleep during a most interesting and quite short address by AVM E.L. Gossage, commanding 11 Fighter Group…these boys appear to have no sense of their own good fortune.'

There is no indication that Jimmy fell into this category. His time in the ATS made him determined to follow in the footsteps of his uncles and his brother and be a pilot in the RAF. He was studying for entry to Cranwell when war was declared.

Jimmy wasted no time in enlisting and on 13 September 1939 he joined the RAF Volunteer Reserve (RAFVR) and reported to the RAF depot at Uxbridge to commence his basic training. With this completed he moved on to the next stage of training and left for 3 Initial Training Wing (ITW) at Hastings. One of a number of ITWs, almost all were located at seaside resorts where the large hotels were requisitioned, plentiful accommodation was available and the promenades provided ideal drill squares. The aircrew trainees were given the rank of leading aircraftman and the course lasted sixteen weeks. The wide-ranging syllabus included basic service training and professional subjects including airmanship, signals, aerodynamics, engines and navigation amongst other flying related subjects. During this period, his cousin Freddie, who was finishing his schooling at nearby Charterhouse, was a regular visitor and they shared many happy hours together.

Whilst Jimmy was pounding the promenade at Hastings and sitting through lectures, brother Johnnie had moved to the School of Army Co-operation at Old Sarum and was flying the Lysander and Hector. Because of the emergency situation in France, the conversion course was compressed and on 20 May 1940, he joined 613 Squadron operating from Odiham. Despite his limited experience, he was pressed into service to assist in the evacuation of the British Expeditionary Force (BEF) from the beaches of Dunkirk. On 27 May, with Aircraftman Gillard as his gunner, he flew across the English Channel at 200 feet to Calais with five other Lysanders to deliver boxes of ammunition and hand grenades to the army. They were escorted by aircraft of the squadron's Hector Flight, which machine-gunned the enemy machine-gun posts. As one journalist commented, 'never did airmen go into battle flying such obsolete machines but the spirit was unequalled'. Later in the day, Johnnie and his Lysander colleagues returned to Calais with more supplies.

Freddie (left) visits Jimmy (centre) at Hastings.

Once the BEF had got back from France, 613 Squadron moved to Doncaster where training with the army was the main task. Johnnie remained there until early 1941 when he fulfilled his wish to be a fighter pilot and he left for 56 OTU at Sutton Bridge, significantly developed since the days his two uncles had been the camp commandants.

After completing his fighter training in early March, Johnnie joined 17 Squadron at Croydon but the squadron soon moved to the north of Scotland and after a few patrols over Scapa Flow, he joined 213 Squadron. Within a week he was on his way to Africa.

At the end of May, Jimmy completed the ITW course and two weeks later he headed for 8 Elementary Flying Training School (EFTS) at Reading to start his pilot training on the Magister aircraft. He had almost completed ten hours of dual instruction when he flew his first solo. At the end of the first phase of his training he was assessed as 'above average and an exceptional pupil'. He progressed to 15 Service Flying Training School (SFTS) at Kidlington to fly the Harvard and in November joined 55 OTU at RAF Aston Down to convert to the Hurricane.

Jimmy was once again assessed as 'above average' and on 4 January 1941 he joined 229 Squadron at Speke near Liverpool to provide fighter cover for the shipping lanes and for the port and city of Liverpool. His time at Speke was brief and on 23 February he was sent to reinforce 615 Squadron at Kenley. The move south provided much more activity and he flew many scrambles and patrols over the Channel. It also offered a more exciting social life with visits to London and local public houses where the handsome Jimmy was not short of girl friends. On Sunday, 9 March he spent all afternoon at thirty-minutes readiness and then 'pushed off to London with two chums'. His diary records great fun at a party, and plenty of drinking, before finally getting to bed in the early hours. The entry for the next day illustrates the life of a teenage fighter pilot:

'Got woken late so consequently missed breakfast at 6.00. Scramble of A Flight at 11.30 in the morning. I am weaver. We see nothing. Do very bad landing as the T is on the wrong runway. Have a hell of a head this morning but is much better after oxygen. On readiness after lunch and all evening. Squadron scramble again at 6 to intercept attack on Hawkinge but, as usual, we are too late. Land in the dark. Go to bed early as I only had a few hours sleep last night.'

With Fighter Command's new offensive campaign of seeking out the Luftwaffe, 'Circus' operations commenced. Small formations of medium bombers were escorted to attack targets in northern France in the hope that enemy fighters could be enticed into combat and Jimmy flew on a number of these operations in addition to the routine patrols over convoys. However, in early May he was recalled to Speke to rejoin 229 Squadron. Just like his brother, he too was on his way to Africa within two weeks.

Margaret (Mattie) Sowrey served in the WAAF.

With her two brothers undergoing their pilot training, Margaret, the surviving daughter of John and Audrey Sowrey, enlisted into the Women's Auxiliary Air Force (WAAF) in June 1940 as an air-woman. She trained as a teleprinter operator at the signal's school at Cranwell before serving at Bomber Command's headquarters at High Wycombe for two years. In those days the teleprinter was the main means of communication to the many bomber airfields and there was a huge amount of signals traffic with the transmission and receipt of air operations directives, intelligence, raid plans and details of the debriefings of bomber crews on their return.

It was during Margaret's time at High Wycombe that Air Marshal 'Bomber' Harris became the AOC-in-C and at the end of May he launched the first of his 'Thousand-Bomber Raids'. With two more to follow in June, there were few departments busier than the signals section, which was almost entirely manned by members of the WAAF.

Over the next three years she continued to serve at various bomber units, and towards the end of the war she was at Biggin Hill, before being released from the WAAF in December 1945 to pursue a long and successful career with Cable and Wireless.

As John senior's three children were getting established in the RAF, his appointment of director aeronautical inspection had become increasingly busy and the value of the measures he had recommended shortly before the outbreak of war became readily apparent. The introduction of many more aircraft and equipments, some arriving from the United States, and the task of inspection at the increasing number of factories and maintenance units rapidly expanded.

In 1940, when the Ministry of Aircraft Production (MAP) was formed, the whole of John's inspection department and its responsibilities were transferred to the new ministry. AID was responsible to MAP for inspection at contactor's works and in all RAF repair and holding units.

On the outbreak of war, John's nephew Freddie was too young to join up and had to complete his schooling at Charterhouse School, another of England's leading public schools, where he had been studying since the summer term of 1936. After the turmoil of changing schools when his father was posted to Egypt, he needed extra tuition in Latin and maths before scraping through the entrance exam for Charterhouse as bottom of the new entrants. From this lowly start, the rest of his life saw him climb steadily to the top of his profession.

During his time at Charterhouse, Freddie developed his life-long love for motor cars and racing. He had been brought up amongst a family of car enthusiasts. His father's great friend from 41 Squadron days, Chris Staniland, raced cars throughout the 1930s and made regular visits to the Sowrey home, which ignited Freddie's racing ambitions. Charterhouse was near the Brooklands track and his grandmother paid the fifty penny annual fee for him to be a 'schoolboy member'. He and three friends made regular visits, cycling in single file with one lamp on the front cycle and the only rear light on the last in the column. During school holidays Freddie stayed with his grandparents at Staines and spent many hours at Brooklands where his Aunt Queenie raced her Riley Kestrel Saloon round the track at 60 mph.

Freddie joined the OTC, which was attached to the Queen's Royal Regiment, and rose to be a corporal. As the evacuation of the BEF from Dunkirk started, it was announced that a Local Defence Volunteer (LDV) force was to be formed from the corps and on 27 May 1940, the Charterhouse Section became No. 7 Platoon of the Godalming Company. The section headquarters was established in the school armoury and initial orders issued:

GENERAL IDEA

To provide a corps of defenders to prevent parachute landings from enemy aircraft and to protect vital points.

SHOULD PARACHUTISTS BE SIGHTED TRYING TO LAND:

Immediately inform the police in all cases. Tel No. Godalming 1400.

Engage single parachutists whilst still in the air. Should large numbers of parachutists manage to land they should be isolated if possible blocking roads round their place of landing.

Inform other groups of watchers in the immediate neighbourhood by messenger.

Freddie (right) at Brooklands with Chris Staniland at the wheel of a Multi-Union.

The orders indicated that duty would be from sunset to sunrise, presumably after a day's work in the classroom.

Freddie was one of the first to volunteer and soon achieved the necessary results on the rifle range. He went on his first night of guard duty three days later. Throughout the summer of 1940, as the Battle of Britain raged overhead, Freddie threw himself into the routine of night guard duty, establishing road blocks and digging trenches. A flavour of the atmosphere that pervaded at the time can be gleaned from the orders for daylight action stations:

DAYLIGHT ACTION STATIONS

These apply between 3.30 am and 10.30 pm or such time as may be notified in orders.

If the siren is sounded, or church bells are heard, the volunteers who are on duty on both succeeding nights will report immediately to the armoury.

Dress and Equipment :- Cap or Battle Bowler. Tunic. Respirator. (If in white flannels, put on a pair of jeans.)

Draw rifles and shotguns etc and proceed immediately to action stations as follows:

ARMOURY 'A'   3 to Mr Morris' garden.
                   3 to Mrs Wootten's garden.
                   4 to armoury trench.

1 on telephone.
1 on guard in Armoury.
1 on guard in or near armoury door.

BROOM & LEES POST 'B'

Post Commander, sentry and messenger in shelter trench.
2 in each positions marked B1, B2 etc.
The post will be approached through Major Thomson's garden. Care must be taken not to trample vegetation in front of positions.

CLOISTER POST 'C'

2 sentries on duty in cloisters.
4 in post near New Block.
Remainder in armoury as reserve.

UNDER GREEN POST 'U'

As arranged by Major Thomson.

When school summer term was over, the LDV became virtually full time for most of the boys when guard duty and digging tank traps featured heavily. As he approached his eighteenth birthday, he started to think about joining the RAF having seen the Battle of Britain overhead. Understandably, his mother was apprehensive but, recognising the long Sowrey family heritage of service in the RAF, she agreed, albeit reluctantly. Finally, five months after his cousin Margaret had joined the WAAF, eighteen-year old Freddie was summoned to Reading. He was placed in a group heading for Oxford where he was enlisted into the RAFVR on Guy Fawkes Night 1940.

Medicals and selection boards were arranged and Freddie had the good fortune to be interviewed by Group Captain Emmett, a contemporary of his father and he was selected for pilot training and 'specially recommended for a commission'.

Within a few days, his group travelled to Torquay where he joined 3B Flight of 1 Receiving Wing at Babbacombe. His luck came into play again when he discovered that in charge of his flight was Corporal Barber who had worked for Freddie's father at Sutton Bridge and Halton. Drill, PT and lectures became the order of the day until the course finished on 30 November.

For the next stage of training Freddie headed for 8 ITW, which had been established at Newquay. It was close to the large RAF Coastal Command airfield at St Eval that, to Freddie, seemed to be constantly busy. Here he went through the same regime that Jimmy had experienced with hours of drill and PT together with many hours studying subjects associated with flying. In mid-February, halfway through the ITW course, the trainee aircrew were promoted to leading aircraftman.

By the time Freddie had completed the sixteen-week course at the end of March, much had changed in the aircrew training system. Soon after the outbreak of war, and with the rapid expansion of the RAF, the demand for pilots and aircrew rose well beyond the capabilities of the RAF's flying training organisation in the United King-

Freddie as an aircrew cadet at ITW.

dom. There was an increasing demand to use the existing airfields for operational units and the skies of the United Kingdom had become a dangerous place for student aircrew.

A series of discussions with the governments of other Commonwealth countries led to the implementation of the Empire Air Training Scheme (EATS) on 29 April 1940 – in 1942 it was renamed British Commonwealth Air Training Plan (BCATP).

The introduction of the EATS provided the facility needed to produce the annual requirement of 50,000 trained aircrew. The flying schools were established throughout the Commonwealth, with the majority based in Canada. By the end of the war, 168,622 aircrew had been trained under the scheme. In early 1941 studies indicated that yet more flying training schools would be required and the British Government agreed a further scheme with the United States under the auspices of the Lend-Lease Act.

Three weeks after the outbreak of war, Prime Minister Chamberlain approached the Canadian Government to consider providing facilities for the training of aircrew. He copied his letter to other Commonwealth governments. The response by Canadian Prime Minister Mackenzie King was immediate. His cipher telegraph of 29 September 1939 included:

> 'I can say at once that our government fully agrees that Canadian co-operation in this field would be particularly appropriate and probably the most effective in the military sphere which Canada could furnish. We would therefore be prepared to accept the scheme in principle.'

Following this positive response there was much to negotiate and agree but it was the beginning of a scheme described by Sir Maurice Dean as 'one of the most brilliant pieces of organisation ever conceived' and one in which Canada would play the major role (and to where Freddie was heading after completing ITW).

With many others, Freddie arrived at Gourock on 3 April 1941 and boarded the *Royal Irishman*, a small Irish Sea ferry, which sailed for Iceland as part of a convoy with a heavy naval escort. After

transferring to the armed merchant cruiser HMS *Derbyshire*, the party arrived at Halifax, Nova Scotia on 17 April and boarded trains for Montreal. Within the hour, Freddie was in a party that transferred to a Canadian Pacific Express for Winnipeg where the aircrew cadets were separated and the pilots headed for Edmonton in Alberta. After three days travelling across Canada, Freddie and his colleagues arrived at the civil airport to start training at 16 EFTS.

Tiger Moths, which were equipped with a hood and cockpit heating to combat the severe Canadian winters, were used for elementary training, which commenced immediately. Freddie noted in his diary:

'Flew practically every day

Many of the flying training schools were in the open spaces of Canada. This is Yorkton.

and did ground subjects when not flying. We fly one morning, getting up at 4 am, working in the afternoon, work the next morning and fly in the afternoon. Pretty strenuous.'

A RCAF Harvard advanced trainer.

He took to flying easily and went solo after twelve hours, the weather having interfered with his early progress. The pace of the training was relentless, sometimes with three sorties in a day, and there was little latitude for those who were slow learners and failed to keep up. Many left to train for other aircrew categories. After just six weeks, the course was over on 7 June and Freddie had sixty hours in his logbook. He was delighted to be one of five selected for fighters and left for 11 SFTS at Yorkton in Saskatchewan.

This offered a very different prospect to the busy and attractive Edmonton. The prairie town was typical of many small communities across Canada to benefit from the BCATP. The influx of personnel and the creation of an airfield with all the necessary facilities and accommodation provided a huge boost to the local economy and provided work for the unemployed. The people of Yorkton embraced the whole project with great enthusiasm.

Within a week of leaving Edmonton, Freddie had his first flight in a North American Harvard advanced trainer. He made rapid progress and his diary entry of 1 July sums up his feelings about Canada and the joys of flying perfectly:

'After a stupendous graduation dinner and dance at the Mac, which I took Babs to, we left on Sunday 8 June for Yorkton among fond farewells and promises to return. The people of Edmonton were very nice to us and made us feel terribly at home.

'Yorkton is extremely dead and nothing doing at all. I soloed after seven hours on the Harvard and they are great fun after Tigers and perfect wonders to fly, in fact they are a dream. I now have thirty hours and spent yesterday in the clouds which were at 6,000 feet rushing up the valleys and shooting over the crests. It was so marvellous and I felt like staying up for ever but after enjoying myself more than ever before, I came down after two hours. The thrill of playing in the clouds beats everything else into a cocked hat and is miles more fun than low flying.'

The exuberance of an eighteen-year old is clear to see.

Freddie completed the advanced course in just eight weeks, having flown ninety-three hours in the Harvard. He was assessed as above average and on 16 August he was one of fifty students to be presented with his wings. He also put up his sergeant's stripes but a week later learnt that he had been awarded a commission.

On 28 August he boarded the 10,000-ton *Port Huon* at Halifax and was back in England as a pilot officer and fully-qualified pilot just four months after departing for Canada.

Unlike some of his colleagues, Freddie did not have to wait long before starting his operational training. Instead of heading for his preference of advanced training on fighters, which his training in Canada

Freddie's graduation. He is extreme left, second row down.

and his excellent assessment warranted, he found himself off to the School of Army Co-operation at Old Sarum, following in the footsteps of his cousin Johnnie. There was a rumour that the top two or three on a course were 'creamed off' for army co-operation, but this gave little comfort to a disappointed Freddie.

He accepted the disappointment and was immediately immersed in a concentrated period of flying. After a brief familiarisation flight he flew a Lysander solo on 1 October and within a month had completed most of the photography and navigation phase of the course. During November he completed the air-to-ground firing phase with his gunner. He finished the course in two months then remained for a few weeks as a temporary staff pilot before progressing to the Tomahawk. He summed up his feelings about the current state of army co-operation when he wrote in later years:

'After being taught to fly in Canada ending on Harvards, 41 OTU at Old Sarum equipped with Lysanders seemed a bit of a backward step. The photographic exercises of vertical and obliques were very relevant for intelligence gathering in real time as were spotting fall of shots from field artillery. Air to air and air to ground firing, however, did not give much confidence in the destructive power of 2 x .303 machine guns.

'The dilemma had been faced by 1942 and the previous Lysander squadrons were being re-equipped with the Tomahawk and ultimately the Mustang I, a six-gun fighter whose Allison engine was fine at low level. However, the pattern of flying undertaken in support of the army followed very much the pattern of the previous twenty years.'

Freddie with a Tomahawk aircraft.

In February 1942, Freddie converted to the Tomahawk and by the end of March he had moved on to the Mustang and a posting to 26 Squadron based at Gatwick.

Chapter Sixteen

AIR WAR IN AFRICA

After a brief period in Cairo, Bill travelled to Nairobi on 19 April 1940 to take up the post of OC RAF East Africa with its headquarters at the RAF station at Eastleigh. The northern borders of Kenya reached to Abyssinia (Ethiopia) and to the north east was the colony of Italian Somaliland, both part of the expanding 'new Roman Empire', which also included Eritrea.

With the collapse of France in June 1940, and the loss of facilities in southern France and French North Africa, there was an increased risk to Allied shipping in the Mediterranean. The entry into the war of the Italians on 10 June changed the whole strategic situation in the Middle East and the availability of the Red Sea routes and the Suez Canal became crucially important. The huge Italian presence in East Africa posed a major threat to this route but the strength of the Imperial forces in the region left much to be desired.

The RAF presence in Sudan, Aden and British Somaliland was also weak and the forces were equipped mainly for policing and garrison duties with no permanent operational presence in Kenya. Italy's East Africa Empire was huge, six times the size of Italy, and was an inhospitable and rugged area, much of it at 6,000-8,000 feet above sea level. Internal communications were very poor with few good roads and just two main railway lines; one ran to Addis Ababa and one from the Red Sea port of Massawa to Asmara in the north of the region.

The most significant factor was the region's total isolation from Italy with its sea and land routes able to be cut easily by British forces, leaving only a very tenuous aerial route.

The Italian military force level was considerable with almost 330,000 ground troops available with a small, but old, naval presence at Red Sea ports. The Regia Aeronautica seemed substantial with almost 200 operational aircraft, some with only a modest performance, and there were few modern aircraft available. There was a large transport force and almost 100 reserve aircraft in maintenance and storage.

The performance of the few squadrons of RAF aircraft was similar with three elderly Wellesley bomber squadrons in the Sudan. In Aden there was a small force of Blenheims and Vincent aircraft for bombing and a flight of Gladiators for air defence. In Kenya, to the south of the Italian territories, there were no RAF units. Fortunately, South Africa and Southern Rhodesia were able to deploy a mixed force of fighters and bombers and these units came under the control of Bill when they started to deploy to Kenya in May.

The Rhodesians sent a squadron of Hawker Hardies, Harts and Audaxes and the three flights of the Kenya Auxiliary Air Force were available for communication flights. By the end of May, the South African Air Force (SAAF) units had arrived in Kenya. These consisted of thirteen Junkers 86 airliners, converted to the bombing role, from 12 SAAF Squadron, twenty-four Hartebeestes of 11 SAAF

A Junkers 86 of 12 (SAAF) Squadron converted into the bombing role (Andrew Thomas).

Squadron to be used as light bombers and six Hurricanes and six Furies of 1 SAAF Squadron in the air defence role. These units made up 1 Bomber Brigade under Lieutenant Colonel S.A. Melville.

On the day Italy entered the war, Bill faced the problem of how to use this small force against the closest elements of a much superior force. Kenya was very vulnerable to attack with Nairobi in easy range of airfields in Italian Somaliland and Abyssinia. Bill, and his senior air staff officer, Colonel H.C. Daniel of the SAAF, planned to hit the airfields at the earliest opportunity. However, the SAAF's first offensive raid, which came on 11 June, was against a 'banda' camp when four Junkers 86 bombers attacked the Somali irregular force's camps. The following day, the campaign against Italian airfields opened with a reconnaissance by Hartebeestes and the following day the Junkers 86s mounted their first attacks against airfields in the south of Somaliland.

As the air war gathered pace, Bill maintained a policy of aggressive action against Italian facilities and positions in the south of Abyssinia and in Somaliland. A series of frontier airstrips were developed near the Kenyan border allowing the SAAF units to extend their range into enemy territory. The aim remained to eliminate the Regia Aeronautica. There was also a need to maintain reconnaissance flights to monitor shipping movements in Somali waters.

By August the bombing campaign had been stepped up and the arrival of twelve Fairey Battles for 11 Squadron provided a welcome increase to the SAAF's bombing capability. These aircraft soon proved their worth with a spectacular attack against Mogadishu, the capital of Somaliland, where a vehicle park was bombed with an estimated 800 vehicles destroyed. Further raids, launched from the advanced landing grounds, accounted for five Caproni Ca 133 bombers.

By September, Bill and his SAAF planners had turned their attention to more distant Italian airfields, some 500 miles into Abyssinia. Fuel installations were also attacked and, with the Italians' isolation from re-supply and with long lines of communications, the Regia Aeronautica began to suffer from lack of fuel and spares for their aircraft. A quarter of Italy's fuel stocks had been exhausted in the first three months of the war.

The activity in the south of the theatre was matched by equally aggressive action from Sudan and from Aden and this three-prong attack forced the Regia Aeronautica to spread its diminishing resources ever more thinly.

At the end of September, the AOC-in-C, Air Chief Marshal Sir Arthur Longmore, visited Nairobi when he confirmed that his policy was active offence with defensive measures reduced to a minimum. With more SAAF reinforcements arriving in October, Bill's command was growing and on 19 October, his appointment was upgraded to AOC Air HQ East Africa with the rank of acting air commodore.

The arrival, at the end of October, of 3 SAAF Squadron with its Hurricanes added a welcome increase in fighter capability. On 31 October, Lieutenant General Alan Cunningham arrived in Nairobi as GOC East Africa Forces and Bill accompanied him on a flying visit to the forward airfields on the frontier. Whilst en-route to Nanyuki, the formation of three aircraft was mis-identified and the leading Junkers 86 was fired on, fortunately no damage was inflicted.

The November rains limited air operations in the south but the first British offensive of the war was mounted from Sudan. Activity in Bill's area was light for the next few weeks but by mid-December all was ready for the ground forces' new offensive from Kenya. It began on 15 December and was supported by Junkers 86 bomber and Hartebeestes and the following day the fort at El Wak was taken and the Italians withdrew. Whilst a relatively small objective, it was a prelude to the successes that were to follow in 1941 and the effect on morale was a great boost. The army commander, Major General A.R. Godwin-Austen, summed up the air support:

'The SAAF have enhanced their already brilliant record and gained the affectionate admiration of every officer, soldier, and *askari*.'

By the end of 1940, the losses of the Regia Aeronautica had mounted steadily and the precarious supply system and insufficient reinforcements had eroded its capability. In the meantime, the capabilities of Bill's units had been increased, some reinforcements had arrived, there was a secure supply chain and parity with the Italians had been reached. All was ready for the advance into Italian-held territory to begin.

On 14 January Cunningham began the long trek towards the Italian Somaliland port of Kismayu when the Hartebeestes provided close support. If the enemy's resistance in Jubaland could be broken, and the port of Kismayu captured, the advance could be continued to capture the important port of Mogadishu. The air forces in East Africa were tasked to:

'Neutralise all enemy air units within range; assist the army's advance by means of direct and close support and to assist naval bombardments. The air force was to supply aircraft for the evacuation of casualties and for communication purposes.'

This was a significant task for the 100 operational aircraft at Bill's disposal. SAAF Marylands, which had recently arrived, were soon very active flying reconnaissance sorties, Ansons were busy mapping enemy territory and Battles of 11 SAAF Squadron bombed enemy airfields. As the troops were moving into position to begin their advance across very difficult terrain, they were attacked on 3 February by a force of enemy bombers with a fighter escort. Hurricanes of 3 SAAF Squadron based at one of the forward strips took off to intercept. Led by Captain J.E. Frost, the Hurricanes attacked the incoming force resulting in the Italians losing three Caproni bombers and at least one CR 42 fighter. Bill responded by immediately launching attacks against the enemy airfields causing the destruction of more of the Regia Aeronautica's limited bomber and fighter forces.

On 2 February the divisional commander called a top-level conference of all his senior commanders. The ground offensive was due to begin on 10 February when the air force would be heavily tasked with flying close-support operations. Bill stressed that to meet his commitments he would have to move some of his squadrons to new bases, some 200 miles away, a complicated task over difficult terrain. The following day he summoned his staff and squadron commanders to a briefing and detailed the role of the air forces, the new deployments and emphasised the importance of concentrating the limited forces to the right place at the right time. He then issued his orders for the SAAF squadrons to move to their new landing grounds, some only recently prepared by the South African Engineering Corps.

Bill attended the final conference chaired by the GOC in Mombasa and by the 8th, all the squadrons were in position ready to start operations the following day. An Advanced Air HQ was co-located with the Advanced Force HQ at Garissa in order that Bill could command his forces alongside his army counterparts. Often overlooked by historians, here was the birth of the air/land co-operation that was to prove so successful in the Western Desert and later campaigns.

The earlier operations had created almost complete air superiority and this allowed Bill to focus the bulk of his air effort on the close support of the ground forces. He had built up his resources at the two-airfield complex at Garissa, which included large dumps of material and supplies with bombs and fuel parks concealed in the adjacent bush.

As the ground offensive moved towards Kismayu the 24th Gold Coast Brigade headed north to cut the only main road to Mogadishu, the likely route of any Italian retreat. As the advance succeeded, Hartebeestes of 41

Bill meets senior British and South African army officers at a forward airfield.

SAAF Squadron moved into abandoned landing strips and were able to continue the harrying of the retreating Italians.

The capture of Kismayu was completed on the 14th with little resistance and Cunningham decided to continue the advance without delay; launching his troops towards Mogadishu. Rapid progress was made, with the Hartebeestes making a major contribution. The Juba River was crossed and the Italian forces fell back with thousands captured. Squadrons moved to advanced landing strips previously held by the Italians allowing more enemy airfields to be attacked, destroying more enemy aircraft.

The advance to Mogadishu was so rapid that it presented major problems for Bill and his staff. They had to move supplies and support to the advanced airfields so that his limited bomber force could extend their reach further into Italian Somaliland and Abyssinia. Fairey Battles hunted down escaping transports on the few main roads and attacked them. Finally, on the 27th the senior staff of Advanced Air HQ entered Mogadishu and the Hartebeestes of 41 SAAF Squadron flew into the city's airfield which was littered with wrecked aircraft.

This remarkable advance in extremely difficult terrain had been achieved with very few casualties and with the loss of just two aircraft. Much of the success of the campaign was due to the swift occupation of enemy airfields by units of the maintenance parties and the efficient supply chain established to keep them provided with stores, weapons and fuel.

At the same time as these major successes in the south were being achieved, the campaign in the north of Abyssinia and in Eritrea had also gone well and General Cunningham was authorised to advance into Abyssinia. Bill moved more of his squadrons to the airfields around Mogadishu in preparation to support the next advance.

The advance was rapid and by 17 March Jijiga, deep inside Abyssinia, had been taken, some 744 miles from Mogadishu. Bill's advanced headquarters had moved forward and the

Bill (with pipe) at one of his basic advanced headquarters in the bush.

constant move of the aircraft from one landing ground to another continued. Attacks mounted from Aden and the retaking of major ports in British Somaliland increased the difficulties for the Italian forces, many of which had become isolated.

Towards the end of the month the Italians made a last desperate attack against the recently occupied airfield at Jijiga. Dispersal of the aircraft limited the damage but three were destroyed on the ground. This prompted a robust signal from General Pierre van Ryneveld, the South African ground commander, to Bill suggesting that he had underestimated the strength of the Regia Aeronautica and demanding to know why he had positioned so many aircraft so far forward. Bill replied in an equally robust manner pointing out that the GOC had ordered him to transport the Force HQ and the Advanced Air HQ to Jijiga in order to keep up with the rapid ground advance. Bill also pointed out that there was no other means of transport and he copied his signal to General Cunningham. The GOC gave his full backing to Bill's actions.

On 3 April, Bill flew into Khartoum where he was joined by the AOCs Aden and Sudan for a conference with the AOC-in-C Middle East, Air Chief Marshal Sir Arthur Longmore. The C-in-C explained that the situation in other theatres necessitated the diversion of some of their more modern aircraft. The majority were taken from Sudan and Aden leaving much of Bill's small SAAF units intact.

Rapid advances had been made in the north; Eritrea fell at the beginning of April and the Abyssinian capital Addis Ababa fell on the 5th. Attacks against the few remaining enemy airfields continued and most of the remnants of the Regia Aeronautica were destroyed on the ground.

For the next phase, Bill promulgated his objectives as:

- Destroying the few remaining enemy aircraft in Abyssinia.
- Giving close support to the ground forces operating under the orders of GOC East Africa.
- Air defence of Addis Ababa.
- Carrying out combined operations with 203 Group against Gondar area.
- Coastal defence of Mombasa and Dar-es-Salaam areas.

At his disposal, he still had the Junkers 86 bomber force, although it was less effective operating from the airfields in the highlands of central Abyssinia. A squadron of Fairey Battles was still available and the two squadrons of Hartebeestes continued to give an outstanding service for such an antiquated aircraft. The

squadron of Hurricanes, now supplemented with Gladiators, gave every satisfaction and within a few weeks had wiped out the remaining enemy air resistance. Ansons provided coastal reconnaissance work and the flight of Marylands gave valuable service mapping the country.

Bill placed great emphasis on providing close support for the ground forces. He tasked his operations staff with forming a close support flight

A SAAF Gladiator at a forward strip with the 'early warning system' up a tree (Andrew Thomas).

of four Hartebeestes and four Gladiators. To maximise the effectiveness of this small force, the close support controller, with a small air cell, was co-located with the HQ 22 (East Africa) Brigade and the aircraft were tasked to directly support a particular ground action.

Bill moved with his Advanced Air HQ to Harar, between Jijiga and Addis Ababa to remain co-located with General Cunningham and his headquarters. The area of operations for the next phase was in the Abyssinian Highlands where most of the country was 6,000 feet above sea level. The possibility of making a successful force landing was very remote and, to make the flying conditions more difficult, it rained heavily, rendering all the temporary landing grounds unusable.

The ground troops were tasked to pursue the Italian forces retreating to the south and to the south west. Close support aircraft carried out large-scale bombing and ground strafing attacks on enemy positions and the lines of communication. The continued bombing and machine-gun attacks, in conjunction with the artillery fire, forced large numbers of the enemy to surrender. As the close-support aircraft continued to harass the enemy, the bombing force and the Hurricanes operating from Addis Ababa constantly attacked military objectives further afield and most of the Regia Aeronautica's remaining aircraft were destroyed on the ground.

On 4 July 1941 the final surrender of the enemy forces in the area marked the victorious end of the Southern Abyssinian campaign in which the somewhat antiquated air forces under Bill's command played such an outstanding part.

A key element of the victory was the close co-operation established between the air and ground forces throughout the chain of command down to the operational level. General Cunningham was full of praise for Bill's co-operation throughout the campaign and commented in his despatch:

> '...its air force commander with his own communications advanced with the commander
> of the leading troops. The value of this arrangement from the army point of view cannot
> be over stressed. Air support for the forward troops of the nature called for by the situation
> was "on tap", and engendered the greatest confidence amongst both commanders and men.'

This statement is of great significance to the student of aerial warfare, in particular those with an interest in the air/land war. Here is the first example of a co-ordinated form of close support between the ground commander and the airmen providing support. The reference to 'on tap' is a forerunner of the 'cab rank' system used to such great effect by the Tactical Air Forces during the campaigns in north-west Europe. Yet, very little credit is given by historians to Bill Sowrey and his air staff for pioneering this tactic that was to have such a significant influence in the desert wars and in Europe.

After the victories in the south of Abyssinia there remained only one enemy stronghold and the remnants of Italian resistance in its East African empire were concentrated in the Gondar region, just to the north of Lake Tana in Northern Abyssinia. It was now possible to co-ordinate the air support of the ground forces with the forces commanded by AOC Sudan.

A combination of the deterioration of (already aged) aircraft, losses and transfers to other theatres, began to reduce Bill's capabilities. The Fairey Battles were soon to disappear due to losses and unserviceability and the Junkers 86s were in a poor state; they too were withdrawn before the end of the campaign. Nevertheless, over the next two months his squadrons were still able to provide crucial support.

The rugged mountainous country with its heavy rainfall was frequently cloaked by thick low clouds, hampering operations. The main objective in this period was to keep the enemy bottled up in the Gondar region whilst mobile British-led 'patriot forces' established themselves at key positions and harassed the enemy at every opportunity, in particular its lines of communication.

Air attacks were carried out to lower the enemy's morale in the hope that it would surrender, as some chose to do. However, the Italian commander, General Nasi, decided to continue his resistance and this necessitated offensive action to clean up the last remaining enemy stronghold in East Africa.

Operations were spasmodic up to 4 August due to very adverse weather but then attacks intensified.

Almost all were delivered from low level in close support of ground forces and casualties amongst the depleted squadrons began to rise. Bill sent a signal to the squadron commanders stating that undue risks were not to be taken. He told them the operations did not warrant such dangers and he urged more control over the squadrons. Initially little heed was taken of Bill's orders and five more aircraft were lost – on 17 September he sent another signal protesting that 'air losses were very perturbing'.

Following a re-organisation of Middle East Command, it was decided on 25 September that operations in the Gondar region would be the responsibility of Air HQ East Africa and 47 Squadron was transferred to Bill's command to operate with 2 Wing SAAF.

On 17 October, as the campaign was reaching its climax, it was announced that Bill had been appointed a Commander of the Order of the British Empire (CBE). The same award went to his senior air staff officer, Brigadier H.C. Daniels SAAF. Just two months earlier, Bill had been mentioned in despatches. The citation for his CBE concluded:

> 'He arrived in East Africa from the Middle East on 18 April 1940 at the time holding the rank of group captain. He was thus responsible for directing the successful air operations against the Italians from the inception of the campaign in East Africa.'

In the final weeks, the Hartebeestes remained very active dropping bombs and ground strafing and Gondar came under heavy attack. This assault continued into November and Bill left for Asmara before embarking on a ten-day tour of all the SAAF units in Northern Abyssinia. Finally, on the 27th the Italians surrendered unconditionally after the large town had been pounded by bombs and artillery. It was appropriate that two Hartebeestes, aircraft of an earlier era, and that have given so much to the campaign, were circling the town when the white flags fluttered in the evening calm.

The Italian empire in East Africa had been crushed with the complete destruction of the Regia Aeronautica and the SAAF squadrons under Bill's command had played a major part in the Allied victory.

SAAF Hartebeestes operated in the light bomber role (Andrew Thomas).

Bill was loud in his praise of his SAAF units and signalled congratulations to Lieutenant Colonel M.C.P. Mostert who had been in command of the final air operations.

Congratulatory signals flowed into Bill's headquarters. The acting GOC East Africa, Lieutenant General H.E.de R. Weatherall, paid a final tribute in a signal to Bill:

'I am now at Gondar. I hear on all sides of the splendid and gallant work carried out by the air forces. No task was too difficult, no day too long.'

The Dominion success in East Africa was the first major victory in a war that had seen almost two years of constant reversals. Many of the principles of air/land warfare were created, and executed, to great effect and Bill Sowrey played a very important role in this development. In many ways he was ahead of his time, locating his HQs alongside the army, giving tactical control to lower formations and in constant and close contact with the ground commanders. It seems strange that in three volumes of the RAF history of the Second World War, this successful and impressive campaign attracts just a few pages. However, it does at least acknowledge the part played by HQ Air Forces East Africa:

'From Kenya the Dominion squadrons under Air Commodore Sowrey and his South African senior air staff officer, Brigadier Daniel, operated with wasp-like persistence against enemy airfields, dumps, M.T. concentrations and wireless stations. Most of their effort was at first taken up with reconnaissance, but to all their duties – whether in close support, or protecting Mombasa, or scouring the coastal waters of Italian Somaliland – the Dominion pilots brought a spirit so offensive that it almost inspires pity for the Italians.'

Following the announcement of Bill's award, a tribute was paid in the East African publication *Wings over Africa*:

Bill during a rare moment at his desk in Nairobi as AOC East Africa.

'The distinction of being made a Commander of the British Empire was conferred on Air Commodore William Sowrey DFC, AFC, AOC in East Africa to mark his outstanding work in directing the air forces during the successful East African campaign.

'Much has been written in these pages and elsewhere of the valuable part played by the air forces in that campaign, and the latest honour has delighted all who have had the privilege of serving under his inspiring leadership.

'Air Commodore Sowrey has never allowed personality or unit to interfere with the true spirit of service, and he has fostered, by every possible means, a friendly spirit of co-operation between both the air forces under his command, in work and in leisure. It is for that spirit of harmony, no less than for his operational and administrative leadership that he will be remembered by all ranks long after the present conflict is over.'

Praise indeed.

With operations over in the immediate region, HQ Air Forces East Africa became HQ 207 (Training) Group on 15 December and Bill remained as the AOC. Kenya became the home of a number of OTUs and they were controlled and administered by the group. He made regular visits to Cairo for meetings at HQ Middle East Air Force and his nephew Johnnie wrote home in April:

'Seen a lot of Uncle Bill in Cairo recently. He has had malaria, is now very white and is looking tired. I thought he could do with a good rest.'

The pressures of the campaign in East Africa had clearly taken their toll. After two years in Africa, Bill returned home on 21 June 1942 and three months later he retired from the RAF.

During the time that their Uncle Bill was deeply involved in the air operations in East Africa in April 1941, two of his nephews were preparing to move to Egypt. With increasing pressure mounting on the limited air capabilities in the Middle East, and the lessening of activity over the United Kingdom, it was decided to reinforce the RAF's fighter force in Egypt. Both Johnnie and Jimmy's squadrons were earmarked but the two brothers were to arrive by different routes.

Johnnie's 213 Squadron had moved to Turnhouse near Edinburgh on 21 April 1941 to prepare for overseas service. The fitting of two forty-five-gallon drop tanks under each wing suggested Malta as the likely destination but, once all preparations had been completed two weeks later, it was announced that it was to be North Africa.

The squadron was split into three groups. The main party, led by the CO, would fly off aircraft carriers in the western Mediterranean and head for Malta. After refuelling they would travel on to Egypt. A second party, mostly consisting of the ground crew, would sail via South Africa and up the Red Sea to the Suez Canal. The third party consisted of four pilots,

Crated Hurricanes ready for assembly at Takoradi (Air Historical Branch).

including Johnnie, and in early May they embarked on HMT *Highland Express* at Liverpool, with their crated Hurricanes in the hold, and headed for the Gold Coast (now Ghana).

In July 1940, an overland route, which became known as the 'Takoradi Route' had been established from Takoradi through Central Africa to Khartoum in the Sudan and then north following the River Nile to Egypt. Staging posts with refuelling and rudimentary servicing and accommodation facilities were established some 4-500 miles apart along the route. It was a remarkable achievement and by the end of the war in North Africa over 5,000 aircraft had passed along the route.

When Johnnie and his colleagues arrived in the Gold Coast, there was already a severe backlog of Hurricanes and Tomahawks waiting to be ferried to Egypt. Johnnie flew a Tomahawk and was not impressed. He was relieved to find that he would be flying a Hurricane on the long flight to Egypt.

After test flying their aircraft, the four 213 Squadron pilots took off on 6 June. For the flight across the desert they were led by a Blenheim flown by fellow Old Tonbridgian, Flight Lieutenant Peter Farr (later air vice-marshal). Flying in loose formation at 10,000 feet, the aircraft set off for Lagos for the first refuelling stop before heading north to Minna and then on to Kano. After an overnight stop, the formation set off on the most hazardous section of the route across Chad and into Sudan. After refuelling at Maiduguri, the next leg to El Geneina was the longest, involving a four-hour flight over featureless desert. The following day, two stages took them to Khartoum.

Once there, the most difficult phase of the transit was complete and there was a semblance of civilisation. On 10 June, the formation followed the River Nile to Wadi Halfa, a flight of three hours and ten minutes. The RAF pilots encountered a minor difficulty during the overnight stop at the Wadi Halfa Hotel where the Greek manager closed the bar to all except the army. This did not go down well with Johnnie and his colleagues and, with the aid of the burly Peter Farr, Johnnie threw the manager into the Nile. The possibility of recriminations the next day was resolved by the party getting airborne for Abu Sueir at a very early hour. Four hours later, they met up with their colleagues of A Flight who had already arrived in Egypt.

As Johnnie headed south on the *Highland Express*, Jimmy and his 229 Squadron colleagues were embarking on the aircraft carrier HMS *Furious* at Liverpool on 11 May. Had Johnnie not been assigned to 213 Squadron's advance party, he too would have been on *Furious* with the bulk of his squadron who were embarked together with 229 and 249 Squadrons. Below deck were sixty-three Hurricanes. A week later the carrier arrived at Gibraltar and a few days after that it steamed into the Eastern Mediterranean and on 21 May, forty-eight Hurricanes took off and headed for Malta.

Furious returned to Gibraltar to collect the remaining aircraft but was almost immediately diverted to help in the hunt for the German battleship *Bismarck*, which was loose in the North Atlantic. This allowed Jimmy and his fellow pilots to relax and enjoy two weeks in the sun at the famous Rock Hotel.

On 5 June *Furious* set off again for the Western Mediterranean with the remaining Hurricanes. Six of 229 Squadron's aircraft had flown off on the carrier's first sortie. At first light on 6 June, the squadron's CO, Squadron Leader Fred Rosier (later Air Chief Marshal Sir Fred Rosier) rolled down the flight deck and was quickly followed by the remaining eleven Hurricanes. They formed up behind a Fairey Fulmar which was to lead them on the 450-mile journey to Malta.

It was a nerve-racking flight for Jimmy and his fellow pilots. They had to fly near the enemy coast, had insufficient fuel to get involved in any combat if they were intercepted by Luftwaffe fighters and had to complete the flight in radio silence. However, they all arrived safely, and after a night's rest, they set off the following morning for Egypt. After refuelling at Mersa Matruh, the squadron arrived at Abu Sueir, a few days before Johnnie and his so-called 'advance party' arrived as the last of the large Hurricane reinforcement contingent. The brothers were together for what Johnnie described as a 'wonderful reunion'. Sadly, it was to be their last.

When they arrived in Egypt, British fortunes in the Middle East were at a low ebb. Driven out of Libya, and having just evacuated the Balkans and Crete, the situation looked bleak. Rommel and his Panzers had recently arrived and advanced to the Egyptian border and the Luftwaffe brought a new and potent dimension to the air war. Air Marshal Arthur Tedder had just arrived to take over as AOC-in-C Middle East Air Force.

The army commanders had been preparing to launch an offensive in the desert, Operation Battleaxe, in mid June with the aim of relieving Tobruk and capturing forward airfields. Tedder recognised the urgent need to bolster the few RAF fighter squadrons and the recent reinforcements, having arrived ahead of their ground crew, were attached to the resident Hurricane squadrons. This gave Tedder a fighter force of about 100 aircraft to provide air cover for the ground operations.

The frustrated Fred Rosier found that his squadron had been split up and parties of six pilots had moved into the desert to reinforce the three Hurricane squadrons. Jimmy left to join 6 Squadron, a veteran desert squadron that had been in the thick of the fighting and was operating in the tactical reconnaissance role. Johnnie's A Flight of 213 Squadron moved to the forward airstrip at Sidi Haneish to form C Flight of 73 Squadron, another with long-standing experience of operations in the Middle East.

Battleaxe opened on 15 June and Johnnie was in action immediately. He was airborne at the head of his section at 10 am. He described the action:

> 'I was ordered to patrol the Sollum area and took off with my No. 2. We climbed to 15,000 feet. I was lucky to be blessed with exceptional eyesight and could pick up aircraft at a considerable distance. We had the sea on our right and were making for Sollum when in the haze of the desert air I saw a pair of Bf 109s below and to our right going in roughly the same direction. I immediately dived to attack. I don't think we were seen as the e/a took no evasive action. I fired a longish burst into the rear of the two aircraft and pulled away as I was overshooting. I next saw the aircraft explode as it hit the ground and a pall of black smoke went up into the air.'

The pilot Feldwebel Herbert Schädlich was killed. Action on this day was fierce and 73 Squadron achieved further success but two Hurricanes were lost and two damaged. Johnnie was in action again in the afternoon and gained a second success when his section engaged a force of Bf 109s. He was also credited with probably destroying a third.

By the evening of the 17th, Battleaxe had clearly failed and British troops were back on the Egyptian border; a stalemate set in with both sides settling down to recoup and bring up supplies for the next offensive.

During this period the tactical reconnaissance squadrons were busy flying over enemy territory to monitor the enemy build-up and dispositions. On 24 June, Jimmy took off with Sergeant Wesson flying as his number two. The tactical reconnaissance role was highly specialised and very demanding and it was normal for inexperienced pilots to fly as

Jimmy a few days before he was shot down.

cover for the more experienced. Both Jimmy and Wesson were on their first patrol and it is difficult to understand how two such totally inexperienced pilots were tasked with such a demanding sortie, especially without one of the experienced pilots flying with them.

On their way to Sidi Barrani, the two young pilots were bounced by four Bf 109s led by one of the Luftwaffe's top aces Hauptmann Joachim Müncheberg. Nineteen-year-old Jimmy was shot down in flames and killed. Wesson's aircraft was damaged but he managed to limp home. Sadly, this tragedy was to be repeated over the next couple of days when two more of the six raw reinforcement pilots who had joined 6 Squadron with Jimmy were shot down and killed.

Fred Rosier was particularly saddened that his young pilots had been lost in the short period when they were detached to another squadron and not under his command. In a letter to his wife, he gave vent to his frustration and wrote:

'...have just heard that Sowrey has departed to a better land and am cast down about it. Having no control over the chaps' movements and actions is not likely to improve my present temper; still, I have tried my damnedest and am still trying.'

He later wrote:

'His loss was a great shock to us as he had endeared himself to the squadron in a very short time by his personality, cheerfulness and efficiency.'

There were many letters of condolence and the loss of Jimmy was mourned greatly. His headmaster at Gayhurst School, P.J. Campbell, wrote to Johnnie:

'It was a great shock to me to hear about your brother's death and I want to tell you how sorry I am for you all. I was very fond of Jim; no-one could help being. He had such an infectiously happy smile that even when he had been getting into trouble one could never be angry with him for more than a minute. I am sure he was a fine airman and a fine officer. The RAF was the obvious profession for him; indeed we knew that was his whole ambition as long ago as the time he was at Gayhurst.'

Finally, a *Times* correspondent captured the feelings of many when he wrote:

'His many friends at home cherish happy memories of his unfailing gaiety, his cheerful personality, and his adventurous spirit – added to which he was an outstanding pilot and completely absorbed in his work for the RAF.'

Over sixty years later, cousin Freddie made the simple statement in a voice full of emotion, 'he was my favourite cousin'.

Johnnie, who was based on a nearby landing strip, was devastated when he received the news. Just like the earlier generation of Sowrey brothers, the two were very close. A few days later, Johnnie learnt that the Air Ministry had informed his parents that it was he who had been killed. The two brothers had almost identical initials and the authorities had mixed the two when the casualty telegram was sent. Jimmy's loss affected the whole family deeply. In this remarkable family that gave so much service to their country in war, Jimmy was to be the only casualty. Today he lies at rest in the Halfaya Sollum War Cemetery in Egypt near the border with Libya.

Three days after Jimmy's death, Johnnie and two of his close colleagues left for a few days leave in the Delta before re-joining 213 Squadron, which had just moved to Palestine. The squadron's various flights were finally reunited at Haifa on 7 July and attached to 80 Squadron.

The campaign against the Vichy French in Syria was drawing to a close. The main task was strafing Vichy airfields and Johnnie flew on these, on one occasion providing support to twelve Hurricanes of 3 (RAAF) and 260 Squadrons. He attacked the airfield at Aleppo, but on the 15th, the Syrian Armistice was signed. The following day a goodwill flight of nine Blenheims and nine Hurricanes, one flown by Johnnie, flew over Beirut and Tripoli.

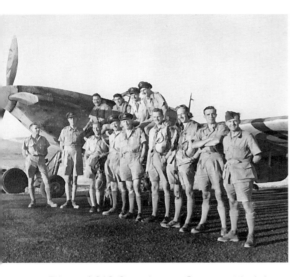

Pilots of 213 Squadron in Cyprus with Johnnie seated on the wing on the right.

After the Germans' lightning successes against Greece and the occupation of Crete, there was a great risk that they would next mount operations against Cyprus. To bolster the modest air defences of the island, 213 Squadron moved to Nicosia on 19 July and started to mount shipping and air patrols. The Regia Aeronautica mounted a few desultory bombing raids against the island and within a few days of the squadron arriving, Flight Lieutenant George Westlake had shot down two enemy bombers.

For over two months, 213 Squadron had operated as part of other squadrons but, finally, the ground crew caught up with their pilots and on 16 August, the squadron was once again a complete unit and tasked with the air defence of Cyprus.

The squadron mounted a readiness flight but there were few scrambles although one or two enemy bombers were shot down. One of the newly-arrived Hurricanes had been donated by the people of Ceylon and an appropriate insignia was painted on the nose of the aircraft. Johnnie posed in the cockpit for a photograph that was distributed widely.

At the end of October, two flights, including Johnnie's, returned to Egypt to become part of 243 Wing and to be based, initially, at El Khanka near Cairo to provide air defence for shipping and the port of Alexandria.

Johnnie shows off the experimental camouflage of his 213 Squadron Hurricane.

On 18 November, the land forces launched Operation Crusader but the squadron was very much on the periphery and saw little action. It moved to Idku just outside Alexandria, but the tedium and frustration continued as the squadron's Hurricanes were unable to climb high enough to intercept the occasional high-flying German reconnaissance aircraft.

The new training programme of dive bombing, air-to-ground gunnery and flying in larger formations, gave an insight into the next phase of the squadron's operations in the desert. However, that was still a few weeks away and, with Operation Crusader grinding to a halt near Gazala, the Luftwaffe was able to divert some of its bomber force to longer-range operations and more Junkers 88s started to appear over Alexandria. Finally, in March 1942, new Hurricane IIc aircraft with four 20-mm cannons started to arrive.

The squadron mounted many patrols but successes against the enemy bombers were few. On 15

April Johnnie chased a Junkers 88 out to sea but was unable to get close enough to open fire. Finally, success came on 21 May.

Johnnie and his No. 2 (Sergeant W.H. Stephenson RCAF) were scrambled to patrol Alexandria and were vectored on to a bandit which they identified as a Junkers 88. It dived as soon as it saw the two Hurricanes, which pursued it and shot it down. The enemy bomber crash landed near Bourg-el-Arab and the crew evacuated the aircraft. As an Egyptian police patrol arrived, the German crew opened fire. In the return fire one of the crew members was killed and another wounded.

Two days later, Johnnie and Stephenson enjoyed another success, which he later described:

'Seagull Camp, our ops centre, was plotting a high-flying aircraft approaching from the north. We climbed as swiftly as possible to our altitude at 30,000 feet only to be called by ops to say that the plot had faded. It could only mean one thing. We were over the sea at that time and I looked down – there, hardly discernible, was the speck of an aircraft. What gave it away was the wash from its propellers, twin plumes fanning out on the water. We immediately gave chase, caught the Ju 88 skimming the surface of the sea and we carried out an attack from the rear. After a short engagement the aircraft crashed into the sea. There were no survivors, though I did see some sort of fluorescent dye in the water.'

As a result of these two victories, Johnnie and Stephenson were taken to the offices of the Egyptian State Broadcasting Company to describe these two actions, the last the squadron achieved in the defence of Alexandria.

On 26 May, Rommel launched a major ground offensive in the desert and the squadron moved 200 miles to the west to operate from Gambut Main airfield. This marked the beginning of six weeks of heavy, and often confusing, battle which led eventually to the 8th Army falling back to El Alamein. Such was the ferocity of the fighting that Air Vice-Marshal Arthur 'Mary' Coningham, commanding the Desert Air Force, was asked to concentrate his fighter effort on close support operations.

Immediately after arriving at Gambut on 4 June, the squadron was in action supporting the Free French forces holding Bir Hacheim. These operations were given top priority and the squadron flew at maximum effort. Early on the morning on 10 June, twelve Hurricanes of 73 Squadron covered 213 Squadron engaged on a ground-attack mission. The Hurricanes were jumped by Italian and German fighters and a defensive circle was formed.

At that point, a force of Junkers 87 'Stuka' dive-bombers with fighter escorts were sighted so Johnnie and his No. 2, Pilot Officer A. Hancock, broke away. Johnnie engaged the rear Ju 87 and shot it down before diving to low level. Two Bf 109s chased the pair wounding Hancock in the arm and damaging Johnnie's aircraft, forcing him to crash land. The Bf 109s turned to strafe his aircraft and Johnnie, luckily, escaped without being hit. When all was quiet, he started walking back to Allied lines and was flying the next day.

Two days later, there was intense air activity by both sides and 213 Squadron was in the thick of the action. Johnnie damaged a Bf 109 when the squadron intercepted a large force of Ju 87s and their fighter escort. Finally, on the 14th, the prolonged resistance at Bir Hacheim broke and the Commonwealth forces began a retreat. Johnnie was airborne in the late afternoon and reported that the German Panzers were advancing – he could see a cloud of sand rising from a column that had broken through as its right hook swept round towards Tobruk.

The squadron moved back from one landing ground to another, sleeping under their aircraft and eventually finding their ground crew. Johnnie slept under the wing of his Hurricane on an inflated bed but it was punctured by camel thorn and became useless. At one location they learnt that the NAAFI stores were to be blown up so they sent a three-ton truck to secure as much beer, provisions and clothes as possible before it was destroyed. He summed up the feeling of many who had been in the desert from the early days:

'Throughout my time it was ding/dong up and back. Wavell went then we had Auchinleck, then Ritchie and finally Montgomery. It was all very disheartening under these conditions going nowhere and we used to meet the "Pongos" (army) in Cairo and ask them "which retreat were you in?"'

On the 16th Johnnie was on patrol over Tobruk when his section was jumped by three Bf 109s. He engaged one and 'fired everything I had into one with no visible effect and I could only claim a damaged'. The intense activity continued and the hard-pressed ground crew were forced to pack and retreat on virtually every day. Tobruk fell late on the 21st and the squadron found itself at Sidi Haneish but operational sorties over the battlefield continued. Air fighting reached a climax on the 26th when twelve Hurricanes were scrambled late in the afternoon and intercepted a force of enemy fighters; five were shot down. Johnnie and his section immediately took off on hearing of the combat and intercepted a large force of Ju 87s and their escort. Three were shot down and Johnnie damaged a Bf 109.

Ground crew at work on Johnnie's Hurricane.

With Rommel advancing to the Egyptian border, the squadron fell back rapidly to a landing ground east of El Alamein. At the end of this hectic phase of fighting Wing Commander Fred Rosier saw Johnnie and told him that he was to go immediately to 80 Squadron to take up a flight commander post. Two days after he left 213 Squadron, having been with the unit for fourteen months, his colleagues were involved in a major action which resulted in the loss of four pilots, including Johnnie's great friend Cyril Temlett DFC. They had been together since their time at Cranwell and Johnnie was deeply affected.

With the situation on the ground stabilised at the El Alamein line, air activity continued but on a less intense scale. Late in the afternoon of 4 July, Johnnie took off to intercept an incoming raid. He described the action:

'On the evening of 3 July we were informed that the "Y" Service had picked up information that there was to be a Stuka party the following day. We prepared to intercept them. I was leading the wing. The controller gave us height and vector and we saw the Stuka formation coming towards us head on. They were at exactly the same height and were closing quickly. Before they reached us they broke off to the right and I think jettisoned their bombs. I turned into them and fired a deflection shot at very close quarters, I was sure I had him.

'The next thing I knew was I'd been in a collision with another as my aircraft was completely out of control in a sort of inverted spin. The only thing to do was to bale out which I did without much difficulty. However, we understood that at that time the Germans were shooting pilots in their parachutes so I carried out a delayed drop. Although my parachute opened correctly, I received quite severe bruising. Fortunately I landed amongst our own troops (4th Hussars) who were very hospitable. After a night with them they kindly returned me to my squadron, then at Alamein.'

As a result of this incident, Johnnie was entitled to become a member of the Caterpillar Club having only a few weeks earlier joined the Late Arrivals Club after being shot down on 10 June.

Throughout his time in the desert, Johnnie, just as his father and uncles had done in the First World War, wrote home regularly. He always felt able to discuss issues with his father and in a private letter in September he felt able to release some of the pent-up concerns that he would never have divulged to his comrades. The letter also gives a powerful insight into the pressures these young men faced but so rarely spoke about. He wrote:

'My dear Dad
    'I haven't written to you for some time but I expect you have gathered most of what has been going on.
    'I'm afraid I had to pull out from actual operations as my nerve was going a bit. As you know one does somewhere in the region of 200 hours before being sent on rest. I had done the requisite number before going back to the desert for this last show but decided to stay on as so many in the squadron knew little about desert warfare. Anyway, I stuck my neck out a bit too far up at Gambut and let myself in for a good pasting by some Me 109s. I got back rather shaken but simply had to carry on as I was leading the squadron every other show.
    'Eventually I was posted to 80, something I didn't particularly want. They had not seen very much action and their spirit was not good. I didn't think I was in the fettle to take on such a job. This I told the CO but the AOC insisted I should stay a month and then go for a rest. So I stayed. Then as you know I was leading the wing one day and found some Stukas and made a head-on attack on them. It was a queer sight being right amongst them and seeing their bombs falling as they jettisoned them.
    'I'm afraid the inevitable happened and I collided with one and only managed to bale out after my a/c had gone over the vertical and thrown me out. That shook me a bit, but when I got back and rang up to let them know I was OK, I found my best friend [Temlett] had been killed and it shook me even more. As my month with 80 was almost up I asked if I could go on rest then. I had a recommendation from the MO and from the CO for my return to England but Middle East are sending me to train pilots before they join their squadron…'

This letter graphically illustrates how even the most stable and effective pilots were affected after months of combat. In addition to the strain of fighting and leading, Johnnie was still affected by the loss of his young brother, to whom he had been deeply attached, and to his closest friend, Temlett.

Johnnie was sent to be an instructor on 244 Wing Training Flight in the Canal Zone where he remained until the end of the year. He had flown 197 operational sorties, shot down five aircraft and shared in the destruction of two and damaged others. To the surprise of many, despite becoming an ace, he received no decoration.

The air war in the desert was intense and conditions for air and ground crews were harsh. Many years later, Fred Rosier captured the realities of life in the desert when he wrote:

'Life in the Western Desert fifty years ago was tough and precarious. We had to put up with the extremes of heat and cold, the flies, the sandstorms. The shortage of water, the muddy tea, the almost daily diet of bully beef and lard biscuits, the fear and the never-ending loss of friends and comrades. Yet, with the passage of time most of us tend to dwell on the brighter side, the camaraderie and the cheerfulness which existed among all ranks, the uplift which came with the arrival of the beer ration, the fun of the squadron parties, the joy of the occasional dip in the sea, the tonic effects of weekends in Alexandria or Cairo, the sing songs, the elation of winning, and that great feeling of being alive.'

A Savoia-Marchetti S.73 in RAF markings at Jijiga.

Early in January 1943, Johnnie left Egypt to join 71 OTU based near Port Sudan where he spent three months training new pilots on fighter and ground-attack tactics flying Hurricane IIAs and the Harvard. On 10 March he moved further south to RAF Eastleigh near Nairobi where he joined the East Africa Communications Flight.

Johnnie spent six months flying with the communications flight, which was equipped with a wide variety of aircraft. In his first ten days with the unit, he flew seven different types of aircraft, many obsolete bi-planes. He soon started to fly the flight's main aircraft, the Hudson, on routes to Somaliland, Aden and Madagascar.

On 19 May he flew a captured three-engine Savoia-Marchetti S.73. The flight had three of these aircraft which, with a capacity to carry eighteen passengers, offered a significant capability. During July and August, Johnnie flew many sorties in the S.73 on long-range flights and on two occasions the centre engine lost oil pressure resulting in a force landing in the bush.

Throughout his life, Johnnie never lost an opportunity to fly and he took full advantage of the availability of all the types on offer. In October, when he was assessed as 'above average', Johnnie returned to Egypt having flown over 400 hours during his time at Eastleigh. He wrote to his father:

> 'Nairobi was a grand interlude. Uncle Bill's name will stay there for some time, he was very much respected by all.'

On 1 November he joined the recently-formed 336 (Hellenic) Squadron, the second Greek fighter squadron in the Desert Air Force, to add to his vast experience on the Hurricane and tactical fighter operations. Flying from Mersa Matruh, the squadron was employed on shipping protection and air defence duties off the Libyan coast. In January, Spitfire VBs started to arrive to replace the Hurricane IIcs. With the Allied armies established in Italy, the Mediterranean and North Africa region was quiet and the squadron saw very little action.

During this quiet period he was able to travel to the Canal Zone and in March was reunited with his father, who was on an inspection tour of maintenance units in North Africa and the Middle East and they enjoyed some time together in Cairo.

On 4 July 1944, Johnnie boarded a Liberator and flew back to England after almost three years away in the Middle East.

Chapter Seventeen

AIR WAR EUROPE

Having converted to the Mustang, Freddie arrived at Gatwick to join 26 Squadron at the end of March 1942. The squadron was the first to re-equip with the American fighter and its much greater capabilities were soon apparent. For a number of months, it was something of a trials squadron providing close support for army exercises.

The squadron also had, on strength, a few Tomahawk and Proctor aircraft, the latter used for camouflage trials. Despite the superior performance of the Mustang, many of the training sorties differed little from earlier days. Artillery shoots, message dropping, and tactical reconnaissance featured heavily in Freddie's logbook. The Tomahawk was used for photographic reconnaissance sorties.

The squadron went on the offensive in late July when tactical reconnaissance sorties were flown from West Malling and, in the space of five days, Freddie flew nine times. In this short period, the

A Mustang I of 26 Squadron.

squadron lost three experienced pilots when two were killed in action and the third became a POW.

This concentrated period of training and operations was a prelude to Operation Jubilee, the ill-fated combined operation against Dieppe, when the squadron had a disastrous day resulting in the loss of five pilots. Freddie missed the operation having suffered a serious eye infection called iritis, a condition where the iris sticks and can tear round the edges unless treated. With the state of medical science at the time, the authorities decided to send Freddie to the RAF Convalescent Hospital at Torquay for treatment.

The hospital was in the Palace Hotel, requisitioned in 1939, and displaying a large red cross painted on the roof in accordance with the Geneva Convention. Staffed by service and civilian medical and nursing staff, the hospital was used extensively for aircrew recuperating from wounds and injuries.

Freddie's admittance coincided with a new Luftwaffe tactic, the 'tip and run' raids. Through their intelligence networks the Germans were aware that the RAF had requisitioned many hotels on the south coast to house aircrew training units. The Luftwaffe adapted some of their fighter aircraft to carry bombs and formed them into special units. Flying singly or in pairs, the aircraft crossed the English Channel at very low level to avoid radar detection, before attacking these seaside resorts with bombs and cannons.

On a quiet, summer Sunday morning the Palace Hotel was targeted. Freddie recounted the event:

'On Sunday 25 October 1942, I was going into Torquay to take a girl out for lunch but 11 am found me in the billiard room watching a very capable Polish player and standing by the large sash windows looking out to sea over the lawns and woodland in front of the Palace Hotel.

'Two aircraft appeared head-on low, and I thought that they were Me 109s. When gun flashes appeared on the leading edges of the wings and strikes could be heard on the upper storeys, I decided it would be safer to lie down under the window. There was a gigantic flash and I found myself head down under rubble, able to move only my left foot through approximately fifteen degrees.

'After an unpleasant time with the weight increasing and other problems, my (barely) twenty years decided that there was little future in this so started shouting "get me out of here!" Ultimately, I heard a voice say "there's one over here" and digging started. A hole appeared and a wonderful British soldier found my hand which he held until my head was clear when a Woodbine or similar was stuck between my lips! I think that we were stretchered to the entrance hall and then to a local hospital for a few days treatment before a hospital train was organised to take the survivors up to Loughborough.'

Freddie was one of the fortunate ones. Two bombs had been dropped with one a direct hit on the east wing, which was wrecked and where most of the casualties occurred. Nineteen patients and nursing staff were killed and forty-five wounded. Amongst those killed were a group captain and three female nurses. The hospital was extensively damaged and never returned to use.

Freddie's injuries delayed his return to operational flying and it was not until the end of November that he was able to rejoin 26 Squadron. During his absence, the squadron had been employed on patrol duties off the south coast in an attempt to intercept the tip and run raiders, a task Freddie relished after his ordeal earlier in the year. A number of sightings of Focke Wulf 190s were made and Freddie chased six of them on 15 December but could not get within firing range. These operations continued for a few weeks but Freddie thought that their Mustangs could have been used more extensively:

'Whilst serving on 26 Squadron, I wondered why more use was not being made of our Mustangs against the Luftwaffe "tip and run" daylight raids during 1942-43. We were patrolling offshore at about 2,000 feet – Brighton to Beachy Head being one of our assigned "beats".

'Standing patrols are an inefficient use of flying hours at any time, but against raiders at wave-top height and low-level overland, they may be the only counter. Certainly the inhabitants of the south coast towns were vociferous in their demand for protection.

'The Mustang I had good low-level performance; it had an endurance better than any other in-service RAF fighter with sorties up to two-and-a-half hours possible; and being based at Gatwick's grass airfield we were about five minutes flying from the coast. With the introduction of the faster Typhoon, the window of opportunity closed.'

After a few patrols, and a week's concentrated flying at 1526 Beam Approach Training (BAT) Flight on Oxfords, it was clear that Freddie's eye problem had not cleared up sufficiently and he was taken off flying for a further three months. When he returned, in early April, the squadron had stopped operations to begin a period of intensive training in 83 Group of the Second Tactical Air Force (2TAF). Freddie explains the background in a letter to the author:

'The 1st Tactical Air Force in the Western Desert had built on the East African campaign in putting army and air force commanders side by side together with their staffs. This was now being transported to England to prepare for the invasion of the continent. We had three highly-decorated and experienced pilots from North Africa attached – Tony Bartley, Ronnie Gilmour and Tommy Tinsey – to prepare the squadron for sustained operations. Advice such as "never fly straight and level in the combat area" and "fly like a sack of s—t"'are still remembered some seventy years later and were borne of hard-won experience. Army co-operation was now mainstream and although we still shared a ditch with our army formations when sent off as "air liaison officers" we were not alone. That summer the squadron moved through Fighter Command to 123 Airfield of 83 Group, 2nd Tactical Air Force, a composite, all-abilities formation where co-located joint staffs met the army requests for air support with understanding and alacrity.'

Freddie was following in the footsteps of his Uncle Bill and two cousins as 2TAF started building on the foundations they had laid for what would develop into one of the most crucial aspects of the air war during, and after, the invasion of Normandy.

To celebrate the RAF's twenty-fifth birthday, Freddie met his long-term girlfriend Anne Haviland, who was a planner in the Airwork factory, and sensibly married her in 1946.

After the frustrations of his eye problem, Freddie had a period of intensive flying as the squadron practiced its tactics for the air/land battle. In addition to tactical reconnaissance,

Freddie poses on his Mustang.

air-to-air combat and cine-gun exercises were increased, as was tactical formation flying. Air-to-ground firing also featured regularly.

Finally, the squadron returned to operations on 1 July. The following day, Freddie flew on a 'Rhubarb' operation (a small-scale fighter attack in search of targets at low level) led by Flight Lieutenant 'Kit' North-Lewis DFC when three locomotives were attacked near Ghent. Freddie recorded 'much flak' in his logbook. Three days later he was taking photographs of Boulogne harbour.

Having just returned to operations, it came as a surprise when the squadron was ordered to Bally-herbert in Northern Ireland to exercise with the army. They also provided day fighter cover for any enemy intruder operations, but all remained quiet.

After eighteen, somewhat interrupted, months on 26 Squadron, Freddie finished his tour in mid-November 1943 with 200 flying hours on Mustangs and Tomahawks, and with an above average as-sessment as a fighter-reconnaissance pilot. He then joined 55 (War) Flying Instructor Course at RAF Upavon. Despite all his single-seat aircraft experience, he was the victim of 'the exigencies of war', having to go where you are most needed, and he found himself training to be an instructor on the twin-engine Oxford.

Six weeks after commencing the course, he had flown sixty hours and qualified as a 'B' Cat instructor. Two weeks later he was instructing at 18 (Pilot) Advanced Flying Unit at Snitterfield near Stratford-upon-Avon. The role of the unit was to acclimatise pilots trained on the various overseas schemes to conditions flying over a darkened countryside and with the vagaries of the British weather.

By this time, John senior had been in his post as DAI for five years, most of it as a civil servant. The scale of aeronautical inspection had risen dramatically, not least because of the many RAF units that

John senior as director of Aeronautical Inspection Services.

had developed world wide. John had recommended that the Air Ministry should resume inspection control at overseas establishments, where the majority of inspectors were service-men, and this suggestion was imple-mented in January 1944 by the formation of the Directorate of Aeronautical Inspection Services (DAIS). All overseas inspection was transferred from MAP to the Air Ministry and John was appointed as the director. As head of a largely serv-ice-manned organisation, it was de-cided that the director should be in a blue uniform and on 27 December 1943, John was made an air com-modore in the Reserve of Air Force Officers (RAFO). The reorganisa-tion meant he needed to travel over-seas extensively providing an opportunity for him to spend a few days with his son Johnnie in Egypt.

The responsibility for inspection within the United Kingdom remained with AID, which was still under the control of MAP. This was the situation until April 1946 when DAIS took over AID in all RAF units – John was still in post to put this measure into effect.

Like many distinguished officers of the First World War and inter-war years, his two brothers were frustrated at the lack of opportunities to 'make a contribution'. Towards the end of 1943, an opportunity arose which Fred and Bill responded to immediately. The Air Training Corps (ATC) had established a number of gliding schools throughout the country and these were organised on a regional basis. On 4 August 1943, Bill was appointed as the command gliding officer for the south-west district with nine squadrons and a headquarters at Exeter. Two months later Fred was appointed to command the south-east area with six squadrons and a headquarters at Sevenoaks.

The Elementary Gliding Schools had been set up following a meeting on 23 May 1941 to give cadets some experience of 'hands-on' flying. The first school was opened in 1942 after the first instructor's course and, later in the year, the Kirby Cadet glider was approved as the standard ATC glider. Arrangements were made for the supply of material by MAP and the gliders were inspected by John Sowrey's AID inspectors during construction. Almost 300 gliders were manufactured, some by woodworking firms.

Bill and Fred supervised the build-up of the schools and made many visits to see them in action. On one visit to the Portsmouth School, a spot-landing competition was in progress and Fred was invited to participate. With virtually no experience on gliders, he was winched into the air and his landing was the closest to the landing marker, as much to his surprise as it was to the onlookers.

In July 1944, Johnnie returned from the Middle East and completed some refresher flying at a fighter OTU at Kirton-in-Lindsey before joining 131 Squadron at Friston a few miles west of Eastbourne. The squadron was equipped with the Spitfire VII and had recently arrived from Culmhead. Johnnie flew on its first operation from the new airfield on 31 August when he escorted a force of Lancasters attacking the V-1 launching sites in the Pas de Calais region.

Bomber escorts and high-level sweeps were to be the squadron's main task as the bomber offensive over Germany was resumed after its extensive use during the operations in Normandy. Johnnie escorted Lancasters on a daylight raid to Emden. Approaching the German border the Spitfires were at their maximum range and had to return, but USAAF Mustangs arrived to take over the close escort of the bombers.

At this stage of the war, the Allied bomber force mounted a major campaign against the German oil industry and Bomber Command joined in the daylight attacks against the synthetic oil plants in western Germany. On 11 September, 131 Squadron was one of twenty Spitfire squadrons escorting a force of 100 Halifax bombers attacking the plant at Gelsenkirchen. Johnnie recorded 'intense flak'.

The following day, another large daylight attack was mounted when the plant at Wanne-Eickel was the target. Johnnie was airborne for over two hours and after a short rest he was up again to escort Lancasters to the plants around Dortmund. Again heavy flak was encountered.

Johnnie's next close-escort operation was during the ill-fated Operation Market Garden, the Allied airborne operation to capture the bridges at Nijmegen and Arnhem. On 21 September he provided cover for a stream of Dakotas attempting to drop supplies to the beleaguered ground forces. A few days later he gave close escort to Dakotas landing at a forward airstrip near Nijmegen.

By the end of September, 131 Squadron had resumed bomber escort missions. Johnnie escorted thirty-six Marauders of the USAAF's 9th Air Force on a mission to bomb bridges near Arnhem. During October, he took Lancasters to Kleve and Halifaxes to Gelsenkirchen where, once again, the force ran into heavy flak.

Johnnie flew his last operational sortie of the war when he took off from Friston on 30 October. As the Allied armies advanced into Holland, a large pocket of fierce enemy resistance had been established on the Dutch island of Walcheren, at the entrance of the River Scheldt which led to the vital ports of Vlissingen (Flushing) and Antwerp. 102 Lancasters, with support from the Pathfinder Force, attacked the gun batteries and they were escorted by the Spitfires of 131 Squadron. On landing, Johnnie's air war was over.

In the postwar years, Johnnie summed up his time with 131 Squadron:

'On arrival in the UK I was posted to a Spitfire squadron operating from the south of Eng-

Ground crew prepare a Horsa glider.

land. We flew the Spitfire VII, the high-altitude version with a pressure cabin; a beautiful aeroplane. We carried out escort work to heavy bombers deep into Germany, medium bombers operating over Holland and cover for Operation Market Garden, the parachute drop on Arnhem. During all these operations I never saw a single German aircraft; our control of the skies was total apart from the V-2 rockets which we could see being launched.'

On 31 October, 131 Squadron was withdrawn from operations to prepare for service in the Far East theatre. Since Johnnie had only recently returned from a long period overseas, he left the squadron for HQ Fighter Command on promotion to squadron leader to join the training staff where he remained for almost a year.

On 13 April 1945, the *London Gazette* announced that Acting Squadron Leader John Adam Sowrey had been awarded the DFC. The citation read:

'This officer is a skilful and resolute fighter. He has participated in a very large number of sorties including many attacks on enemy airfields and lines of supply. In air fighting he has destroyed five enemy aircraft. Squadron Leader Sowrey has invariably displayed a high degree of courage and, throughout a long period of operational flying, his devotion to duty has been unfailing.'

In the eyes of many, this was a long-overdue recognition of his sustained service and courage. It is surprising that his successes in North Africa did not receive recognition at the time and the reference in the citation to his gallant service in the desert war indicates that someone had realised the omission and was determined to rectify the situation.

Throughout the summer months Freddie had been at Snitterfield instructing on the Oxford, and later the Anson, before he received an unexpected posting. Instead of returning to a fighter squadron (he had hoped to be posted to Typhoons), he was sent to fly gliders.

There had been heavy losses of experienced glider pilots during Operation Market Garden and, with other large-scale air landings anticipated, there was a need to increase rapidly the output of trained glider pilots. At this stage of the war, there was a surfeit of trained powered pilots and many RAF pilots were sent to fill vacancies in the glider force. On 10 October Freddie reported to the Glider Instructor School at Shobdon in Herefordshire and, in the course of the next three days, he flew twenty-one sorties in the Hotspur glider, fourteen of them solo. On 21 October, he arrived at 22 Heavy Glider Conversion Unit at Keevil in Wiltshire. After just one familiarisation sortie on the Horsa glider, he started instructing RAF pilots.

For the next twelve months, Freddie instructed on the Horsa and the American Hadrian glider and flew the Albemarle tug aircraft. In the build-up to the Rhine crossings in March 1945, the intensity of training increased and some exercises involved 'balbos' of eight Hadrians. In mid-March, he flew on a number of exercises towing Hadrians in large formations on long-range exercises, some at night.

Throughout his time at Keevil training RAF pilots and men of the Glider Pilot Regiment, Freddie met senior army officers and discussed with them his experiences, and philosophies, on air/land operations and co-operation. Years later he recognised the value of these meetings:

> 'I had the opportunity to talk with the senior officers of the Glider Pilot Regiment (Brigadier George Chatterton, Colonel Billy Griffith) about the need for air superiority, and flak suppression, in glider operations and their subsequent re-supply. This was an apprenticeship for subsequent postwar tours in the chief of staff secretariat and as a station commander in Transport Command.'

Twelve months after joining the unit, Freddie flew his final sortie when he spent all day flying an Albemarle as he towed twenty-four Hadrians to Shepherds Grove in Suffolk where they were to be stored. He left Keevil in mid-October with an above average assessment as a tug and glider pilot. In the New Year's Honours List announced on 1 January 1946, he was mentioned in despatches.

Chapter Eighteen

AUXILIARY SQUADRONS

In the aftermath of the war, personnel inevitably found themselves filling short-term appointments until repatriation and demobilisation plans had taken effect. Both Johnnie and Freddie spent short periods at various units. By October 1945, Johnnie was at Merryfield in Somerset in the operations wing and Freddie was at HQ 38 Group in the Accident Investigation Branch. In the summer of 1946, both moved to more settled appointments.

The first austere months of peace were ones of relief but it was also unsettling from a career perspective. As an ex-Cranwell cadet, Johnnie was serving on a permanent commission and he decided to remain in the RAF. Freddie had also decided to make the RAF his long-term career but he was still waiting for confirmation. However, his personal life and long time happiness had been assured when he married Anne Margaret Haviland on 9 March 1946 at Crowborough.

On the outbreak of the war, the Auxiliary Air Force (AAF) squadrons had been embodied into the RAF 'for the emergency' but when the war ended, their number plates passed to squadrons of the regular RAF. However, on 2 June 1946, the AAF was re-formed as a force of thirteen day-fighter squadrons, three night-fighter and four light-bomber squadrons. All were converted to day-fighter squadrons shortly afterwards.

Freddie and Anne marry at Crowborough.

Unlike the pre-war auxiliaries, only trained air and ground crews were to be recruited initially. To establish the squadrons quickly and effectively, each had a small cadre of regular officers, which included the adjutant, flying instructor and engineering officer. Both Johnnie and Freddie were posted to AAF squadrons to fill one of these regular appointments. Johnnie headed north to Scotland and Freddie to London.

After a brief spell flying the Spitfire with 164 Squadron, Johnnie, who had reverted to his substantive rank of flight lieutenant, left for Edinburgh to be adjutant of 603 (City of Edinburgh) Squadron, arriving at Turnhouse on 1 July. With the squadron building up from scratch, this was a busy appointment. Most of the pilots joining the squadron had not flown since the end of the war so Johnnie spent many hours in the squadron Harvard giving refresher training to the new arrivals. To add to his numerous responsibilities, he also filled the post of acting station commander of the airfield which had just been transferred from Fighter Command to Reserve Command.

On 3 October, General Dwight D. Eisenhower, the wartime supreme commander in NW Europe, visited Edinburgh to receive the freedom of the city. Johnnie led the squadron contingent in the parade mounted for the occasion.

The pattern of squadron activity was very similar to the pre-war days with flying at the weekends and ground training conducted one night each week at the squadron's town headquarters. The first Spitfire arrived on 27 October and, by the spring, the squadron had six Spitfire LF XVIs on strength, rising in the coming months to nine. Some of the wartime pilots returned in ranks two or three lower than their wartime rank. These included an old squadron stalwart, Group Captain 'Sheep' Gilroy DSO, DFC & Bar, who came back to command the squadron in the rank of squadron leader. There were numerous recruitment drives and in April 1947 an intensive one-week effort was launched with the assistance of the editors of the local newspapers.

One of the traditions of the pre-war era to be resurrected was a two-week summer camp and in June the squadron left for Woodvale near Southport taking two Harvards and eight Spitfires. Training included opportunities to fire on the weapons range at Jurby on the Isle of Man and air firing on a drogue towed by a Martinet.

Just before leaving the squadron at the end of August, Johnnie met up with an old chum from his wartime days, Jack Meadows. An experienced night-fighter pilot with the DFC, Meadows had left the RAF as a wing commander but was one of the first to jump at the chance to return to flying, albeit as a flying officer. A letter he wrote years later captured the essence and spirit of the postwar auxiliaries:

Pilots of 603 Squadron with Johnnie on the extreme right.

'I had just joined 600 Squadron at Biggin Hill when my firm sent me to Edinburgh. I thought that was that but the squadron adj wrote to John Sowrey, adjutant of 603 in Edinburgh and told him to contact me. After a boozy "selection board" in L'Aperitif in Rose Street, with John, Count Stevens and another 603 "old boy" – all ex-group captains – I became Flying Officer J.P. Meadows, AAF. Dropping several ranks was happily accepted by ex-regulars and auxiliaries at that time. Quickly the routine was established as before, flying every weekend, with two evenings a week ground school at Town HQ.'

Johnnie's time with the Edinburgh auxiliaries came to an end in the autumn of 1947 when he was promoted to the substantive rank of squadron leader and he moved to Hendon to join the staff of HQ 65 (London) Reserve Group, where he had responsibility for operations and training of the RAFVR flying schools, auxiliary squadrons and the Air Training Corps in the London area.

Cousin Freddie joined 615 (County of Surrey) Squadron at Biggin Hill in May 1946 as the training officer. Winston Churchill, whose home at Chartwell was just a few miles from Biggin Hill, was the squadron's honorary air commodore and he always showed a great interest in their activities. The squadron soon became universally known as 'Churchill's Own'.

The squadron was commanded by Battle of Britain ace Squadron Leader R.G. Kellett, DSO, DFC. Initially, equipped with two Harvards for continuation training, it was not until the beginning of November that the first Spitfire XIVs started to arrive. Freddie had the task of collecting them from Keevil before giving each an air test.

The severe winter of 1947 curtailed flying seriously but on 7 March Freddie and his CO, Ronald Kellett, left for Dublin on board an Aer Lingus Dakota. To encourage recruiting, they had decided to acquire an aircraft that could be used to give the ground crew an opportunity to fly. Kellett had purchased a Walrus amphibian (G-AIZG) for £150 and the day after arriving in Dublin, they flew the aircraft back to Biggin Hill.

The first three Spitfire XXIs arrived in early April and Freddie carried out an acceptance check on each but a great deal of his time was instructing on the Harvard. The weekends were always busy and it was normal for him to fly at least five sorties a day with new pilots and those under training.

On 30 July Freddie became a father when his daughter Susan was born but twenty-four hours later he took off for Horsham St Faith in Norfolk for the squadron's summer camp. In addition to the Spitfires and the two Harvards, the Walrus was also flown to Horsham St Faith where it was used to give flights to the ground crew, including trips to the nearby beaches. On one occasion the aircraft put down in the sea causing pandemonium with rescue rockets being fired and resulting in the launching of the Lowestoft lifeboat. A donation of £5 to the RNLI funds avoided further embarrassment.

Freddie leads a formation of Spitfire XXIs over Biggin Hill.

Summer camps were very popular with the men of auxiliary squadrons and the two-week period offered concentrated training including air-to-air and air-to-ground sorties flown on the weapons ranges in the Wash. Some of the targets used by Freddie had been constructed and developed during the time that his father and his Uncle Bill had been the commandants at Sutton Bridge.

On return to Biggin Hill on 16 August, the eight Spitfires flew over Chartwell in formation to salute their honorary air commodore. To commemorate the Battle of Britain, RAF stations held an 'At Home' day when the gates were opened to the public and these annual events became a major feature in the calendar of almost all RAF stations. With its deep association with the Battle, and its proximity to London, Biggin Hill's Open Day was immensely popular and attracted large crowds.

September was largely taken up with formation and display practices and on Battle of Britain Day, 15 September, Freddie led formations of aircraft over local towns in Surrey. The station was opened to the public on the 20th and 615 Squadron provided many of the displays culminating in a flypast by twelve aircraft with Churchill taking the salute.

In addition to the posts of squadron commander and flight commander, all fighter and fighter-bomber squadrons had two other specialist appointments. One was the qualified flying instructor (QFI) who was responsible for continuation training and instrument-flying practice. The other post was the pilot attack instructor (PAI) who was responsible for supervising weapons and tactical training. These were two much sought after duties with most squadron pilots aspiring to qualify for one or the other. Freddie was a very experienced flying instructor and at the end of November he was selected to attend a PAI course.

He set off to join 85 PAI Course at the Central Gunnery School (CGS) based at Leconfield in East Yorkshire. Throughout the three-month course he flew the Spitfire XVI with a Packard-built Merlin 266 engine. Optimised for ground-attack operations, the aircraft had two 20-mm cannons and it could carry two 500-lb bombs under the wings or six 3-in rocket projectiles (RP) with 60-lb warheads.

The pace of instruction on the ground and in the air was intense. In the first month of the course, which included Christmas, Freddie flew thirty-two air exercises, a pace that continued for the rest of the course. All facets of day-fighter operations were taught, discussed and then practiced in the air. The air exercises started with the basics but all were debriefed in great detail and many soon discovered that there was rather more to being a fighter pilot than they had perhaps thought.

Use of the gyro-gunsight figured largely in the early exercises before manoeuvres and interceptions against other fighters and bombers were practiced. The next phase included air-to-air firing against a drogue target towed by another aircraft and many of these sorties concluded with attacks against ground targets on the nearby Skipsea weapons range.

As the course progressed, the exercises became progressively more advanced. Attacks against bomber formations became more complex and tactical exercises were flown. Rocket firing against targets at Skipsea was introduced towards the end of the course and each student flew with an instructor in a Master aircraft when instructional techniques had to be demonstrated.

An essential part of any weapons sortie was the pre-flight briefing and the subsequent de-briefing after landing. It was also important to be able to assess weapon scores achieved during the flying exercises, which included interpreting the camera-gun film. In addition to displaying proficient flying skills, the PAI had to be able to impart his knowledge and critical analysis of sorties to his fellow squadron pilots. Throughout the course, and on each flying exercise, students had to demonstrate these numerous skills.

At the end of the course, Freddie was awarded a Category 'A' (distinguished) pass and was assessed as an above average fighter combat leader and instructor.

At the beginning of March 1948 he returned to 615 Squadron, which was now part of the Royal Auxiliary Air Force following the announcement on 16 December 1947 that King George VI had given permission for the 'Royal' prefix in recognition of the outstanding wartime service of the twenty-one auxiliary squadrons.

With his newly-acquired qualification as a PAI, Freddie found his training task significantly increased. He continued to instruct the new and less-experienced pilots on the Harvard, but now had the additional responsibility for the operational weapons and tactical training.

At this time Freddie was suffering with an increasing stiffness of the back, which had been diagnosed a few months earlier as ankylosing spondylitis and was worsened by the injuries he suffered during the bombing of the Palace Hotel in October 1942. The vertebrae progressively fused together and this was treated by deep X-rays at the Westminster Hospital, but with only modest success. Freddie was comfortable seated and the ailment did not affect his flying. Whilst recognising that he might suffer severe injuries if he was ever forced to eject from his aircraft, he elected to take the risk and his flying career was not affected. He attracted great respect for this courageous decision and for the rest of his career, he was known throughout the RAF with great affection as 'Bent Fred'.

The summer of 1948 passed in much the same way as the previous year. Summer camp was held at Manston and in September the formation flypasts over the towns of Surrey and the Battle of Britain 'At Home Day' were major events in the squadron's routine. There was an even greater event for Freddie and his wife Anne when their son Peter arrived on 18 November.

After two-and-a-half years, Freddie's tour with 615 Squadron came to an end in November. He had played a major part in the re-formation of the squadron, serving as the training officer and, in the latter period, as the squadron PAI. He well deserved his assessment as an above average fighter pilot and exceptional in air gunnery. To crown his success, he was given one of the plum postings for a fighter pilot. He was to return to the Central Gunnery School to be an instructor.

From pre-First World War days, the Sowrey family, men and women, had a great sense of adventure

Freddie and Anne in the HRG at the Eastbourne Rally.

and motor cars and motor cycles figured large in the lives of all the family.

During the immediate postwar years, Freddie had a variety of cars, bought depending on the state of his finances. A Fiat 500cc gave way to an Austin 7 Ruby and then a 1932 MG Midget. The purchase of 1939 HRG in April 1949 offered him the chance to take part in races when he achieved considerable success. To improve performance, he spent many hours 'under the bonnet' and his racing times improved. The next few years, with the encouragement of his wife Anne, he competed in many sprints, hill climbs and races.

Johnnie, also with a great interest in cars, turned to gliding in 1947. With his posting to 65 Group, and then to Hornchurch, there was little opportunity to fly so he spent much time at the gliding school at Hornchurch. On 4 October 1947 he had four dual flights in a Falcon III glider before flying solo from a winch launch. By the end of the day he had completed eleven flights.

In June the following year, he joined a RAF Gliding and Soaring Association (RAFGSA) expedition to Oerlinghausen, Germany. He flew a number of different types of glider and on 9 June 1948 he was winched into the air flying a Minemoa (a German sailplane). He soon contacted thermal lift and remained airborne for five hours and twenty minutes. Towards the end of the flight he climbed in a cumulo-nimbus cloud to 8,000 feet. This flight gained him two legs of the Fédération Aéronautique Internationale (FAI) Silver award. Two days later, flying a Weihe, another German glider, he completed the third and final leg for the Silver award by making a sixty-kilometre flight to the wartime Luftwaffe airfield at Rheine. To gain this prestigious award in just thirty-one flights was an outstanding achievement.

In 1949, Johnnie joined the Surrey Gliding Club at Redhill where he met and flew with some of the country's finest glider pilots and where he enjoyed a busy social life. For the next few years gliding was to be one of Johnnie's main interests.

Chapter Nineteen

TRIALS AND TESTING

Having recently enjoyed the stimulating challenges of his PAI course, Freddie was delighted when he heard that his next appointment was a return to CGS, but this time, to join the staff as an instructor. His arrival at Leconfield coincided with the delivery of the first Meteor jet fighter and on 21 January 1949, he took off in a Meteor III for his first flight in a jet. There was no two-seat version at the time so he had to read the pilot's notes, sit in the cockpit for familiarisation and then take off in the single-seat fighter. The first two-seat, dual-control Meteor, the Mark VII, arrived a few months later.

Initially there were few Meteors and the students flew the majority of their exercises in the Spitfire XVI with an occasional instructional sortie in the Master. The Meteors were used for air-to-ground strafing sorties.

Freddie had been made an acting squadron leader in March when he was appointed as the air armament development officer at CGS but in June his flying was interrupted by a recurrence of his eye problem. For some time he had been flying with a patch over his eye but it was a worrying time as the specialists struggled to find a cure. Over the next few months, he had to endure two more lengthy periods of treatment and Freddie feared that his flying career was over. Eventually, he decided to visit a Harley Street specialist and a new treatment started to take effect.

By the middle of 1949, Fighter Command's second main fighter, the Vampire, had arrived at CGS. On his return to flying, Freddie flew his first sortie in the single-engine jet, the fourth aircraft type he flew routinely during his time as a PAI instructor. In November he added two further types to his logbook.

The value of a two-seat trainer for teaching air combat and air-to-ground firing had long been appreciated and in November 1949, Freddie was tasked as the trials officer to assess the merits of the piston-engine Boulton Paul Balliol and the Avro Athena as air armament training aircraft. The cockpit configuration of both aircraft was side-by-side seating for the two pilots.

In the space of two weeks, Freddie flew twenty-two sorties to assess each aircraft. The trial included cine-gun exercises, air combat and ground-attack sorties, the latter using a fixed .303 wing-mounted Browning machine gun. The trials were useful but, with the two-seat Vampire expected to be available in the near future, it was decided not to order the two piston-engine trainers for air armament training. However, it was not the last that Freddie would see of the Balliol.

By the middle of 1950, most RAF squadrons were equipped with jet fighters and the Vampire FB V progressively took over the role of the Spitfire at CGS. However, in late August, Freddie was tasked with a fascinating project that would take him to the United States for three months.

The USAF's training aircraft all employed the tandem seating arrangement for the instructor and

Freddie and his team in the United States with the Balliol.

his pupil and they wished to evaluate the side-by-side configuration preferred by the RAF.

During August a small team was formed with Freddie in command and Flight Lieutenant Graham Hulse DFC as the second pilot. A small servicing party, led by a flight lieutenant, was formed for the project. Initially, the idea was to fly the aircraft to the USA but, with the onset of poorer weather, it was decided to send them as deck cargo. Five Dakotas carried various spares.

The team arrived in the USA at the end of August and the two Balliols were taken to Mitchell AFB on Long Island. On 1 September the aircraft were ready for an air test and Freddie tested VR 601. With long transit flights between the various airfields to be visited, the aircraft were fitted with overload fuel tanks mounted on each wing.

Over a two-day period the two aircraft headed for Randolph AFB near San Antonio, Texas staging through three USAF airfields. Randolph was the home of the USAF's training organisation and the two pilots demonstrated the aircraft and gave air experience to a number of senior officers and instructors. Freddie, an attack instructor, demonstrated the combat training aspects and Hulse, who was a QFI, demonstrated the flying training elements. In addition to these tasks, they were able to fly the latest USAF trainers to make a comparison. During the detachment, Freddie flew in three of them, including the North American T 28, Beechcraft T 34 and the Fairchild T 35, in addition to the well-proven Harvard.

On 2 October the RAF team arrived at Nellis AFB, Las Vegas, the centre of USAF weapons and tactical training. During the time one of the Balliols was being fitted with bomb racks, USAF officers were given clearance to evaluate the second aircraft. Freddie took advantage of the free time to re-acquaint himself with the Mustang. He was able to fly four sorties including two air-to-air firing sorties against a towed flag target. He had not previously fired on a flag (the RAF was still using a drogue as a target) and he was very impressed, so much so that he managed to acquire one and take it back to CGS for evaluation.

With the Balliols back on line, dive-bombing sorties on the nearby weapon ranges and more demonstration flights were flown. After a visit to Indian Springs to carry out ten dummy deck landings with a colonel of the US Marines, Freddie and Graham Hulse flew a sortie that attracted a great deal of publicity.

On 10 November, Hulse took off in the Balliol with Freddie flying 'chase' in a North American T 28 with Sergeant Ross, a USAF photographer, in the back seat. The aircraft flew down the Grand Canyon below the lip of the spectacular feature as Ross took many photographs. Flying at a very low height, but 7,000 ft above sea level, some spectacular photographs were obtained.

Over the next two weeks, the two Balliols made their way back to Mitchell AFB and the detachment was home in time for Christmas. Freddie described the three-month tour, 'It was a fascinating detachment, an eye-opener and we had an excellent time professionally and socially'.

It was also clear that the visit had been valuable from the USAF's standpoint. A few years later they introduced a pilot and weapons training aircraft, the Cessna T 37, which had side-by-side seating and it remained in service for many years.

The year 1951 got off to a good start for Freddie as he learnt that he had been promoted to substantive squadron leader and, over the next few months, he was kept very busy. The flag target he acquired during his visit to the USA was soon being tested and it was not long before a similar towed target was introduced by the RAF. This replaced the drogue that had given long service. The new Dive Bombing Sight 2 (DBS 2) was fitted to a Vampire and Freddie flew many trial sorties, which required him to write detailed reports after each one. In the event, the sight was not adopted by the RAF and the gyro-gunsight was modified for use on ground-attack sorties. In addition to writing reports on the airborne trials, Freddie was kept busy preparing operational and tactical notes for issue to the RAF's fighter squadrons.

At the beginning of April, the prototype de Havilland DH115 (later called Vampire T 11) arrived at CGS for evaluation. The aircraft had first flown six months earlier and at the end of the company test flying programme it went to 204 Advanced Flying School for evaluation before arriving at Leconfield. Over the next three weeks, Freddie flew it extensively on typical weapons training profiles. With its side-by-side cockpit arrangement, it proved to be an ideal training aircraft and it went on to give many years service with the RAF and numerous foreign air forces.

Freddie's time at CGS came to an end in June when he was assessed as an exceptional PAI. He had found it professionally invigorating and rewarding but he was not sorry to give up the daily ride on his Corgi motor bike from his rented accommodation in Hornsea to Leconfield fifteen miles away. In the winter months he needed some time draped over a radiator to thaw out before he was ready to start work.

Freddie delivers the de Havilland DH115 back to Hatfield.

A ground tour beckoned as he left CGS and he headed for the Air Ministry to work in the Directorate of Operational Requirements where he had responsibility for the design and fitting of fighter cockpits. He became involved in the design and ergonomics of the cockpit for the new Hunter fighter and visited Hawkers on numerous occasions to assist with the design and modification of the cockpit mock-up. He was very aware of the importance of being able to see behind when in a combat situation and he was not sure that adequate provision had been made for this crucial requirement. At one meeting, the aircraft designer turned to Freddie and said: "I am giving you the fastest f…..g fighter in the world and all you do is talk about the rear view."

Freddie had hardly got his feet under his Air Ministry desk when he was told that he was to return to Biggin Hill to take command of 615 Squadron, which he had left three years earlier.

In the meantime, after spending two years on the staff of 65 Group, cousin Johnnie had moved to Hornchurch where the RAF's Officer's and Aircrew Selection Centre was based and he spent eighteen months on the selection boards. Both of these appointments could be described as routine with civilised working hours. This allowed Johnnie plenty of scope for his hobbies and social life.

At the end of the war, the British gliding movement developed rapidly and the country's crop of outstanding pilots soon started to gain national and international honours. Johnnie spent a great deal of his spare time at the Surrey Gliding Club travelling to and from the site in his pre-war Bentley. Having gained his FAI Silver award, he had already established himself as an excellent glider pilot and he embarked on a series of cross-country and duration flights, often flying the EoN Olympia, one of the first British postwar high-performance gliders. He also found the social life much to his liking and skiing figured largely in his winter calendar. He also found time to join a syndicate restoring a Comper Swift light aircraft.

In August 1949 he had joined three colleagues from the Surrey Gliding Club and they entered the National Gliding Championships held at the Great Hucklow gliding site in Derbyshire. Plagued by poor weather, the competition is best remembered for the social events. These were not restricted to periods away at competitions but were a regular part of the club's activities. His friend, Wally Kahn, one of Britain's foremost glider pilots for decades, commented:

> 'John was a great guy and we had a lot of laughs together. His pride and joy was his vintage Bentley which we used on many occasions for our visits to numerous pubs. One sortie, which I organised, resulted in some famous family separations but John came out smelling of roses as always and the rest of the night's activities are best forgotten!'

By late 1950 the activities of the club and the RAFVR were increasing at Redhill, and the expanding club needed to find a larger location. The old wartime airfield at Lasham near Basingstoke was chosen. Before departing, a final party was held and Wally Kahn captured perfectly the spirit and fun of the gliding world, a feature that lives on:

> 'The social life at Redhill left nothing to be desired. We had built a cosy snug bar in the clubhouse. The Surrey Flying Club had a well-appointed bar for their wealthier members and the RAF Volunteer Reserve had their mess close by. It was a case of "throttle to bottle" in a very meaningful way.
>
> 'Our parties enlivened the long winter evenings and were always well attended. One evening a fancy dress party was arranged with all participants having to wear something with an aeronautical theme. Tony Goodhart came as a CuNb (a cumulo-nimbus thunder cloud) wearing a strange structure made of cotton wool on his head. In the centre a lighted candle served as a lightning strike, but inevitably his magnificent creation was soon alight.
>
> 'There were many other ingenious costumes. John Sowrey, the son of one of the famous Sowrey Brothers cheated a bit by arriving in his father's First World War RFC uniform, albeit with the right trouser leg cut vertically to provide room for the plaster cast from toe to knee acquired on a recent Surrey Club skiing expedition.
>
> 'As a member of the RAFVR, I suggested that a visit to their dining-in shindig being held that night might liven things up, so off we went. The CO and his guests cheered or booed depending on our costumes but John held back as he wanted to make a grand entrance. Flinging the door open with such gusto that it nearly came off its hinges, he shouted, "I say you chaps, can some of you help? I have just pranged my Camel". Unfortunately, the very old air commodore who was an honorary member of the mess, on seeing this apparition and hearing the shout, fainted clean away.'

At this time, Robin, the youngest Sowrey, who had followed his two brothers to Tonbridge School, entered the RAF College, Cranwell to train as a pilot in September 1950. He was withdrawn from training two years later and then embarked on a long career in civilian aviation.

Initially he joined Vickers Armstrong at Weybridge and for five years he flew as a flight test observer during the development of the Valiant as a bomber and on in-flight refuelling trials. He later joined the flight test department of Short Brothers and Harland before spending two years on the Concorde programme. In 1966 he left for Hong Kong and for eleven years he worked in the sales and marketing division of Hong Kong Aircraft Engineering Company before returning to England in 1977 working as a consultant and at the Marshall's Flying School at Cambridge. Throughout his career, a great deal of his work was in support of the RAF and so he continued, in an indirect way, the long tradition of the Sowrey family serving the Royal Air Force.

Above: Robin Sowrey as a flight cadet at RAF College Cranwell.

After three years filling ground appointments, with his flying restricted to gliding and light aircraft, Johnnie was anxious to get back to a full-time flying appointment and he applied to join the 1951 course at the Empire Test Pilots' School (ETPS). The majority of students were drawn from the three British flying services but pilots from Commonwealth and Allied Air Forces also attended. They had to be assessed as exceptional or above average pilots, have recently completed an operational tour of duty and have at least four years to serve on completion of the course. After attending a selection board, Johnnie was successful and offered a place on No. 10 Course.

On 26 February 1951 he reported to the school's home at Farnborough to join thirteen other RAF students, four from the Fleet Air Arm, two each from the USAF and the USN and a single represen-

Below: Empire Test Pilots' Course with Johnnie second from left in the middle row.

tative from the RAAF, RCAF and the Indian Air Force. Amongst the RAF students was Flight Lieutenant Roger Topp AFC who would later gain fame as the CO of 111 Squadron and leader of the 'Black Arrows' aerobatic team, which famously flew the twenty-two Hunter loop at the 1958 Farnborough Air Show. An air correspondent described it as 'the most wonderful aerobatic manoeuvre ever witnessed, a performance transcending all others'.

The commandant of ETPS was New Zealand-born Group Captain A E Clouston DSO, DFC, AFC, a pre-war test pilot who had gained fame for record-breaking flights to South Africa and New Zealand. He had served in Coastal Command during the war in addition to carrying out experimental flying work.

The need for service test pilots in the RAF had always existed but the large numbers of new aircraft that had been developed during the war had created a heavy strain on the limited test-flying facilities that existed at the time. There were few experienced service test pilots and they were largely self-trained. The relatively ad-hoc arrangements of the pre-war and early wartime days had satisfied the demands of the time but the increasing need for production test pilots at the various aircraft factories and the initial testing of new types of aircraft and equipment could no longer be met adequately.

By 1943 it was clear that a more formal organisation was required. The result was the formation of the Test Pilots' School at RAF Boscombe Down under the aegis of the Aeroplane and Armament Experimental Establishment (A&AEE). In 1944 the school was upgraded and was renamed the Empire Test Pilots' School and moved to RAE Farnborough.

The school's task was to train pilots for test-flying duties in the A&AEE establishments within the service and in industry. On graduation they needed to have an adequate knowledge of the basic theories and flying techniques to enable them to start learning about practical test flying. The 'apprentice' test pilot had to have experience of the precise flying necessary for performance testing and to be able to make qualitative assessments of an aircraft's handling characteristics. It is often forgotten that there is always a need for test pilots to evaluate equipments in addition to testing complete aircraft and this type of test flying often requires different techniques.

Each course, which lasted almost a year, involved a great deal of ground school and lectures in addition to flying exercises. These were monitored by a tutor and required the student pilot to fly a sortie and then record the results and prepare a report. This provided the experience of collecting and validating test data in order to draw valid conclusions based on in-flight observations.

Each pilot flew a variety of aircraft ranging from the modern fighters to heavy transport and bomber aircraft. One day a student could be flying a Vampire jet fighter and the next flight could be in a Lincoln bomber. Students also flew high-performance gliders and the basic aircraft that towed them into the air, which included a captured German Fieseler Storch.

The availability of gliders and tugs was particularly appealing for Johnnie who was able to pursue his great interest and he spent many weekends gliding when he was also in great demand as a tug pilot flying an Auster or the Storch. On 17 June he was airborne in an Olympia glider for six hours and fifteen minutes and a few weeks later climbed many thousands of feet in a standing wave east of the Pennines. During the summer break he again entered the national championships, this time flying the ETPS Olympia glider in the team event with his friend Peter Bisgood. Weather again interfered but the two managed a creditable eleventh position in the final standings.

During his time as a student at ETPS, Johnnie flew eighteen different aircraft types, the majority new to him. For a fighter pilot, he had flown an unusually wide variety of aircraft from transport aircraft during his time in East Africa to many flying hours on light aircraft and gliders.

On successful completion of the course, Johnnie was awarded the prestigious 'tp' symbol when the course came to an end on 15 December 1951 with the traditional dinner night. The students left for their various appointments and, for Johnnie, this involved a short trip across the airfield at Farnborough to join the Wireless and Electrical Flight (W&E Flt) at the Royal Aircraft Establishment (RAE).

For one keen to fly higher-performance aircraft, Johnnie often found himself at the controls of

Vikings, Valettas and Yorks, which were used as flying test beds for various radio and radar trials work. Some sorties in a Lincoln and the York were described as 'radio warfare' and included dropping 'Window', strips of tin foil cut to various lengths dropped in bundles to confuse enemy radars. He also flew a number of times in the Storch (VP 546) on 'radio warfare' sorties but the purpose of these flights is not clear. In his logbook there are many other entries of flights in the Storch but these were to tow gliders into the air.

The E&W Flight also used a Meteor, a Firefly and a Sea Fury and Johnnie flew these on VHF homing and instrument landing system (ILS) trials. In April he had a pleasant change from the rather staid work of flying heavy aircraft straight and level. He took off in a Meteor F 4 and staged through Istres, Malta and Cyprus before arriving at the RAF base at El Adem in eastern Libya.

The Martin Baker Company was conducting a series of trials of their ejection seat with firings from the modified rear cockpit of the company's Meteor. It was Johnnie's task to fly alongside the company's aircraft and photograph the ejection sequence as the seat was fired from the rear cockpit. Over the next two weeks he photographed seventeen ejection trials, a series of tests at various heights and speeds.

For an active man like Johnnie, some of his flying was probably dull but, during his time at Farnborough, his hectic and adventurous life as a bachelor took a new and lifelong change. His stepson Gavin explains:

'John entered my life in 1951. My mother, Audrey, a divorcee, was not short of admirers, but there was only one winner. John was tall, dark, handsome, and charming, and being a dashing test pilot with a pre-war three-litre Bentley tourer was thoroughly approved of by a nine-year-old boy.

'John married Audrey on 19 July 1952, a day I remember well being particularly impressed by his bluff when returning a boat hired on the Serpentine claiming that it had only been sent out with the one rowlock. This, in fact, remained in his room in the Savoy Hotel.

'There was further excitement and glamour as friends included Mike Hawthorn, world motor racing champion, who once gave me an exhilarating

Johnnie and Audrey on their wedding day.

ride in a Cooper Bristol sports racing car. John also introduced me to flying and arranged trips in an open cockpit BA Swallow and a flight in a Slingsby T21B glider. Further, he introduced me to sailing, hiring a dinghy on holiday in Cornwall. John was, of course, my hero.

'John and Audrey soon had daughters Julia and Amanda. He became a responsible parent and husband, gave up gliding, sold his Comper Swift share and his Bentley, and enjoyed a happy family life.'

Johnnie and his stepson became great friends and in later life, they spent many hours sailing and flying together in Gavin's yachts and his Bölkow 207 aircraft.

Back at Farnborough Johnnie flew the Canberra for the first time when he completed a number of trials associated with the aircraft's generator and he flew the Gannet on its radio clearance flights.

In December he was transferred to the Structures and Mechanical Engineering Flight at RAE and here he was able to fly a selection of more exhilarating aircraft types including the Brigand, the Hornet and the Vampire. Flutter tests and spinning trials in the Wyvern provided some excitement, as did a complete electrical failure in the Canberra when flying above cloud. Fortunately, a small gap in the clouds appeared and Johnnie was able to make a safe descent and land.

At the end of March 1953 he took off in a Meteor for the RAF airfield at Idris in western Libya where Martin Baker were conducting more tests on their ejection seat. Some of these tests were conducted at 30,000 feet and Johnnie followed the same procedure as before, flying alongside and taking photographs.

The blockade of Berlin and the outbreak of the Korean War caused a dangerous escalation of the Cold War, which led to a rapid rearmament programme. There was now a need to rush a new generation of aircraft into service and the tasks imposed on A&AEE soon grew rapidly. This was particularly so for 'A' Squadron which was responsible for testing and issuing the release to service of fighter aircraft.

As a result of this expansion, Johnnie was transferred in July 1953 to Boscombe Down to join 'A' Squadron. He could hardly have arrived at a more exciting time. The testing of the first generation jet fighters – the various marks of Meteors and Vampires – was coming to an end, and the second generation – Hunter, Swift, and Venom – were beginning to arrive. These aircraft, with their different aerodynamic characteristics, introduced new features such as swept wing handling, powered controls and reheat. It would be a few weeks before Johnnie became involved with the Hunter and the Swift and, in the meantime, he was flying the night-fighter version of the Meteor and conducting armament trials on the Venom.

Johnnie's first experience of the 'new' jets came on 30 September when he flew the Avro 707C Delta aircraft and a few weeks later he flew his first sortie in the elegant Hunter. It was the beginning of a love affair with the aircraft and, over the next few months, he carried out handling trials of the Mark I. In February 1954, he had his first flight in the more capable Mark 6 version.

On 2 March, Johnnie flew his first sortie in the Swift, an aircraft that was to have a troubled life and one that presented the test pilots with many problems and issues. However, trouble was to arrive in a different guise for Johnnie just three days later.

A small group from A&AEE travelled to the Gloster Aircraft Company's airfield at Moreton Valence near Gloucester on 4 March to carry out a brief assessment of the Gloster GA 5, later to be the Javelin. The following day, Johnnie was detailed to fly the fourth prototype making him the first RAF pilot to fly the large delta-wing night fighter. The first two prototypes had crashed and the aircraft Johnnie was to fly (WT 830) was the first to be fitted with powered controls.

After climbing to height over Wales and carrying out some handling tests, the aircraft suffered a failure of the aileron-powered control system. It was later discovered that the hydraulic pump powering the starboard aileron had fractured. After advice over the radio from the company test pilot, Johnnie selected manual control but found the aircraft virtually impossible to master. He was told to eject but ignored the advice since he did not fancy baling out and parachuting into the Welsh mountains on a late winter's day.

He headed for the long runway at Boscombe Down and, despite having virtually no aileron control, he managed to make a safe landing. Eric Absolon, one of the company's senior engineers who later examined the aircraft wrote in his report:

> 'Although rudder and elevator control were still available, without ailerons, directional control would be virtually impossible. Certainly, to attempt a landing would have been courting disaster. But, by some superhuman effort, the pilot managed to gain some control and successfully landed. How he did it still remains something of a mystery. He would have had to be able to, by some means, transmit sufficient load through the control linkage to be able to move the piston in the power control cylinder, overcoming friction in the system and displacing hydraulic fluid.
>
> 'It was my job to determine what had gone wrong. The first step was to interview the

pilot. This was very difficult for me. Here was this man in blue, who had put his life on the line and achieved what, by many standards, was an impossible task in successfully landing a disabled aircraft rather than baling out. Had he ejected, the aircraft would have been lost and the secret of what went wrong probably buried in the wreckage forever. Who was I to ask this man questions about what he did? But we had to determine the problem and find out what happened. In the event, he couldn't tell us very

The Gloster GA 5 that gave Johnnie so much trouble (Jet Age Museum/Russell Adams Collection).

much. He confirmed that he was only able to have some sort of roll control by a massive effort. He had to jam his leg against the side of the cockpit and use all his strength to achieve some movements of the ailerons.'

It had been a brilliant and skilful piece of flying; all the more praiseworthy since it was the first time Johnnie had flown the delta-wing fighter. A few weeks later, it was announced that he had been awarded a Queen's Commendation for Valuable Service in the Air. The Gloster Aircraft Company presented him with a gold watch.

In May 1954, Johnnie and his friend and fellow test pilot, Bill Bedford, were tasked to carry out the flight trials of the prototype Olympia Mk IV high-performance glider. Flying from Lasham, each pilot flew many sorties exploring the whole of the performance envelope in order that the glider could be issued with a Certificate of Airworthiness.

Over the next few months Johnnie was heavily involved in flying the Hunter Marks 1 and 2 on handling trials and the Venom on handling trials with bombs. The Hunter became a great aircraft but the early days were not without some difficulties. In particular, there were problems with the under-fuselage airbrake and a report on 21 May highlighted other issues:

Johnnie tests the Olympia Mk IV glider.

'Great concern is felt about the frequency of occasions in which almost complete loss of power (surging) occurs in high-altitude manoeuvring. This should receive the most serious consideration in relation to the forthcoming C.A. Release.

'Also the very severe criti-

cisms of the aileron stick forces for landing in manual (already put forward on many occasions) has been further emphasised by recent experience of dummy GCA approaches in bumpy air. This aspect gives rise to the greatest concern even to the extent of withholding a release recommendation. The closest consideration will be given to this matter in the next few days.'

On 29 June, Johnnie returned to Moreton Valence and was re-acquainted with the Gloster GA 5, WT 830, and over the next few days he flew three sorties in the aircraft, including one supersonic run. The tests were successful and the detailed report compiled by Johnnie and the engineers concluded, 'The test confirmed the aircraft has great potential'.

Flying the Hunter was still Johnnie's main priority during the summer of 1954 but he continued with his work on the Venom FB 1 and had his first flight in the North American F 86 Sabre, which was entering service with the RAF as a stop-gap fighter. He also joined the Swift testing programme.

From the outset, the Swift had caused numerous problems and the test programme had suffered. It had soon become clear that the Swift Mark 1 was not going to be suitable as a fighter but there was great pressure to introduce the aircraft into RAF service, despite the misgivings of the Boscombe test pilots. The Mark 2 had arrived in March and Johnnie flew it on numerous occasions. During September he flew a number of gunnery trials but problems arose with the engine surging at high altitude and in turning flight, with or without the gun firing, prompting Squadron Leader Pete Thorne AFC, one of A&AEE's most eminent test pilots, to comment, 'The Swift Mk 2 was by far the most troublesome variant'.

In September there was an interesting diversion for Johnnie and Pete Thorne, who had been Freddie's flight commander at CGS; he later recalled:

'In September 1954, John Sowrey and I went to Chilbolton to do a brief handling assessment on the prototype Folland Midge (single-seat predecessor of the Gnat). It was a delightful aircraft with no vices throughout the range, and a good performance from a Viper engine, but there was very little room in the cockpit and, as well as having a non-standard ejection seat, hardly any standard RAF equipment was fitted. We reported some doubt about its suitability for RAF service.'

Both Johnnie and Pete Thorne were tall men and it must have been a very tight squeeze for them. Although the Midge did not enter service with the RAF, the two-seat variant, the Gnat, was to give many years service as an advanced training aircraft and with the Red Arrows. The Midge gave excellent service with the Indian Air Force.

From the end of October, Johnnie became increasingly involved in the Swift programme. The Mark 3, equipped with reheat, showed a considerable improvement. Johnnie flew the Mark 4 in November but the aircraft handling became a major concern. The A&AEE report of 18 November gives a graphic example of the work, and risks, Johnnie and his fellow test pilots had to cope with:

'Further investigations into the use of elevator augmented by tailplane have shown that in a typical recovery from a dive at Mach numbers

Swift Mk 1 (WK 200) which was converted to a Mark 5 and caught fire just after Johnnie had landed.

of 0.93 IMN there is no response to full stick back; upon the application of small amounts of tailplane the initial recovery is good, but as the Mach number reduces a strong pitch up occurs which cannot be held by full stick forward movement. Eventually, the full stick forward which it is natural to retain, produces high negative "g" in the region of M = 0.85.

'These features appear to be associated with nose up trim change with decreasing Mach number combined with sharp recovery in the elevator effectiveness, further accentuated by the pre-stall instability.

'The aircraft is therefore considered unacceptable for service use in the present form.'

Johnnie, Audrey and Gavin after the investiture at Buckingham Palace.

In a more detailed report issued two months later by the performance division, it was recognised that the many modifications embodied as a result of the problems identified by the test pilots had improved the control of the aircraft. However the longitudinal control characteristics were still not considered adequate for the operational role and other major deficiencies remained. It concluded, 'The aircraft still falls short of the qualities needed in a present day operational interceptor'.

It was perhaps some relief to Johnnie that he spent much of December and January flying the Hunter to try and solve the engine surge problems when the guns were fired. During this period he also flew the Sapphire-engined Hunter V, which had just arrived for testing.

Early in 1955, Neville Duke, Hawker's chief test pilot, was injured in an aircraft crash and for two months Johnnie was seconded to Hawkers as a production test pilot at Dunsfold where he tested many Hunters prior to their delivery to the RAF. It was a happy interlude and one where he was immensely popular with his Hawker colleagues.

When he returned to Boscombe in early March, it was back to testing the Venom, Hunter and Swift. With his time at A&AEE coming to an end, he took off on 10 May in a Swift Mark 5 (WK 200), which had been fitted with a suite of cameras in the nose. The aircraft had only recently arrived and the flight was to test the temperatures in the nose bay. After landing, and whilst taxiing to the dispersal, the engine turbine blades disintegrated. They cut the fuel lines and a major fire started. Johnnie evacuated the aircraft in great haste and the machine was written off.

Johnnie's time as a test pilot came to an end just as the Lightning and the Javelin were arriving to start their testing programmes. He had played a major role in testing and clearing the latest generation of fighters for RAF service and in June his services were recognised with the award of the Air Force Cross. He was the fifth member of the remarkable Sowrey family to receive this prestigious award, a unique and unparalleled distinction for one family.

Promoted to acting wing commander on 30 May, Johnnie headed for Wattisham in Suffolk. He was appointed OC Flying Wing with two Hunter day-fighter squadrons and a Meteor night-fighter squadron under his command.

Chapter Twenty

FIGHTER OPERATIONS

Freddie welcomes 615 Squadron's honorary air commodore, Winston Churchill, on a visit to the squadron.

In the late summer of 1951, Freddie had settled into his appointment in the Operational Requirements Branch at the Air Ministry when he was unexpectedly posted back to 615 (County of Surrey) Squadron to be its commanding officer.

The Korean crisis had increased the tempo of testing at Hawkers where Neville Duke had taken over as chief test pilot. He had been the CO of 615 Squadron for some time but, with his new demanding responsibilities at Hawkers, he had to relinquish command and a replacement was sought. As there was no sufficiently experienced auxiliary officer in the squadron it was reluctantly agreed to appoint a regular – and they wanted one whom they knew. With the honorary air commodore now prime minister, Freddie had a series of one-sided interviews with increasingly senior officers wanting to know what strings he had been pulling. Totally innocent, he was nevertheless delighted to be returning to those he knew, admired and was proud to lead. Many years later, he commented:

'The last thing an auxiliary squadron wanted was to be commanded by a regular. The air and ground crews were volunteers giving up their weekends, summer holidays and any spare time in the week. A regular officer is following a career. Auxiliaries are special people and react accordingly. They will respond to leadership and example – in 615 Squadron they were led from the front, occasionally pushed from the back, sometimes persuaded, perhaps cajoled, but accepted that their skills had put them amongst the upper levels of regular air defence fighter squadrons at a testing time in the Cold War. They wore "Fred's Mob" with equanimity and were supremely loyal.'

Freddie returned to Biggin Hill and 615 Squadron on 11 October 1951. There had been a number of changes since he had left three years earlier. The squadron had been re-equipped with the Meteor F 8 and, together with 41 Squadron and 600 (City of London) RAuxAF Squadron, it formed part of the Biggin Hill Wing commanded by Wing Commander Arthur Donaldson DSO, DFC, AFC.

Freddie arrived in the midst of considerable activity with the call-up of personnel in response to the Korean crisis. The squadron strength had built up to twenty-one auxiliary, four regular RAF, ten ground officers and 154 airmen – fifty-five of the latter were regulars. There was also an increase in operational training, which included a wing exercise in December when thirty Meteors intercepted the Waterbeach Wing at 35,000 feet.

Throughout the winter and spring of 1952, the auxiliaries flew at high intensity each weekend and often mid-week. The squadron participated in large-scale Fighter Command exercises intercepting USAF B-29 and B-50 bomber formations. In early April another large exercise involved interceptions over Bel-

gium and France when thirty-six 'enemy' Meteors were intercepted at 36,000 feet. During one bomber affiliation exercise, the 'bomber' turned out to be a Constellation airliner. Sector exercises were a feature of most weekends when a wide variety of fighters and bombers were intercepted. Air-to-air weapons training against a towed target also featured regularly.

Freddie's first few months in command were busy and it was clear that the auxiliary squadrons had become a much more potent operational force during the three years he had been away. Pilots were achieving almost as much flying time each month as their regular colleagues. However, just as the routine of the auxiliary squadrons had not changed, neither had the traditional spirit and social life, which was just as hectic. This extended to frequent gatherings with the other three 'London' squadrons (600, 601 and 604). It all meant that there were few free weekends for Freddie to share with his young family.

Freddie briefs his pilots of 615 Squadron. Hugh Merewether is second left.

One of 615 Squadron's young pilots, Tony Vivian, who had recently graduated from Oxford where he had been a member of the university air squadron (UAS), and was one of the less-experienced pilots on the squadron at the time, captured the spirit of the auxiliary squadrons when he wrote:

'The regulars had always taken it upon themselves to rather look down on us weekend flyers. That didn't matter one bit, since we knew for a fact that we were vastly superior. (It is sometimes difficult to tell the difference between high morale and arrogance, of course, but what kind of unit didn't think it was utterly perfect; pretty second-rate probably.)

'We flew to the same instrument flying ratings as regular pilots and had better air-to-air firing results than many regular squadrons. We also clocked up 180 hours flying time a year. Five of our number were or became industry test pilots, Neville Duke and Hugh Merewether at Hawkers, Peewee Judge at Supermarine, Ian Smith of de Havilland Propellers and Alec Roberts at Shorts. This general level of experience and skill couldn't help but brighten up the rest of us "Bloggs".

'We took our flying standards and flying discipline very seriously – but absolutely nothing else. The trick was to take flying seriously, but above all without appearing to do so. That would have been so non-U! So, for the annual AOC's inspection, some bolder spirits wore their pink socks, trousers nicely hitched up so the AOC could see them, and top button of the uniform jacket undone (the fighter jockey's privilege). This could be guaranteed to raise the old chap's blood pressure quite a few points and prompt a furtive laugh from us rebellious auxiliaries.'

Pilots were still expected to attend summer camp and, at the end of May, the squadron headed for Celle close to the border with East Germany. During the two-week camp, the pilots shared the Battle Flight responsibility with two aircraft at fifteen-minute readiness to scramble. During the camp, the squadron was visited by its former CO, Hawker's chief test pilot Neville Duke, who flew across in the company's Hurricane 'Last of the Many'. With 327 sorties flown, the camp was described as 'most successful'.

July saw the squadron working with the USAF 81st Fighter Wing providing dissimilar air combat training (DACT) with the F-86. October saw one of Fighter Command's biggest air operations; Exercise Ardent, when the Biggin Hill Wing was launched over two weekends to intercept large formations of RAF and USAF fighter forces.

The beginning of November was marked with a special occasion when Queen Elizabeth the Queen Mother, the honorary air commodore of 600 (City of London) Squadron and Winston Churchill, honorary air commodore 615 (County of Surrey) Squadron arrived to inspect their squadrons at a joint parade. Freddie accompanied Churchill during the inspection of 600 Squadron and he then escorted the Queen Mother on her inspection of 615 Squadron. After the parade, the party of distinguished guests retired to the officers' mess where they met the members of each squadron.

Freddie's first year in command had been hectic and successful. Over 2,000 hours had been flown and the operational efficiency of the squadron rated alongside that of most regular fighter squadrons. The New Year brought the announcement that the squadron had been placed second of the twenty auxiliary squadrons for the coveted Esher Trophy awarded annually to the most efficient and operational squadron.

HM the Queen Mother and Winston Churchill visit Biggin Hill to inspect their squadrons.

Ground crew re-arm a 615 Squadron Meteor F 8.

Although the pace of flying changed little during 1953, it was noticeable that there were less major exercises and training was concentrated more at squadron level. This can be put down, in part, to the lessening of international tension. The summer camp at Oldenburg in northern Germany was another great success with a constant series of exercises flying sweeps and air interception exercises against large formations of Germany-based RAF Vampires and Meteors and NATO fighters. An added bonus was the availability of air-to-ground live firing on the weapons range at nearby Meppen.

Air-to-air firing was a major feature of the year's training and the success rate increased every month and in September the squadron diarist wrote:

> 'The squadron average has once again been raised and stands at 13.79 per cent. This is a record for the squadron and we believe is also a record for any auxiliary squadron. Cine, however, was not so successful. Somehow we have got to overcome the pilot's dislike of cine!'

After the series of annual autumn exercises, the pace of flying dropped but Freddie insisted that all the training should be directed towards operational efficiency. This is reflected in the number of practice interceptions and air-to-air firing exercises flown. Finally, on 21 December, Freddie flew his final sortie with the squadron when he indulged in some low flying, a rare opportunity for something different.

On 2 January 1954, he handed over the squadron to Squadron leader R.A. Eeles who invited him to take the salute as the squadron marched past. That evening he was dined out in the squadron's town headquarters. The events of the 2nd were given greater poignancy the day before when it was announced in the New Year's Honours List, that Freddie had been awarded the Air Force Cross for his leadership of 615 Squadron. There was added celebration when it was announced that the squadron adjutant, Flight Lieutenant R.G. Shillingford had been appointed MBE and Flight Sergeant W.L. Agate had been awarded the BEM.

On leaving, Freddie was assessed as an exceptional fighter pilot and his station commander, Wing Commander D.G. 'Splinters' Smallwood wrote:

> 'There can be little doubt at the moment that 615 Squadron is the most efficient of all the

auxiliary squadrons and although I have not heard officially, I should imagine that you stand a very good chance of winning the Esher Trophy for this last year. I certainly think you deserve it. My heartiest congratulations on a splendid year's performance.'

The station commander was correct. A few weeks later it was announced that 615 Squadron had been awarded the trophy and Freddie received a flood of congratulations including those of the AOC-in-C of Fighter Command and Winston Churchill who wrote:

10 Downing Street
22 January 1954

'My dear Sowrey
    'I should like to thank you for all that you have done for 615 Squadron during the time you have been its commanding officer. I know how much the squadron owes you for its keenness and well being. Let me also congratulate you on your award in the New Year's Honours List.
    'I take this opportunity of wishing you success at Staff College and good fortune in the future.

Yours sincerely

Winston S. Churchill'

Freddie spent the next twelve months as a student at the RAF Staff College, Bracknell where his first-term tutor was Wing Commander Neil Cameron (later Marshal of the RAF Lord Cameron of Balhousie). He developed a deep respect and admiration for Cameron and their paths would cross again. In addition to demonstrating his talent for writing and discussion, Freddie managed to add forty hours to his logbook, most of it flying the Balliol and Meteor. He even managed to take his instrument-rating test and be awarded a master green rating, a qualification allowing him to fly in the most demanding weather conditions.

A posting to the Defence Research Policy Staff in the Ministry of Defence reflected his success at Bracknell and his ability, indicating that his potential for higher rank had been recognised. This was reinforced six months later when he was promoted to acting wing commander (just four-and-a-half years after his substantive promotion to squadron leader) and transferred to the chiefs of staff secretariat.

As Freddie moved to his new appointment in London, Johnnie was settling in at Wattisham where the station commander was Group Captain Hughie Edwards VC, DSO, DFC. The two resident Hunter squadrons

Johnnie with his personal Hunter F 5 at Wattisham.

(257 and 263) were equipped with the Sapphire-engined Mark 2 and 152 Squadron flew the Meteor NF 14.

The Hunter had entered RAF service in July 1954 and would eventually equip twelve squadrons in the UK and a further twelve in Germany. Others served in Aden, Cyprus, Hong Kong and Singapore.

As wing commander flying, Johnnie flew with all three squadrons and became a fully-operational pilot flying on all types of training sorties and exercises and he regularly achieved fifteen to eighteen flying hours each month. In addition to his responsibilities for ensuring the operational efficiency of the squadrons, he also commanded all the various flying support functions such as air traffic control and fire and crash rescue services.

In September 1955, the Mark 5 version of the Hunter started to replace Wattisham's older Mark 2s and Johnnie selected WP 189 as his personal aircraft. The Mark 5 was also powered by the Sapphire engine but had a greater endurance. Cine-gun and air-firing exercises still dominated but each pilot

Johnnie leads the Wattisham Wing over London for the queen's birthday flypast.

had to complete a series of standard exercises each month and these included battle drills and formation flying with some sorties ending with an instrument let down to a precision ground control approach (GCA). Air defence exercises, some on a very large scale, were an important feature of the annual programme.

Of course, fighter pilots enjoy flair and panache and formation flying so aerobatics were an important feature of a squadron's life. During the 1950s, numerous fighter squadrons formed formation teams that gained worldwide admiration. The most famous was 111 Squadron's 'Black Arrows' and 92 Squadron's 'Blue Diamonds'.

For the traditional Battle of Britain flypast over London on 15 September, forty-eight Hunters flew over in four formations with Johnnie leading the Wattisham Wing. In the spring of 1956, many flying hours were devoted to formation flypast practices in anticipation of a number of events, the most significant being the visit of the new Soviet leaders, Marshal Bulganin and Nikita Khrushchev. The Soviet party visited RAF Marham on 23 April and, during a short air display, Johnnie led the Wattisham Wing of twenty-four Hunters, flying in six boxes of four.

The visit of the Soviet leaders opened the way for further high-level visits and when a Soviet Air Force delegation, led by Marshal Zhigarev, visited RAF Manby on 6 September, Johnnie led a formation of the Wattisham Wing in salute.

Exercises to test the air defence of the United Kingdom were regular activities for fighter squadrons, and these culminated in a major annual exercise involving the whole of the air defence system. Exercise Stronghold started on 22 September 1956 and Johnnie was airborne on each of the seven days. One of the main aims of the 1956 exercise was to counter a surprise attack against the UK when Fighter Command's task was simply to intercept as many raids as possible. After four days, Stronghold was co-ordinated with a large NATO exercise under the direction of the supreme allied commander Europe (SACEUR) and raiders from the continent were intercepted over the UK.

These exercises involved a considerable amount of time on standby waiting for a scramble. Under the control of a ground control interception (GCI) unit, the fighters climbed for height to attack the target. Apart from an advance in technology and aircraft performance, little had changed from the wartime days. As wing commander flying, Johnnie had to spend much of his time in the station's operations room but he still found time to fly on each day.

The 1956 Exercise Vigilant took place in May and its purpose was to resist an atomic attack when the large force of attackers would fly at speeds to simulate those of a potential enemy. It was recognised as the most demanding test of Britain's air defences up to that time. Over a four-day period, just over 3,000 attack sorties were flown against the United Kingdom with Bomber Command and NATO forces providing the 'enemy'. Wattisham fighters were heavily engaged and Johnnie, despite his heavy commitments controlling the squadrons, still managed to fly numerous sorties to intercept the high-flying raiding force.

After two years in his appointment, and a few weeks before the two Hunter squadrons were disbanded (following the savage cuts stemming from the Duncan Sandys 1957 Defence White Paper), Johnnie left Wattisham to attend a course at the Joint Service Staff College (JSSC).

The Sandys White Paper included three statements crucial to the future of the RAF. First it stated the importance of the national nuclear deterrent provided by the V-Force. Secondly, it was announced that a force of ballistic missiles would supplement the bomber force and, thirdly it stated:

> 'The defence of the bomber airfields is an essential part of the deterrent and it is a feasible task. A manned fighter force, smaller than at present but adequate for this limited purpose, will be maintained and will progressively be equipped with air-to-air missiles. Fighter aircraft will in due course be replaced by a ground-to-air missile system.'

The White Paper also foreshadowed far-reaching changes in the RAF's strength and role with an all-regular force by 1962, reduction in certain commitments, and the accelerated replacement of aircraft with missiles. The main casualties were the squadrons of Fighter Command and the disbandment of the Royal Auxiliary Air Force.

The massive cuts in aircraft strength were soon implemented. By 1960, Fighter Command was reduced from its 1956 strength of 600 aircraft in service with thirty-five squadrons to just 272 aircraft. Two years later this figure had been further reduced to 140 fighters in just eleven squadrons.

The British aircraft industry was another casualty of the new policy as was the next generation of supersonic fighters to meet the increasing high-level bomber threat posed by the Warsaw Pact. The English Electric P1, which would become the Lightning, was spared, only because it was too far advanced to justify cancelling.

Freddie re-entered the fighter world at the beginning of February 1958 as the effects of the White Paper were starting to materialise.

Freddie repeats the photo on page 98 and shows son Peter a 46 Squadron Javelin.

After three years in the chiefs of staff secretariat at the Ministry of Defence (MOD) (described in detail in the next chapter), he arrived at 228 Operational Conversion Unit (OCU) at RAF Leeming to convert to the Javelin all-weather fighter prior to taking command of 46 Squadron. The conversion course lasted five months and involved seventy-two flying hours on the Javelin and Meteor night fighter.

At the beginning of May, Freddie assumed command of 46 Squadron at RAF Odiham in Hampshire where he teamed up with Squadron Leader Norman Greenhalgh, the squadron's navigator radar leader. The squadron was one of three equipped with the Javelin F (AW) 2, which was fitted with the US-designed AN/APQ-43 (AI 22) airborne intercept radar, housed in the nose. Powered by two Armstrong Siddeley Sapphire Sa.6 jet engines giving 8,000 lb of thrust each, the aircraft took ten minutes to climb to 45,000 feet and had a service ceiling of 52,500 feet.

With this performance at high level, practice interceptions were routinely carried out above 40,000 feet. On a 'Bomex' he intercepted a Vulcan at 46,000 feet and some months later a Canberra photographic reconnaissance variant at 48,500 feet.

Freddie had hardly got his feet under the table when 46 Squadron deployed to the RAF base at Brüggen on the Dutch-German border for a NATO air defence exercise. Meteors, Hunters, USAF fighters and NATO jets appeared in Freddie's gunsight.

A major event in the British aviation calendar was the annual SBAC Airshow held at Farnborough in September. Those held in the 1950s attracted huge crowds and it was in that era that the range of British aircraft on show highlighted the depth, and skill, of the British aircraft industry and the test pilots that demonstrated the aircraft.

The RAF played a major role in supporting the air show. For the 1958 event, Fighter Command provided a flypast involving forty-five Hunters and forty-five Javelins flying in ten formations. Much of August was taken up with practices culminating in two dress rehearsals with a final route check. The large formation appeared at the show on 1 September, the first of five appearances finishing on the public day. As soon as the SBAC show was over, practice for the Battle of Britain flypast commenced with Freddie leading the Javelins over the Mansion House in London on 21 September.

The squadron routine of practice interceptions, battle formation and cine-gun attacks was the same for UK-based Javelin squadrons, much of it above 40,000 feet. After attending the squadron commander's course at the All Weather Fighter Combat School at RAF West Raynham in February 1959, Freddie led 46 Squadron to the airfield on the island of Sylt off the coast of Schleswig Holstein. For many years, Sylt, with its off-shore weapon ranges, was the home of the RAF's Armament Practice Camp, which operated in much the same way as the pre-war camp at Sutton Bridge with RAF fighter squadrons based in the UK and Germany making annual visits.

Another feature of the annual cycle of training was to carry out an exchange detachment with a NATO squadron. Soon after returning from Sylt, the squadron flew to the French air force base at Tours on 20 April. Situated on the River Loire, this detachment offered social and cultural benefits in addition to the professional advantages of operating with an allied squadron. Dissimilar air combat training is a particularly valuable exercise for air defence squadrons and the crews of 46 Squadron were able to develop their skills against the resident Sud Aviation Vautour IIN interceptors of the 1/30e Escadre de Chasse Tous-Temps.

Whilst at Tours, the squadron introduced their French colleagues to the renowned 'schooner race', which involved a team of relay drinkers consuming a large quantity of beer in competition with another team. The contest was set up during a visit to the cellars of the local vineyard but Freddie and his crews were surprised when they discovered that their French hosts, and opponents, had decided that the beverage should be the local Vouvray wine!

Soon after returning from France, the squadron became involved in an unusual role for an all-weather fighter unit. Trials were conducted to assess the effectiveness of the Javelin attacking fast patrol boats using their four 30-mm Aden cannons in a shallow dive. After a few daylight sorties, the tactic was repeated at night under flares dropped by Shackletons. The trial was concluded with Exercise Half-

The successful Ingpen Trophy team. Freddie is in the centre and his navigator, Dick Dawes, on his right.

back when Freddie attacked three fast patrol boats at night.

A few weeks later it was back to the familiar operational heights above 40,000 feet when four crews left for Horsham St Faith to compete in the Ingpen Trophy, the annual air-to-air firing competition for all-weather fighter squadrons. Having come second in 1958, the squadron was determined to go one better. Freddie, flying with Flight Lieutenant Dick Dawes as his nav/rad, led the team. Each crew flew cine-gun sorties followed by two live air-to-air firings. An excellent team effort resulted in 46 Squadron winning the trophy, which was later presented to Freddie at a formal parade by the AOC-in-C Fighter Command, Air Marshal Sir Hector McGregor.

The RAF's fighter force based in the United Kingdom was a key element of the deterrence strategy, always ready, willing and able to meet the threat, which was the most likely to develop from the north and the east. To combat this threat and keep reaction times to a minimum, air defence squadrons were relocated to the eastern side of the country.

This resulted in a move for 46 Squadron and on 13 July, Freddie led a formation of ten Javelins to their new home at Waterbeach, a few miles north of Cambridge, a move that offered many advantages both operational and training. There were numerous weapon ranges situated in the east of England, and a number of other fighter squadrons were based in the area providing an opportunity for mutual training.

A further advantage of being based in the east of England was the proximity of the V-bomber bases and the opportunity to intercept the bombers as they headed for their airfields from the north east. Most were intercepted above 40,000 feet and sometimes as high as 48,000 feet. Some exercises were flown in pairs without the aid of ground control when the Javelins would fan out and search ahead on their radars before carrying out head-on attacks. Other sorties were flown in an electronic jamming environment.

The squadron had little time to settle at Waterbeach before participation in the Farnborough Air Show loomed again. This time, there was greater pressure since Freddie had been tasked to lead the large Fighter Command formation with 46 Squadron. It was a big responsibility and challenge and Freddie went about the preparation with his typical enthusiasm and thoroughness. Precise timings and accurate navigations were essential with a force of eighty-nine aircraft behind him.

Preparations started two weeks in advance when Freddie flew the route in an Anson to check the key visual navigation points and to take photographs. He then organised sorties for leaders only to practice the rendezvous timings before the first route check followed by two dress rehearsals. During his planning, he had recognised that, whilst the navigators in the Javelins would be able to direct their pilots to a diversion airfield in the event of an emer-

gency, the single-seat Hunter pilots would be concentrating entirely on keeping formation and not always aware of their precise position in relation to diversion airfields so, he detailed his No. 3 to broadcast, at frequent intervals, the distance and bearing to the nearest airfield.

On 7 September the formation of ninety aircraft flew over the show and repeated the performance over the next six days. The delta-wing Javelins flew in formation and, as they approached the president's tent, they overtook a group of the delta-wing Vulcans with an overtake speed of 100 knots. The whole exercise went without a hitch and was a credit to Freddie's meticulous planning and leadership and also the skill of the crews who took part. His foresight in using his No. 3 to relay positions paid handsome dividends. During one show, a Hunter suffered an engine problem and was given an immediate heading for Duxford airfield where the aircraft's engine stopped on the landing run.

Freddie encountered very few mishaps flying the Javelin but he experienced an engine failure on 8 January 1960 when flying at night. The port engine shed a compressor blade, but the destruction was contained within the engine (there were a few instances when fuel lines were cut resulting in a fire). The engine was shut down and after a GCA the aircraft was landed safely.

Freddie leads the formation of ninety aircraft over Farnborough.

After a series of air defence exercises, some involving the aircraft at readiness on the operational readiness platform (ORP) connected to a tele-scramble, Freddie's tour in command of 46 Squadron approached its end. He finished on a high note. He took off on 16 June on an air defence exercise and intercepted two Valiants at 40,000 feet, a Victor at 45,000 feet and gained contact on a Vulcan at 46,000 feet. A few days later he handed over command of the squadron unaware that his days as a fighter pilot were over.

Chapter Twenty-one

STAFF APPOINTMENTS

As Johnnie was coming to the end of the six-month course at the JSSC, he was warned that a posting to Aden was in the offing. Shortly afterwards, there was a suggestion that this could be changed to Addis Ababa in Ethiopia as the air attaché. He had just purchased the necessary tropical uniforms when he was informed – in the perverse way of the services – that he would be going to Norway.

NATO's Allied Command Europe (ACE) was divided into three regions under the command of the supreme allied commander Europe (SACEUR) with his headquarters at Fontainebleau just outside Paris. On the flanks of the Central Region were Allied Forces Southern Europe (AFSOUTH), with its headquarters in Naples, and Allied Forces Northern Europe (AFNORTH) at Kolsås near Oslo.

Johnnie was posted to the tactical air operations cell of AFNORTH where he shared an office with a Royal Norwegian Air Force (RNoAF) officer and a USAF officer. His Norwegian colleague, Hal Christensen, became a lifelong friend and they and their families shared many activities and social events together.

AFNORTH was a large region stretching from Schleswig Holstein in the south to the Norwegian-Soviet border near the Kola Peninsula well north of the Arctic Circle. Apart from Turkey, Norway was the only NATO country to share a border with the Soviet Union.

Defence of this vast region was beyond the capabilities of the two host nations, Denmark and Norway. Norway was particularly difficult to defend and its military forces were far too small to protect all of the territory against a major aggression. Its strategy was designed to protect key areas, especially in the north, until forces from other members of NATO could arrive. The main air force contributions came from the UK and the USA. The huge region also presented uniquely different terrain and weather patterns requiring very flexible forces. The tactics for air operations in the most northerly part of Norway were very different to those appropriate in the temperate areas of Denmark and the Baltic.

Johnnie's responsibilities included the preparation of plans for basing the reinforcement squadrons but his main activity was to monitor the activities and effectiveness of the air defence and tactical air support squadrons during routine training and the numerous national and multi-national exercises. Most of the resident squadrons operated US and UK-built aircraft so there was a large measure of standardisation and the air forces of both countries were modelled on similar lines to the RAF. There was a very strong affiliation with local commanders; the great majority having served in the RAF during the war and the younger pilots had all been trained in the United States or with the NATO scheme in Canada.

With Johnnie's great love of the outdoors and adventure, his posting to Oslo provided many opportunities for him and his family to enjoy the pleasures of Norway. Working hours at Kolsås could best be described as 'gentlemanly' and there was no shortage of time to take advantage of all the pursuits on offer. He enjoyed many adventures with Hal Christensen including cross-country skiing and visits to his mountain hut. There were also opportunities much nearer to home that he could share with his young family and they enjoyed the winter snows with skiing day and night on illuminated runs to the door of their house, gentle downhill skiing only a tram ride away, and skating on the fjord.

He retained his fondness for cars and was able to take advantage of the duty-free arrangements for those posted abroad. He purchased a new Mercedes Benz 220S, which he collected from the factory in Stuttgart. Renowned as a furious driver, he took great pride in it and the car served him well for many years.

In March 1960, his very happy two-year appointment was over and he returned to the UK to join the Flying College Course at the RAF College of Air Warfare at Manby near Louth. The students were very experienced senior wing commanders and the many lectures and classroom tactical exercises were interspersed with a great deal of flying on various aircraft types. On completion of the six-month course, the graduates were ideally suited to take command of an operational station.

Johnnie was promoted to group captain and was looking forward to commanding a flying station but it was not to be and he was appointed to command RAF North Luffenham in Rutland, one of the new Thor inter-continental ballistic missile stations. Initially disappointed, Johnnie was to enjoy a fascinating and enjoyable time in Rutland.

Prior to commanding 46 Squadron, Freddie had served in London for over two years at the new MOD, then situated in King Charles Street. After six months as the staff officer to the RAF representative on the Defence Research Policy Staff, he had moved to the Chiefs of Staff Secretariat (COSSEC) on promotion to wing commander.

Working as a secretary at the twice-weekly service chiefs meetings provided him with a detailed insight into matters of defence policy. It also reinforced his views on the value, and need, for 'jointery'. Whilst he recognised fully the need for strong leadership of the single services, he was convinced that the individual services had to work together at all levels, not least the operational level. It had been a feature of his wartime career and many of his future appointments were inextricably linked with the other two services.

This time at MOD was also a busy period for Freddie on the motor racing track and hill climb circuits. In December 1955 he had bought a Cooper 1100cc with a view to creating a standing start speed record over a mile course for the International Class 'G'. Many modifications were made, including a new streamlined body, and Freddie obtained permission from the Ministry of Supply to use the long runway at Thurleigh Airfield near Bedford.

Freddie's partner in the attempt, Peter Hughes, was killed just before it was due to take place but Freddie decided to press on alone. Trial runs were carried out at Biggin Hill and, by September, all was ready. Specialist timing equipment was obtained from Switzerland but it was only

Freddie (second right) and his team with the Cooper at Thurleigh Airfield for his world record.

available for one weekend. Fog descended on the airfield on 21 September 1956 and the attempt had to be delayed a day. Royal Automobile Club timekeepers had arrived at Thurleigh and, on the Sunday, Freddie encountered a few problems on the first runs but then achieved 93.88 mph for the mile and 87.64 for the kilometre. He was clocked at nearly 200 mph as he crossed the finishing line. Both speeds were world records, the first car speed records in Britain since the war. That afternoon, it was champagne with his team and his wife Anne, his strongest supporter.

Soon after this record, Freddie left the MOD and his motor racing activities had to take a back seat as he went off to command 46 Squadron, but cars continued to be his great fascination. He had achieved much on the racing scene and competed amongst some of Britain's best drivers. Years later, he said:

> 'I reckoned that I would never make world champion so decided to stick to flying jet fighters. I made up my mind to pursue built-in obsolescence and the veteran car scene so bought a 1903 Riley Forecar. Two years later I exchanged it for a 1901 Darracq 6 ½ hp, which was a four-seater so more family friendly!'

It was the beginning of a new chapter in Freddie's motoring achievements. He completed his first London to Brighton rally in 1962 and has not missed many over the past fifty years.

In 1960, the original plan for Freddie was to join Johnnie on the Flying College Course at Manby and they were both looking forward to sharing experiences, and most likely flying, together. But it was not to be as Freddie was selected to be the personal staff officer (PSO) to Chief of the Air Staff Air Chief Marshal Sir Thomas Pike, a distinguished wartime fighter pilot and recent AOC-in-C Fighter Command. Pike had clearly been impressed with Freddie's leadership of 46 Squadron and, when he took over as CAS, he selected him to be his PSO and they soon established a close rapport.

Although the RAF continued to have major commitments overseas, much of Freddie's two years with CAS were concentrated on Cold War issues. Following the major cuts to Fighter Command in the wake of the Sandys Defence Review, the RAF's role centred on Bomber Command and the overseas commands. Freddie was aware of his specialist operational experience and recognised the need to learn more about other roles. Hence, one of his first acts on taking up his appointment was to visit the V-bomber stations for briefings and to fly sorties in the Valiant and the Victor.

Bomber Command with its V-bombers and Thor intermediate range ballistic missile (IRBM) force provided the British strategic nuclear deterrent. At the time, it was estimated that the current level of expenditure on the deterrent, inclusive of capital and running costs of the V-force, its airfields, nuclear weapons, together with the running costs of the Thor force and research and development, represented about 'ten per cent' of the defence budget.

Years later, when he was asked what had been the dominant feature of his time with CAS, Freddie unhesitatingly said 'Skybolt'. The British Blue Streak strategic missile system, on which so many hopes had been based as the successor to the V-force, had recently been cancelled. As a result, an agreement had been reached on 29 March 1960 with the USA for the British participation in the Skybolt air-launched ballistic missile (ALBM) development and acquisition programme. The missile was to be carried by modified Vulcan aircraft.

The memorandum accompanying the 1961-62 Air Estimates confirmed the intention to introduce Skybolt in the mid-1960s, to be carried by the Vulcan B 2, and the missile would be fitted with a British warhead. Issues regarding Skybolt continued to be a regular feature of CAS's work but in December 1962, just after Freddie had left his appointment, it was announced that the Skybolt programme was to be cancelled and replaced by a submarine-launched missile, the Polaris. This decision was a watershed for the RAF and Bomber Command with the responsibility for the strategic nuclear deterrent, held by the RAF since the mid-1950s, handed over to the Royal Navy. The noted air historian Air Commodore Henry Probert commented:

'This was a body blow to Tom Pike and the RAF, and growing doubts about the viability of TSR 2 on cost grounds only made things worse. As Pike himself had commented: "It was a splendid aircraft but the RAF was asking too much."'

Another initiative implemented by CAS was to increase the number of surveillance flights made by RAF signals intelligence-gathering aircraft with flights into the Baltic region. In addition to this important task, the flights, recommended by CAS and authorised by Secretary of State for Air Julian Amery, also tested the Soviet's air defence reaction capability. The intelligence gathered was of great value and reflected the professionalism of the force. Freddie commented later:

'Occasionally I would send in a little folder to CAS recommending an AFC, which would have no citation, so the boys got recognition for their important work.'

In the 1960s, the RAF continued to enjoy a worldwide reputation for excellence and influence. The RAF's presence in Germany was second only to the USAF with a force of 55,000 personnel spread over eight large airfields in addition to forces in Berlin. RAF squadrons fulfilled all the tactical air support roles in addition to mounting quick reaction forces for air defence and nuclear strike operations. CAS was much in demand for overseas visits, particularly to NATO organisations, Commonwealth air forces and the United States. Freddie accompanied him on some of these, one he remembered well was to India, but he often found himself 'minding the office' when his chief was away.

In addition to the RAF's NATO and worldwide commitments, the RAF units based in the UK amounted to a very large force with eight major commands. CAS made regular visits to them and once a year he held a conference to brief the home and overseas Cs-in-C and to seek their views. All this liaison and co-ordination placed heavy responsibilities on Freddie. At the end of 1961 he was promoted to group captain but remained in his post.

Air Chief Marshal Sir Thomas Pike arrives at Westminster Abbey with Lady Pike.

During Sir Thomas Pike's tenure as the CAS there were considerable pressures placed on the RAF. In addition to the on-going issues of Skybolt, the ending of National Service was causing major recruiting problems. There were growing pressures for a stronger central defence structure, an initiative that CAS disliked and which he fought against. Although it was a relatively quiet and stable period for the RAF commands overseas, international pressures and treaty obligations did flare up. At the beginning of July 1961 the ruler of Kuwait requested assistance following threats to his country from the Iraqi prime minister. The RAF became heavily involved in providing support with fighter squadrons deployed to the area and a major airlift was mounted to transfer army reinforcements to the region.

Stemming from his time as a student at Staff College, Freddie developed an increasing interest in international affairs. His appointments in the MOD and with CAS had provided further stimulus and he joined the International Institute for Strategic Studies (IISS), recognised as one of the world's leading authorities on political-military conflict.

Founded in 1958, with its original focus nuclear deterrence and arms control, the IISS established strong establishment links with former US and British government officials. The institute was very influential in setting the intellectual structures for managing the Cold War.

On 13 May 1962, Freddie had a most enjoyable and nostalgic evening when he accompanied his father to the celebrations for the fiftieth anniversary of the formation of the Royal Flying Corps held at Lancaster House. About 600 former members of the RFC and the RNAS attended including many of Fred's friends including his greatest John Leacroft. The guests were received by Lord Carrington, Julian Amery and the service chiefs. The following day, a Remembrance Service was held at St Clement Danes after a wreath-laying ceremony at the cenotaph. Fred was able to meet his old chief from their Iraq days, Marshal of the RAF Sir John Salmond.

After two years in post, Freddie left at the end of June. He had developed a great admiration for Sir Thomas Pike who he considered to be a 'thinking man's CAS'. He admired his resolve to seek the best position for the RAF, and defend it, and to ensure it remained a highly efficient force.

Freddie's time with CAS had broadened his experience considerably and had been an invaluable guide to the workings of the RAF at its highest levels. He was highly regarded and had enhanced the potential to reach the higher ranks that he had displayed in earlier appointments. CAS felt that he would benefit further if he was given experience in another operational role and so he was selected to take command of the large air transport station at Abingdon, a very different position for a predominantly fighter man.

Chapter Twenty-two

OPERATIONAL COMMAND

There was a certain sense of irony when Johnnie assumed command of RAF North Luffenham on 29 December 1960. His long and distinguished career as a fighter pilot had suffered as a result of the cuts to the air defence force resulting from the Sandys White Paper and, now, he was to command one of the RAF's four wings of ballistic nuclear missiles, one of the main pillars of that same White Paper.

Stemming from Sandys decisions was an initial US Government offer in mid-1956 to provide the UK with Thor IRBMs. The decision to add it to the RAF inventory was taken in 1957 and, on 22 February 1958, an agreement was concluded between the UK and USA to install sixty Thors in eastern England for a five-year period. Under the terms of the agreement, Project Emily, the USA furnished the missiles and warheads with the UK providing operating sites and associated installations. The missiles were to be operated and maintained by RAF personnel; launching the missiles was to be via a 'dual-key' system involving RAF and USAF officers.

The first RAF Thor squadron had formed in August 1958 at Feltwell, Norfolk, and the Thor force was completed when North Luffenham became operational in March 1960 under the command of 3 (Bomber) Group. Each of the four major bases (Feltwell, Hemswell, Driffield and North Luffenham) had four satellites established on nearby disued wartime airfields with three missiles on each site. The satellites under Johnnie's command were at Folkingham, Harrington, Melton Mowbray and Polebrook. To provide an area defence for the vulnerable ground sites of the North Luffenham Thor

A Thor missile in the launching position during an exercise (Air Historical Branch).

complex, the Bloodhound Mark 1 surface-to-air missile (SAM) system was deployed to Woolfox Lodge, a few miles to the north east and to Warboys, south east. The Bloodhounds were controlled by 151 (SAM) Wing HQ at North Luffenham.

With twelve Thor missiles and two SAM sites dispersed at six locations under his command, Johnnie had a huge responsibility over part of the United Kingdom's strategic nuclear deterrent, a force with the capability for massive destruction.

Command of one of the four main Thor bases presented a range of problems unique for an RAF station commander. Postings to the Thor force were not seen as career enhancing and the need for twenty-four-hour manning at a high state of readiness, allied to the routine work and regular training drills, proved monotonous. Unlike flying stations and maintenance units, there was no 'end product' at the end of a day or night shift and facilities and amenities at the satellite sites were modest in comparison with main RAF bases. Morale was an issue that station commanders had to be aware of constantly.

Johnnie had 1,200 personnel under his command and this included seventy members of the USAF. The individual squadrons were located some distance from North Luffenham and many personnel had long daily journeys to get to and from work. Some chose to live locally but they felt remote from the RAF. The severe winters of the early 1960s presented particular difficulties, not least transporting personnel and equipment. Soon after arriving at North Luffenham, Johnnie discovered the realities of operating from distant and remote sites. Harrington was virtually cut off and the hungry police dogs had to be rescued and transferred to North Luffenham since there were no adequate welfare facilities for dogs on the dispersed site. The severe weather and very low temperatures on the exposed sites presented some difficult engineering and security issues and hampered training.

A welcome break for some of the launch crews was a visit to Vandenberg AFB in California to conduct a 'Combat Training Launch' of an RAF missile selected at random and flown to Vandenberg in a USAF C-124 Globemaster. The aim of these firings was to verify the operational capability of the launch teams and the system's overall reliability. A successful firing gave confidence in the RAF's operational, training and maintenance capabilities. Only two of the twenty-one test firings were classed as failures.

In June 1961, a North Luffenham crew travelled to Vandenberg and on the 20th they achieved a successful firing. This launch was also a landmark since it was the first undertaken solely by RAF personnel and without the assistance of their US counterparts.

One of the few occasions for the Thor crews to break from the daily routine was a result of the Cuban Missile Crisis in October 1961. On the 27th the C-in-C Bomber Command, Air Marshal Sir Kenneth Cross, ordered a higher alert condition as a precaution. Readiness State One-Five (fifteen minutes to launch) was ordered and, whilst this may appear to be a significant escalation, it was little more than normal readiness. Some training was halted and more personnel were on standby. The state was held until 5 November when normal routine was resumed. Most people involved remember the 'crisis' as largely uneventful.

By mid-1962 it was clear that Thor would not remain viable for much longer. The US had decided not to extend the operational life of their force and, without an upgrade, the RAF's force of sixty missiles would become increasingly expensive and vulnerable to air attack.

Just before a formal decision was announced in August, a team from North Luffenham left for Vandenberg and on 19 June 1962 they successfully launched a missile. In the event, this was the last launch of an RAF Thor.

On 1 August an announcement was made in the House of Commons that the Thor force would be run down. This was received with mixed feelings. There were many, including senior politicians and RAF commanders, who had questioned the value of Thor. Of more concern to Johnnie and his fellow station commanders was the need to maintain operational efficiency following the announcement of the draw-down.

On 15 August 1963, North Luffenham's five squadrons were declared non-operational and they disbanded a week later with the missiles returned to the USA. There was little ceremony in the RAF to mark the end of the Thor era. At North Luffenham a disbandment party was held in the NAAFI

Horseshoe Club and Thor, after a short-lived existence, passed into RAF history.

Throughout his time at North Luffenham, Johnnie maintained his flying currency and made regular visits to the RAF College at nearby Cranwell to fly the Meteor and Vampire trainers. He and his family enjoyed their time in Rutland where they purchased a cottage one mile away from the RAF station in the nearby village of Edith Weston. The family vacated the official residence on the station to live in the cottage. Johnnie and Audrey's two daughters attended the local school in Oakham and kept their ponies near the airfield where they set up a jumping course. Julia, the eldest daughter, summed up the family's feelings:

> 'We kept the cottage at Edith Weston when my father was posted away as we had all fallen in love with the area and my brother, sister and I always considered Rutland to be our home.'

In August 1963, Johnnie left North Luffenham to attend a series of briefings at the Foreign Office and Air Ministry in preparation for his next appointment as air adviser on the British High Commission Staff in New Delhi, India.

As Johnnie was embarking on his final year in command of North Luffenham, Freddie was completing a flying refresher course on Provost and Varsity aircraft at Manby. In September he joined 242 OCU at Thorney Island near Chichester to convert to the Blackburn Beverley transport. The large, ungainly machine was a far cry from the sleek fighters that he was familiar with. It was a new experience for Freddie, as was the luxury of flying with a large crew. On 3 October he flew his first solo on the type and two weeks later went solo at night.

On 3 December, Freddie took over command of RAF Abingdon from Neil Cameron. He commented: 'Neil Cameron was a hard act to follow since he had achieved a great deal and was highly respected.'

Abingdon was a large station with two resident heavy-lift Beverley squadrons (47 and 53), tasked with providing tactical airlift and re-supply for the army and a flight of Hastings for duties with the special forces. His two years in command proved to be a highlight for Freddie and for his wife Anne.

Many of Freddie's responsibilities at Abingdon brought him into contact with the army and his attitude and belief in 'jointery' attracted admiration from

Johnnie presents trophies to ladies of the winning team in the station bowling competition.

Freddie kitted out for a parachute jump.

army units, commanders and the personnel who were under his command in the air dispatch units and with No. 1 Parachute Training School. The latter conducted a wide range of courses for all three services and it was a unit that generated a lot of visitors, many from overseas. To understand the role of the two units he flew many sorties with the dispatchers and, soon after taking command, he made two parachute jumps, one from a Hastings and a second from a Beverley. He later made another jump when the Argosy entered service. During his time as station commander he established the RAF Sport Parachuting Association.

Soon after his arrival, the severe winter of 1963 presented Freddie with a unique task. The airfield was soon snowbound but he was determined that flying should continue. He acquired two redundant Derwent jet engines, mounted them on the front of a heavy lorry and blasted the ice and snow off the runway. This allowed aircraft to take off, many in order to drop food supplies to stranded livestock on Dartmoor and in the Cotswolds.

Freddie introduces his wife Anne to Princess Margaret.

Freddie flew whenever time allowed, most as captain, and his flights included long-range re-supply sorties to the Mediterranean and to Libya in addition to flying on parachute training sorties, exercises and tactical support sorties. In October 1963, he flew to El Adem in Libya for Exercise Triplex West and shipped army personnel and equipment into remote desert strips.

The Beverley, with its large cargo hold, was in constant demand to carry supplies for all three services. Unlike the rest of the transport force, it was able to carry bulky and unusual loads including small tanks and stripped-down helicopters. Beverley crews never suffered from a monotonous existence.

As the station commander, Freddie had many responsibilities. Situated relatively close to London, and commanding a station with many diverse activities, there was a heavy programme of visitors and many VIPs, including HRH Princess Margaret, so the duty and social programme for Freddie and his wife was demanding. They also played an important role in the local community and were frequently invited to attend events and activities in addition to the formal occasions when the station exercised its freedom to march through Abingdon town.

He established a warm friendship with the local MP Airey Neave (later killed by an IRA bomb), a man with a distinguished army record and one of the few POWs to escape from Colditz Castle.

A particularly important and welcome visitor was Sir John Salmond who arrived in his marshal's uniform on 4 July at Freddie's invitation. After a tour of the station, the aircraft, and the parachute training, Sir John was entertained at a formal lunch before being flown back to his home in Sussex. A few days later he wrote to his old friend Fred senior to compliment him on Freddie's hospitality and achievements:

'My dear Fred
    'I went over a week ago by invitation to your son's station, driven there from the RAF Club by a car to Abingdon.
    'Personally I was amazed at what I saw, the immensity, the detail and the precision, and

it fairly woke me up. The Beverley's staggering number of instruments to watch and control in flight – all of which your son takes like a duck to water. I was truly astounded at that young man. I am quite sure he will go a very long way.

'I was sumptuously entertained. It was one of the pleasantest and certainly the most instructive visits I remember having.

Yours ever
Jack

PS. Best wishes and congratulations to you both on a wonderful son.'

The winter of 1963/64 witnessed increased tension in Cyprus and the Abingdon squadrons were heavily committed. An armoured car squadron was taken to Cyprus and helicopters were airlifted from Gütersloh to Akrotiri. Freddie flew a number of sorties into Malta, Libya and Cyprus with reinforcements and the airlift was completed on 25 February.

A month later there was a requirement to ferry a Beverley to the squadron based in Singapore and Freddie joined Flight Lieutenant Hugh Crawley's enlarged crew as second pilot. The aircraft left Abingdon 23 March on the first stage to Orange in southern France. It was to be a trip full of surprises and adventures.

After a night stop in Malta, the crew flew the short leg to El Adem to prepare for a 1.10 am departure the next morning. This early take-off time allowed the aircraft to arrive over the large rocky outcrop on the Egyptian-Sudan border, known as 'Nasser's Corner', at first light, obtain a fix and head for Khartoum in time for breakfast. Starting the engines at Khartoum for the flight to RAF Khormaksar in Aden was the beginning of a series of troubles. Freddie was the first pilot for the leg to Aden but the starter motor for the two port engines failed. It was decided to rush down the runway with the starboard

MRAF Sir John Salmond visits Abingdon.

engines running in order to windmill the two propellers on the port side and hope that the engines would burst into life. It was successful and Freddie was able to take off. An engine failed en-route and a successful three-engine landing was made.

Freddie took advantage of the enforced four-day delay needed for repairs to their aircraft and flew two re-supply sorties with the local Beverley squadron (his Uncle Bill's 84 Squadron) to desert strips in up-country Aden. In the meantime, Crawley fell ill and had to return to the UK so Freddie assumed command of the aircraft and decided to press on to Singapore. Another member of the crew was also taken ill and a signaller had to be borrowed from 84 Squadron. On the 29th, the crew took off for RAF Masirah and, after a night, they headed for Bombay. After a brief lunch, it was then on to Calcutta. It was a long day with Freddie and his young co-pilot at the controls for over nine hours without an autopilot, which had become unserviceable soon after leaving Masirah.

More repairs were needed in Calcutta, which caused further delay. Anxious to press on, Freddie was concerned with the meteorologist's forecast of storms so he set off on a night flight to Rangoon when the risks were likely to be less. By now, two of the crew were suffering from food poisoning and, after the minimum crew rest time at Rangoon, he headed for RAF Seletar in Singapore, arriving on 2 April with the survivors.

The summer of 1964 passed in a similar manner to other years with a mixture of command, flying, social and community activities. With many visitors, including General Lemnitzer, SACEUR, and General Joseph Mobutu, the C-in-C of the Congolese National Army, in addition to plenty of entertainment, the Sowrey residence was a busy household supervised by Anne who was at ease, and very popular, with all ranks. On arrival two years earlier she had introduced a training schedule for the house staff. It was so successful that the staffs were 'head hunted' for the CAS's residence in London.

Freddie and Anne found their time at Abingdon one of the most enjoyable and fulfilling throughout their long time in the RAF. Many years later he commented:

'As a station commander, it is the last opportunity in which you and your wife can put your personal imprint on a unit. We enjoyed our time at Abingdon immensely although it was testing. However, we faced it with the knowledge that one had good training and many experiences to draw on.'

At the end of his very successful tour, Freddie was appointed a Commander of the Order of the British Empire (CBE); a recognition that he always considered was a 'station' award. With his selection to attend the 1965 course at the Imperial Defence College (IDC), his career continued its upwards trend.

Attendance at IDC was reserved for a select few drawn from all three services, the civil service and the emergency services. Many of the students would have dealings with each other in later appointments and this was one of the principal benefits of the course. Another was to listen to and question the many visiting speakers from the political, international, military and industrial sectors. Visits, overseas and at home, provided another

Freddie and his family at Buckingham Palace after Freddie was invested with the CBE.

opportunity to broaden interests.

Freddie took full advantage of the chance to escape the pressures of command and staff work. Since his days at Staff College, he had become increasingly interested in politico-military affairs and IDC gave him an ideal opportunity to study in more detail and develop his own ideas, some of which he committed to articles in learned journals. He described his time at IDC as 'mind stretching'.

For the four-week overseas visit, Freddie elected to join the African tour. Starting in Libya, the party travelled to Nigeria and Ghana in the west, on to Kenya and then south to Southern Rhodesia, Botswana and South Africa. It was a fascinating experience and would pay handsome dividends a year later when Freddie took up a senior appointment in Aden.

During his year at IDC Freddie became very involved in the fortunes of the RAF Club. Situated at 128 Piccadilly, the club was walking distance from Seaford House, the home of IDC in Belgrave Square.

The club bulletin of October 1964 had alerted members to the alarming and precarious state of the club's finances and it was proposed to increase the annual subscription fee significantly. This brought about many resignations and, with less than ten per cent of serving officers as members, drastic action was needed. This came from Air Vice-Marshal Lewis Hodges and Group Captain Neil Cameron, both serving in Paris, who suggested that the former should write to all serving officers to ask them to help redeem Lord Cowdray's gift of the club in 1920 to the flying services. Enough support was gathered to call for an emergency general meeting, which took place on 14 December when it was agreed that Cameron, soon to return home, should chair a new membership sub-committee. He immediately set to work to co-opt members and one of the first to accept was Freddie Sowrey. Two colleagues about to join him at IDC, Group Captains Ivor Broom and Ronnie Webster, were also co-opted. What had become known as the 'Colonels Revolt' was under way.

Much of Freddie's 'study time' at IDC was devoted to work with the membership committee who recognised immediately that there was a need to modernise the club and give it a new look if they were to attract the younger serving officers. At the annual general meeting held in March 1965, a draft report was presented which resulted in Neil Cameron being elected as chairman of the RAF Club and it was agreed that Freddie, Ivor Broom and Ronnie Webster would join him. As the historians of the RAF Club wrote:

> 'So now "the Colonels" were not just putting their ideas together but were also on the inside, charged with tackling the immediate practical problems still confronting the club. They were immeasurably strengthened by the knowledge that their scheme was backed by the Air Force Board and by all the commanders-in-chief – the kind of moral support that the club had never before been given.'

The committee had many hurdles to negotiate during 1965, some erected by its own members, but Cameron and his team campaigned vigorously to make the necessary changes needed to prevent bankruptcy. By October, initiatives to encourage serving officers to join were beginning to take effect and Cameron re-directed his key henchmen to form a 'Way Ahead Committee' chaired by Freddie. Hodges returned from Paris to take up an appointment at MOD and he now joined the committee. The team to take the RAF Club forward was now in place.

Freddie's committee was encouraged to 'let boldness be its guide' with the key aim of making the club more attractive to the younger members. The new initiatives soon bore fruit and by April 1966, service membership had risen ten-fold to almost 12,000. The club employed a professional manager and slowly the drastic measures, including a major refurbishment, began to take effect. By this time, Freddie was on his way to the Middle East and his work at the RAF Club came to an end – but he would be returning in eighteen months.

Chapter Twenty-three

FOREIGN SERVICE

Johnnie left for India on 3 September 1963 from Stansted where he was seen off by his Uncle Bill and cousin, Heather before boarding a British United Airways Britannia for his flight to Aden. He spent the evening with his brother's old wartime CO, Fred Rosier, before flying to Delhi to take up residence at 24 Golf Links Road in New Delhi where Audrey and their two daughters joined him a few weeks later. He was made an acting air commodore and was one of three military advisors to the British High Commissioner, Sir Paul Gore-Booth.

The Indian Air Force was modelled along very similar lines to the RAF and the two air forces enjoyed a close relationship. This was reinforced during Johnnie's time in the country by his close personal friendship with Air Chief Marshal Arjan Singh, his colleague from their days together as flight cadets at Cranwell. Singh was deputy CAS and a year later became CAS of the Indian Air Force. They were to meet officially, and socially, on many occasions.

Although the Indian Air Force had started to purchase some aircraft from the Soviet Union, it had a force of eighty Canberra bombers and six squadrons of Hunters. It had recently re-equipped some of its Vampire fighter squadrons with the Folland Gnat built under licence by Hindustan Aeronautics Limited of Bangalore. One of his first visits was to see the Gnat assembly line and the large maintenance facility for Vampires, Canberras and the Indian-designed and built Hindustan HF 24 fighter. He described his visit as 'most impressive'. With the Indian Air Force's heavy reliance on British aircraft, Johnnie had many dealings with the aerospace industries in both countries. His experience as a fighter pilot and as a test pilot gave him a very authoritative view and valuable input, which was respected by the industry and the IAF.

Johnnie had barely settled into his appointment when he provided support for a major detachment by 64 Squadron Javelins to the IAF airfield at Kalaikunda to take part in Exercise Shiksha, a major air defence exercise. He visited the airfield to meet the IAF commanders and review the facilities. The twelve aircraft were supported by Valiant tankers and arrived on 28 October. This was the first time RAF combat aircraft had been stationed in India since independence. Squadrons of the USAF and RAAF also provided forces.

The exercise was designed to test India's air defence organisation and the Javelins were used to intercept large forces of IAF and RAAF Canberras. Johnnie flew down to spend a few days observing the exercise, which was widely regarded as very successful. On 21 November, five of the Javelins, with Valiant tankers, took off for Singapore to reinforce the resident 60 Squadron and the remaining aircraft returned to the UK.

During his time as air advisor, Johnnie had a Dakota at his disposal; later replaced with an Andover, and he was able to travel widely to IAF bases, in addition to other diplomatic visits. On numerous occasions he used the aircraft to transport the many VIPs and government dignitaries who visited the country including Lord Mountbatten, Alec Douglas-Home and Barbara Castle.

On 24 May 1964, India's prime minister since partition in 1947, and leader of the Indian Congress Party, Jawaharlal Nehru, died. His funeral attracted many British mourners and Johnnie and his wife were heavily involved in hosting.

Johnnie and his wife Audrey are introduced to Lord Mountbatten.

Life as a foreign representative also involved a very hectic programme of protocol and social activities. In addition to celebrating British and Indian anniversaries and events, Johnnie and Audrey were invited to many similar occasions and receptions at the other international delegations. There was a steady steam of official visitors to the Sowrey home and Audrey had to manage her staff and the complex arrangements, not least dietary, for the many and varied guests to dinner parties, receptions and overnight visits.

Life in India was a great adventure for Johnnie and the family. Exotic birds filled their garden and all the family enjoyed riding, swimming and skiing in the winter. His two daughters attended an English school and enjoyed many friendships in the international community. Stepson Gavin was at boarding school in England and was able to share in the excitement and adventures only during school holidays. He wrote:

'The family experienced a fairy tale life of privilege. They saw wonders, such as the Taj Mahal, rode with The Delhi Hunt, shot duck with princes and maharajahs and enjoyed countless rounds of social events, often three parties a night. To me, staying in Britain, they appeared to enjoy an inordinate number of lengthy holidays in Kashmir skiing in winter, and on the houseboats on lakes there in the summer. Many years later, when John talked about the aircraft activity in the area, it became clear to me that the Kashmir trips had also been in the line of duty.'

Johnnie and family enjoy the ski slopes in Srinagar.

When Prince Philip visited India in March 1965, Johnnie personally piloted the Dakota transport in which he flew, and accompanied him to social events.

In May 1965, a joint US/UK Mission visited India in an attempt to establish a measure of air defence support. This included deployment of USAF and RAF fighter squadrons to participate in exercises and to advise on development and tactics. This involved Johnnie in considerable liaison and staffing duties. In the event, however, the regional international situation and readjustments of the Indian domestic political scene, in the post-Nehru era, proved to be too difficult and no specific plans and arrangements were made.

Johnnie's very hectic two years came to an end in September 1965 and he and the family sailed from Bombay by Lloyd Triestino to Venice, where Gavin and his wife Charlotte met them to drive back to England in their brand new car. After a period of leave, Johnnie reported to MOD to begin his next appointment.

Within a few months of Johnnie's return to the UK, his cousin Freddie set off for Aden to continue the many years of foreign service that had been a feature of the Sowrey family since the earliest days of their RAF service.

There had been an RAF presence in Aden since the 1920s and in 1928, the policy of air control, instituted in Iraq following the Cairo Conference of 1921, was extended to Aden. For the next forty years, the RAF was regularly in action against dissident factions in the protectorate.

In the late 1950s the deterioration of relations with Egypt following the ill-fated Suez operation and the worsening of Arab/Israeli relations had created increasing concern about the political situation in the Middle East. As a result, the British Government had begun to reinforce the garrisons east of Suez. The force levels in Aden were increased rapidly in size and responsibility and, in 1959, it was decided to create a unified military command, the first such overseas organisation. The success of HQ Middle East prompted other unified commands to be established in Cyprus and the Far East.

Aden became the pivot of our military power in the Middle East with the dual role of defending the oil-rich dependencies in the Persian Gulf and acting as a staging post on the island route to Singapore. The command stretched from Bahrain to Botswana and Uganda to Madagascar with Eastern and Western Aden Protectorates providing an absorbing series of operations on the doorstep. Khormaksar was the biggest and busiest airfield in the RAF with over 100 aircraft, of eleven different types, permanently based there. It was also a busy staging post for Transport Command and for carrier-borne Fleet Air Arm aircraft operating in the area.

In 1964, the Conservative Government announced that South Arabia would be granted independence 'not later than 1968', but that it was intended to maintain a military base in Aden. However this policy was changed after the Labour Government's Defence Review was published on 22 February 1966. It was announced that the British military would be withdrawn when independence was granted. This caused shock waves amongst the federal rulers who saw themselves highly vulnerable to their enemies and they recognised that the tempo of terrorism would almost certainly increase. To President Nasser of Egypt, the Yemen government and the nationalists it came as a welcome surprise.

Freddie arrived at HQ Middle East Command to take up the post of senior air staff offi-

Joint staffs in Aden with the AOC, AVM Andrew Humphrey (centre) and Freddie two to his left.

cer (SASO) two weeks after the Labour Government's announcement. He arrived to find a truly 'joint' headquarters. The C-in-C was Admiral Sir Michael Le Fanu and the AOC was Air Vice-Marshal Andrew Humphrey. Freddie worked alongside the Brigadier General Staff (Brigadier Charles Dunbar) with a shared office and their respective staffs alongside.

RAF squadrons were based in Bahrain and Sharjah, in addition to those at Khormaksar. There were staging posts in Oman, the Persian Gulf and along the South Arabian coast. Small British units were also based in East Africa. The unexpected and demanding commitments of enforcing the United Nations oil embargo on Ian Smith's Rhodesia following his Unilateral Declaration of Independence (UDI), in November 1965 was an additional responsibility for the SASO. Now, added to this was the planning for withdrawal of British forces from Aden by the end of 1967, just eighteen months away.

Freddie summed up his position:

'There was a small war up-country, the deterrence against the Yemeni air force, an increasing terrorist war; control of units in the Persian Gulf; an oil lift into Zambia following the declaration of UDI in Southern Rhodesia; support of a Javelin squadron, a radar unit and the RAF Regiment in Zambia. It was a lot to look after. We opened up an airfield at Majunga in Madagascar to take a Shackleton squadron, which was monitoring the oil embargo flying on the Beira Oil Patrol, and then there was the withdrawal from Aden.'

Before leaving the UK he had completed a conversion course on the Hunter, a brief helicopter introduction and refresher flying on the Beverley and the Argosy – this allowed him to fly regularly. He was determined not to be tied to his desk but to visit his large parish. Soon after arriving, he flew to the staging posts en-route to the Persian Gulf followed by a visit to Nairobi. He flew on a supply drop to forces at Beihan in the north of the protectorate and flew re-supply sorties into airstrips at the forward army posts. For the next eighteen months, he continued to fly on these support sorties in addition to regular visits to the overseas stations.

Not everyone was keen to serve in Aden but Freddie and his family enjoyed their time there despite the increasing risks. He wrote:

'In spite of the heat, humidity and risks, Aden could be a happy place for families. Ours came out in the holidays from school or university by air or sea and like-minded young people did the same. Our daughter Susan much enjoyed the swimming and water-skiing with the Hunter pilots of 8 Squadron whilst Peter made flights up-country, inconspicuous in his Charterhouse CCF khaki. Everyone also had an opportunity of a fortnight in Kenya either at a coast resort or independently. In those far-off days you could hire a Land Rover and go, literally, anywhere. We did just that.'

Acts of terrorism did increase and British casualties, military and civilian, mounted. Initially, the majority of attacks were unsophisticated, usually hand grenades thrown into compounds. However, by the beginning of 1967, families became targets in addition to military personnel and the terrorists started to use booby traps and mail bombs in addition to mortar and gun attacks. Many personnel lived 'off base' and Freddie and his wife stayed in an official residence at Steamer Point that bordered the sea. RAF regiment patrols were introduced to secure the airfield at Khormaksar and helicopter patrols were mounted, some at night when a searchlight was used as a deterrent.

The already difficult situation up-country also started to deteriorate. The Radfan Campaign had come to an end only a few months before but the rival nationalist organisations became more aggressive and some aircraft were placed on a high state of alert. Hunters flew daily air defence patrols along the Yemeni border and continued to support the army and federal units in the Radfan and Dhala areas. The transport force of Beverleys, Argosies, Twin Pioneers and the Wessex helicopters were in constant

An 84 Squadron Beverley damaged by a mine at the up-country Habilam strip.

demand to support the troops. Up-country there was always a threat from mortars, automatic fire and mines and there were casualties. A Beverley was wrecked by a mine at an advanced landing strip and a number of aircraft suffered damage from small-arms fire.

Planning for withdrawal became an increasingly important task for Freddie. At a seminar of the RAF Historical Society in 1997 he summed up the scale of the task:

'The task was to withdraw in safety and good order in the face of an increasing terrorist campaign; to maintain, as far as possible, law and order in the Protectorate until independence; and to try and leave something constructive for the new nation state whilst ensuring the smooth transfer of our own military responsibilities elsewhere – notably the Persian Gulf.

'So an early decision was made that as well as planning for an administrative withdrawal, it could also be opposed on the basis that whichever of the two terrorist groups – FLOSY or the NLF – was most successful in seeming to eject the British (whatever the reality) they would have stronger credentials in the eyes of the population of post-independence Aden in forming a government of sorts. The approach to all planning therefore had to be flexibility and inventiveness.'

During 1966 stocks of ammunition, technical spares and barrack stores started to be run down. A team began to address the re-deployment of units to the Persian Gulf and plans for the evacuation of families were drawn up. Heavy stores were to be evacuated by sea but it was soon realised that there would have to be a massive airlift and the single runway at Khormaksar would need to be resurfaced. Unnecessary expense was to be avoided and the materials had to be obtained for work that would have to be undertaken in the cool of the night when traffic was limited. It was a risky, but necessary, task and the AOC gave his approval.

With the main evacuation built around the airlift, it was realised that the bases in the Persian Gulf were vital, in particular the RAF airfield at Muharraq in Bahrain. This was the 'elbow' between a tactical airlift from Aden and a strategic lift to the UK. Andrew Humphrey decided that he should transfer his headquarters there for the final month.

The Operation Order (11/67), signed by Freddie, was published on 23 May 1967 and this large document outlined in great detail the instructions for every aspect of the withdrawal. At this stage, it was still the intention to complete the withdrawal in 'early January 1968'.

'The run down of RAF Khormaksar is to be in phase with the withdrawal of British Land Forces into Aden during 1967 and their subsequent withdrawal from the Aden Base.

'All army units except for some small detachments will have withdrawn into Aden by July and, in turn, from Little Aden by October. This latter will entail the RAF communications facility at Hiswa being moved to RAF Khormaksar by 1 September.

'To enable our final withdrawal to take place within seven days of Independence being granted it is planned to reverse the polarity of AFME.

'Instead of the main base area being in Aden, the Gulf will assume this responsibility with Aden functioning as a forward operating area for the minimum air forces remaining.

'From 1 October RAF Khormaksar will come under command of HQ Air Forces Gulf with the aircraft operating as detachments from Gulf units stationed at Muharraq and Sharjah...'

'The task of helicopter support for any contingency intervention by British Forces in the Federation will pass on 1 November from RAF to RN Wessex in HMS *Albion*.
IS helicopter tasks remain a responsibility for the specially-fitted RAF Wessex Mk 10.

'HMS *Eagle* arrives in Aden on 23 October and will begin an air defence work up and assume this role, and that of retaliatory strike, from the RAF on 15 November.

'The JMC at Barrack Hill will be closed and the secure teleprinter channels to Comcen Khormaksar transferred to Government House and/or Sheba.

'It is hoped to close RAF Steamer Point on 31 October.

'By 1 December all army forces, stores and vehicles to be recovered will have been moved out of Aden, except for those remaining in the Khormaksar area to cover final tasks.

'The total RAF compliment remaining on 31 December is estimated at 350. If the security situation permits, all personnel will be withdrawn by air from RAF Khormaksar. This lift will be by RAF aircraft at approximately three-hour intervals and could begin at 0001 hours on Independence Day.'

Notification that a Naval Task Force led by the aircraft carrier HMS *Eagle*, with two commando carriers of helicopters and marines to cover the final withdrawal, was a great load off the minds of Freddie and his planners. Royal Navy Sea Vixens and Buccaneers would provide the air defence and retaliatory attack capability in the event that threats developed after the departure of the Hunters and over the period of the final withdrawal.

The air transport plan for the withdrawal was based on a tactical lift by the Argosy, Belfast, Beverley and Hercules. Troops, embarking with rifles and ammunition, were to be flown to Muharraq before a Britannia or VC 10 flight back to UK. The staffs were determined not to leave any hostages to fortune. To avoid the possibility of leaving a transport aircraft behind, only those that could take off empty on three engines would remain until the end. That ruled out the Belfast for the final phase.

The first major airlift was families – Operation Relative. By the end of April 1967, 2,691 passengers had been flown out and, as the security situation worsened, the move was accelerated. By July, 9,706 from all services had been evacuated. With the families departed, Freddie, who already shared an office with Charles Dunbar, moved into a bungalow with him on the basis that a call-out for one would inevitably be a joint service one.

Following a significant increase in terrorist attacks in June and July it was obvious that the Federal Government was rapidly losing what little control it had over the terrorists and it was becoming clear

Basic precautions were taken to provide some protection for 8 Squadron's Hunters.

that an orderly transition to a stable government, backed by the South Arabian Army, on 1 January 1968 had virtually disappeared. To withdraw in an orderly manner was essential and the date to leave was brought forward to the end of November.

As withdrawal grew closer, there was an increasing amount of industrial unrest and this was particularly damaging at the port and the fuel depots. The supply of aviation fuel presented a major problem and Freddie flew to nearby Djibouti to make emergency arrangements with the French authorities.

From July onwards a steady transfer of responsibility to Bahrain took place and in September the new HQ British Forces Gulf was formed relieving Aden of much of the responsibility for routine operations. The Argosies of 105 Squadron moved to Muharraq and the tasking for maritime and transport operations passed to the new HQ. The Hunters of 8 Squadron, to which the Sowrey family had a deep attachment, also moved to Muharraq leaving 43 Squadron to provide air defence cover for Aden until this responsibility was passed to the Naval Task Force.

As the 'thinning out' of personnel and stores continued throughout the late summer, the requirement for regular flights by Argosies and Beverleys to support the British military detachments in East Africa and Majunga continued. The Shackletons of 37 Squadron left Aden, as did the Twin Pioneers of 21 Squadron, both squadrons to be disbanded.

On 27 October, the AOC, Andrew Humphrey, departed for Bahrain to take overall command of the operation and Freddie remained as commander RAF Aden responsible for executing the final withdrawal. By 31 October the concentration of the remaining units and sections into Khormaksar was complete. Freddie established his HQ in the vacated secondary school, which allowed Steamer Point to be evacuated. Finally, a date was set for the final withdrawal and 'WE' Day was given as 29 November.

The hard-working Beverleys of 84 Squadron departed in early November and a large transport force started to gather at Muharraq for the final lift. A force of fifteen Hercules was deployed to the Gulf to join the Argosies for the tactical lift from Khormaksar. It was to be the Hercules first major task since entering RAF service a few weeks earlier.

Operations started in earnest on 26 November and the intensity increased until the 29th. The last ceremonial took place on W-1 when High Commissioner Sir Humphrey Trevelyan, flew in from HMS *Eagle* (he had left Government House a few days earlier). He inspected a magnificently turned out Joint Service's Guard of Honour with Admiral Sir Michael le Fanu, Freddie and the station commander,

Freddie discusses the loading of one of the final Hercules sorties.

Khormaksar in attendance. The remaining Hunters of 43 Squadron flew overhead in salute as they departed for Muharraq. As Sir Humphrey boarded his aircraft for the UK, the Royal Marine Band from *Eagle* struck up with 'Fings Ain't Wot They Used to Be'.

During this day, over 1,300 service personnel and civilians left in twenty aircraft. Freddie recorded the final events:

> 'On the next day, "W" Day, the skeleton joint HQ on the airfield closed and 45 Commando was lifted by helicopter to the Naval Task Force. This left 42 Commando holding the shrinking perimeter around the airfield with armed helicopter support.
>
> 'The last aircraft into Khormaksar were a freight Hercules, a freight Argosy for ground equipment and a passenger/freight Hercules with two Hercules overhead as airborne reserves. The RAF airfield was closed down between the landing of the last Hercules and its departure at 1345, after a twenty-five minute turn-round, with seventy-five passengers. These included two air traffic controllers, two radio operators, a mobile Air Movements Section, police and an Argosy/Hercules rectification team. With Desmond Brown, the station commander, went the commander Aden Brigade, Dick Jefferies, and last in, Charles Dunbar and myself.
>
> 'I always considered that my time in Aden was one of the most successful periods of my career.'

Since April, 24,000 servicemen had been airlifted from Aden, 6,000 since the beginning of November, 800 in the last nine hours with all arms, ammunition and freight.

So ended 128 years of British rule in Aden and, for the RAF, forty-eight years of occupation. The final withdrawal without a shot fired or a life lost under the most dangerous and trying conditions must rank as one of the best planned and executed operations in British military history. Marshal of the RAF Sir Michael Beetham, who had commanded RAF Khormaksar until 1966, commented: 'The planning and execution of the withdrawal was a model'.

Chapter Twenty-four

MOD POLICY

At the end of 1965, Johnnie took up an appointment in the MOD as deputy director of organisation (Establishments), a far cry from the attractive life in India and the excitement of front-line flying. For some unexplained reason Johnnie managed to persuade the authorities that a pre-requisite for his desk job in London was to complete a flying refresher course! For six weeks he enjoyed flying the Jet Provost at RAF Manby before settling into life in London.

Soon after arriving in his new appointment, he decided that he needed to make a visit to the Far East air force to discuss personnel and manning issues. Whilst at RAF Changi, he joined a Hastings crew on a re-supply drop to troops in the Borneo jungle during the Indonesian Confrontation Cam-

The Sowrey family celebrate John and Audrey's (centre) Golden Wedding Anniversary.

paign, before visiting the RAF elements at Labuan and Kuching.

As 1967 began to draw to a close, events unfolded that saw the beginning of the Sowrey family's unprecedented service to the RAF begin to fade. Notwithstanding a number of visits to overseas bases, Johnnie had for some time been unsettled in his appointment in the MOD. A man of action, both in and out of the service, he found the mundane nature of his job frustrating and started to turn his thoughts to taking early retirement.

Sadness descended on the Sowreys when John senior died on 9 October aged seventy-five. He and his wife Audrey had celebrated their Golden Wedding just twelve months earlier when all the family, except Freddie whose commitments in Aden prevented him from travelling, had gathered for a family party. John had been ill for a short time and he was buried in the family vault at Staines where his parents had been laid to rest.

Susan Sowrey with her five children at the turn of the last century.

By the end of the year Freddie had returned from Aden and there was cause for celebration when it was announced in the New Year's Honours List of 1 January 1968 that he had been appointed a Commander of the Order of the Bath (CB) for his services in Aden, an award that was usually reserved for more senior officers. But, within six weeks, the family suffered the loss of Bill when he died on 15 February aged seventy-three after a short illness. As he was reunited with his parents and brother John in the vault at Staines, his surviving brother Fred stood at the salute with tears in his eyes. He had been immensely fond of his younger brother.

On 27 October, Freddie's father played a round of golf with his great friend John Leacroft. (He had been credited with twenty-eight victories in the First World War.) Soon after returning home he felt unwell and retired to bed where he suffered a heart attack and died. He was seventy-five years old. From the earliest days of childhood, throughout wartime, during their service careers and into retirement, the three brothers had always been very close and shared many common interests and experiences. Born over a two-and-a-half year period, they died within twelve months of each other. Fred was cremated but his ashes were interred in the family vault with the remains of his parents and brothers.

Soon after arriving in London, Johnnie and his wife had bought a mews house in Earls Court in need of refurbishment, and where the family virtually camped out as the work progressed. During their time in India, Audrey had become interested in Indian embroidered silk and had returned home with some wonderful clothes that she had designed herself. These were much admired by many people and as both their girls were now at boarding school, she decided to chance her hand and start a small business. Early in 1968, Johnnie made the decision to leave the RAF to support Audrey's business and he retired in July.

With the loss of his father and two uncles, and the retirement of his cousin, it was left to Freddie to continue the family's remarkable years of service in the RAF. For the next twelve years, he served in a series of increasingly senior and important appointments.

Towards the end of his time in Aden, Neil Cameron, who was assistant chief of defence staff (policy) (ACDS Pol) in MOD, called Freddie and asked him if he would be prepared to take over as chairman of the RAF Club. Freddie responded, 'It will depend where I am going and who I will be working for'. A signalled reply arrived immediately: 'You are going to be in London and you will be working for me.' As Freddie pointed out, it was game, set and match!

Cameron had recently been working for Dennis Healey, the secretary of state for defence, in a small team looking at long-term defence policy – The Programme Evaluation Group (PEG) – an organisation that created friction in the single-services and one the chiefs of staff found irksome. There already existed within the MOD organisation a Joint Planning Staff but daily pressures gave them little time to look at long-term defence issues. The eminent defence analyst, Sir Michael Howard, wrote:

> 'To say the joint planners were working far too hard to have time to think would be only slightly unfair as a description of men who often worked sixteen-hour days, six days a week. But it is undeniable that they had to give total priority to immediate problems of daunting logistical complexity, for which ministers required answers within a matter of hours. Men under this kind of pressure are not the best qualified to produce well-matured consideration of what British defence policy ought in fact to be.'

It was just this situation that Healey was trying to resolve when he created the PEG but, with his imminent departure from MOD, he agreed to the formation of the Defence Policy Staff. Responsible to the chiefs of staff committee, they were to replace the unpopular PEG and he insisted that Cameron should be in charge. The policy staff had five divisions tasked to handle different aspects of policy and Cameron handpicked his team. Howard described their role:

> 'So far from being a secret cell at the centre of some sinister web, the policy staff, if it is to do its work properly, needs to be the most accessible of all the departments in the MOD. It needs to spread its antennae as widely as possible to attract new ideas, and the generosity of its hospitality to unorthodox concepts must be equalled only by the rigour with which it analyses them.'

On his arrival in MOD on 1 Feb-

Freddie (right) with Neil Cameron (centre) and Ted Hawkins.

ruary 1968, Freddie was appointed to lead the tri-service Team 'C' dealing with Britain's military activities outside the NATO area. Following the significant defence cuts announced a few weeks earlier, it was clear that he and his team would be spending most of their time reviewing, and creating, policy and plans associated with the withdrawal of British forces from the Far East (except Hong Kong), and the Persian Gulf. The cancellation of the Royal Navy's next generation of aircraft carriers and the RAF's F-111 bomber force also had a profound effect on future policy outside NATO.

In addition to reviewing military withdrawal and its impact on the global and international scene, there was also the need to develop contingency plans for the 'withdrawal from empire'. This could require the evacuation of British civilians from unstable parts of the world and there was a possible need for intervention operations.

As a director, Freddie sat on the committee with his fellow directors (Commodore Colin Dunlop, Brigadier David Fraser, Dr Eddy Benn and Michael Quinlan) and they were charged with reviewing the size and shape of UK armed forces. Unlike their MOD colleagues in the single-service plans directorates, the defence policy team were more concerned with looking conceptually and beyond the ten-year long-term costings programme.

After a year with Team 'C', Freddie transferred to Team 'A', which dealt with future plans for the structure, capabilities, and equipping of all three services to fulfil defence policy. In order that single-service equipment plans could be directed appropriately, it was important that Freddie and his team highlighted, to the individual service departments, the capabilities of the others so that their future plans could be complementary and appropriate within the constraints of a tight budget.

This feature of Freddie's work was particularly important. The introduction into RAF service of a new range of very capable 'fast jets', the Harrier, Phantom and Buccaneer, soon to be followed by the Jaguar, offered the other two services a significant increase in the capabilities of the support they could expect to receive. This would impact on their own capabilities and procurement plans. Freddie highlighted the example of the RAF's newly acquired responsibility for the land-air support of maritime operations following the eventual demise of the aircraft carrier and the introduction into RAF service of the Phantom air defence and Buccaneer strike-attack aircraft. He commented:

> 'We had the task of convincing the other two services that our re-equipment was to their advantage. I was also pleased to convince my naval opposite number that an extra squadron of Harriers would be as much to their advantage as ours.'

Freddie was not only fulfilling a big job at a time of major defence re-structuring but he was very busy on other fronts. He and Anne bought their first house, 40 Adam and Eve Mews in Kensington, which had been neglected for many years and needed a considerable amount of work. This was very much a family effort and one all-night interior painting session ended at 5 am on the day the carpets were to be laid! This created a pleasant family connection since cousin Johnnie and his family were living close by and they were able to spend time together. The two cousins always enjoyed each other's company and they shared a number of interests.

Freddie's other major activity at this time was his chairmanship of the RAF Club. As one of the 'colonels', he now found himself implementing the measures agreed following the 'revolt' in order to develop the club and make it financially viable. At the top of the list of priorities was the commitment to extend the club's amenities and a five-phase 'Three-Year Plan' was adopted. Additional accommodation was provided and the public rooms were extended and refurbished, in addition to raising general standards throughout the club.

To celebrate the fiftieth anniversary of the formation of the RAF, a reception was held in the presence of Her Majesty the Queen and the Duke of Edinburgh in November 1968. Some 700 people attended and the event was described as just a 'memorable and a fitting conclusion to the metamorphosis which had begun four years earlier'.

As mentioned earlier Freddie was very keen to attract the younger officers to the club. He is well re-membered for a remark he had made at an earlier EGM when he suggested:

> 'One idea for attracting young members would be to provide them with some music and a pocket-handkerchief-sized floor where they could stand next to a girl and prop themselves up; I believe they call this "dancing" these days.'

This was done and a disco was opened on 11 October 1968 and proved very popular.

After two stimulating years working for Neil Cameron in the MOD, Freddie left in April 1970. He completed a flying refresher course at Manby on the Jet Provost before spending a week at CFS flying five familiarisation sorties in the Gnat, subsequently taking up the appointment of SASO at HQ Train-ing Command at RAF Brampton near Huntingdon. He was promoted to acting air vice-marshal.

Chapter Twenty-five

THE TRAINING WORLD

Freddie had hoped to be appointed as SASO at HQ Transport Command, an appointment that he was well qualified to fill. However, the CAS, Air Chief Marshal Sir Denis Spotswood, wanted Freddie to go to Training Command.

His arrival at Brampton on 11 May 1970 did not get off to a good start when he discovered that the ex-officio married quarter, the Old Rectory, was still occupied and unlikely to become available for some time so Freddie spent five weeks in the officers' mess. There were one or two other issues, 'which rankled a bit'. It was an early indication that his time as SASO would be one of his less satisfying appointments.

There were, however, many aspects that were rewarding and enjoyable, not least the opportunity to fly some of the command's aircraft. One of his responsibilities was to recommend approval of the Red Arrows for their formation aerobatic sequences prior to the air show season and Freddie flew with them on a number of occasions. He also took advantage to fly the Jet Provost on some of his visits to the flying training stations.

Soon after taking up his appointment, Freddie became heavily involved in the major changes being introduced at the RAF College, Cranwell. The air member for personnel (AMP), Air Marshal Sir Andrew Humphrey, had recognised that more young people aspired to go to university and obtain a degree and he proposed some radical changes for the future of Cranwell. In 1964 the Air Force Board had recognised that the possession of a degree, or its equivalent, should be the basic qualification for direct entry to the General List of the main executive branches of the RAF. This would mean ultimately the

Freddie ready for a sortie in a Jet Provost.

phasing out of the long-established flight cadet entry scheme but it would ensure that every new officer
was exposed to the ethos and excellence of the college.

Such a radical change was recognised but it raised a great deal of questioning and doubt amongst
the traditionalists, of which there were many. Freddie recalled:

> 'It took a lot of persuasion in some quarters to sell the graduate entry scheme and there was
> a degree of misunderstanding of Andrew Humphrey's motives.'

The scheme was adopted and it created an uneasy transition period at the college. The mixing of flight
cadet and officer student entries was not without some difficulties and friction. The last cadet entry
entered in the autumn of 1970 at the same time as the first graduate entry. A key element of the graduate scheme was attendance at a university air squadron whilst studying, where flying and general
service training were key features.

As these major changes to the RAF officer entrance system were being announced HM the Queen
and Prince Philip visited Cranwell to
mark the Golden Jubilee of the RAF
College. Shortly afterwards came the
announcement that the Prince of Wales
would attend the college to begin his
flying training on the Jet Provost.

Presentation of wings at Linton-on-Ouse.

In January 1971 three Jet Provost
Mark 5s arrived to form Golden Eagle
Flight in readiness for the arrival of the
prince. This involved meticulous planning and the careful selection of instructors. As Freddie commented, 'we weren't
going to be popular if we killed the heir
to the throne'.

To qualify for his wings, the prince
would need to fly solo. Freddie and his
staff analysed thousands of circuits to
identify where the critical points occurred so that risks could be overcome.
Doctors were approached to identify
what, if any, was the likelihood of a fit
young man becoming incapacitated in flight. Teams of instructors, ground crew and radar operators
to monitor the royal flights were handpicked. Squadron Leader R.E. Johns (later Air Chief Marshal
Sir Richard Johns and CAS) was appointed as the prince's personal instructor. Once the prince had
gone solo, then he completed the rest of the training to wings standard by flying with experienced instructors and navigators. The project was a success and on 20 August 1971, the Prince of Wales received
his pilot's wings from the CAS, ACM Sir Denis Spotswood, in the presence of Prince Philip.

Events at Cranwell occupied much of Freddie's time. The Varsity aircraft was phased out, women
officers were on parade for the first time and the headquarters of UASs moved to the college and came
under the instruction of the commandant. Towards the end of his time, Freddie and his staff made the
initial plans to transfer the RAF College of Air Warfare from Manby to Cranwell.

In addition to these specific, and unique, tasks, Freddie was responsible for the routine job of the
administration of a large flying training undertaking that produced over 300 new aircrews each year
in addition to those on post-graduate flying training at CFS and the RAF College of Air Warfare.
Flying training also included the ATC gliding schools, the air experience flights and sixteen UASs, in

addition to the flying training schools situated on ten airfields and the Red Arrows.

Freddie continued to take to the air when possible and, in his final month at Brampton, he flew a general handling sortie in a Varsity and an aerobatic sortie in a Jet Provost Mk 5. A few days later, on 19 October 1972, he left for Latimer.

Since his days working for CAS in the early 1960s, Freddie had maintained his keen interest in international and politico/military affairs. He had joined the International Institute for Strategic Studies (IISS) at that time and his later MOD appointments and attendance at IDC had developed this interest significantly. Hence, his appointment as commandant of the National Defence College (NDC) was much to his liking. He had hoped to be appointed AOC of 38 Group but he described his time at Latimer as 'wonderful'. It was also a happy and stimulating time for Anne.

The well-established Joint Services Staff College, which had run unbroken for twenty-five years ended in 1971, and the change to a one-year course was not greeted with universal acclaim. There were some who thought that the lengthened course, on a national basis, directed specifically towards high-grade appointments in the MOD and other headquarters, would alter the character of Latimer. Freddie did not agree and in a foreword to the college magazine *Cormorant* he wrote:

> 'Inevitably things must change, as it is a new and different course under changing pressures in defence. However, although the loss of the overseas students is to be regretted, the course has gained much in other respects and is an undoubted success. A recent survey of those who attended the first three NDC courses shows that they regarded the year at Latimer as fitting them well for the wide range of posts they had undertaken so far. And it is worthwhile emphasising that the NDC provides a year's mind broadening and mental stretching that is of great value in any post in any of the three armed services.'

During his time as commandant, Freddie wanted to identify a method that would enable him to assess the success of the course. He wanted to measure the improvement of the students as they progressed through careful monitoring by the directing staff. He recognised that this method was adequate for those of the lower and middle capabilities but he was less sure that it suited the brilliant students. He knew this was a difficult task but it was particularly important to stretch these officers more in order to develop further their undoubted ability and equip them for the most important and demanding appointments on graduation. To achieve this, Freddie insisted on having high grade officers posted into NDC as directing staff.

To get the best out of the students, Freddie recognised the importance of instilling confidence in the students and this came from a combination of good tutoring and leadership, exposure to important individuals in the military, political and industrial fields and a demanding set of stimulating exercises. In his foreword, he went on to say:

> 'Confidence will be in great need in defence in the future. There is the confidence borne of friendship with individuals in the other services, and our civil service colleagues; the knowledge of the way in which these other services operate; and the certainty of their support if the need arises.
>
> 'Then there is the individual confidence, which will be needed to state defence requirements unequivocally and with complete conviction. The further the experience of large-scale war recedes, and the less war itself appears likely, the more necessary it is for those who have to press the needs for defence in a bleak economic climate to have confidence based on their own professionalism and the knowledge that they are good at their job.
>
> 'The confidence of those in the armed services is also particularly important in encouraging informed public support for the military profession. The fact that Latimer students are well able to dominate the cut and thrust of university seminars on the more esoteric as-

pects of defence is encouraging. However, unless the services are ready to articulate the risks that face the Western alliance and the collective needs to meet them, whenever the opportunity arises, our own case may go by default.

'In the postwar period the contribution that serving officers have made to the public debate on the development of military strategy has been swamped by the product of academic pens from both sides of the Atlantic. This cannot be good either for defence or the image of the military profession, and in a small way we have tried to redress the balance.'

These comments, penned almost forty years ago, remain valid to this day; some would claim that they are even more apposite.

Amongst many VIPs who visited Latimer was General Alexander Haig, SACEUR.

The rural calm and tranquil routine of Latimer was shattered by the sound of an explosion at 9.12 am on 12 February 1974 as the NDC joined the growing list of IRA targets. The instructional block was beginning to stir when a bomb was detonated causing considerable damage. Three ladies in the documents room, a member of the directing staff and two junior NCOs were seriously injured and four others suffered minor injuries.

The emergency services were soon on the scene and the media were not far behind. As always, an incident of this nature brought out the best in people with an immediate upsurge in team spirit epitomised by the enthusiastic acceptance of extra, and sometimes menial, duties. As one student remarked, 'It will take more than a bomb to change this place'. Despite two weeks of painstaking enquiries and analysis of the debris, no major successes were achieved although a number of outstanding petty crimes were resolved!

In September, Freddie hosted a residential seminar on the subject of Western European defence. A distinguished gathering of serving officers, members of the administration, senior civil servants and academics, from both the UK and the USA, spent three days debating the problems of decision making in the defence environment. The seminar provided a forum for stimulating discussion on a subject of considerable importance in an age when technological development, combined with rapidly escalating costs, made it even more important to obtain cost effectiveness.

Despite the inevitable disruption to college activities, and a heightened sense of security following the bomb attack, Freddie found his time at Latimer very stimulating and rewarding. The stream of high-profile military and political lecturers, the spirited debates with very talented students, drawn from a wide variety of backgrounds and experiences, together with an enjoyable social life was a welcome respite from the demands of the policy appointments that Freddie had tackled for a number of years. It was also a very happy time for Anne whose encouragement and friendly manner inspired the wives to make substantial efforts for charity with one initiative resulting in the purchase of two guide dogs for the blind.

Throughout their numerous senior positions, Freddie and Anne always recognised the value of support from talented colleagues and loyal and dedicated staff. With senior rank came the commitment to accommodate official visitors and, at Latimer, they were blessed with excellent staff under a *major domo*,

Sergeant Sloan. Freddie commented, 'we were running a high-class hotel and we needed them all'.
After almost three years, Freddie left Latimer in July 1975. The editor of the *Cormorant* wrote:

> 'The National Defence College very sadly said goodbye to Air Vice-Marshal Freddie Sowrey
> and Mrs Sowrey…His influence, particularly on the intellectual aspects of the syllabus, was
> considerable.'

On a fine morning, Freddie and Anne were 'piped' into their polished Bentley as they made their
farewells and, with his driver Corporal Page at the wheel, departed down an avenue lined by members
of the staff.

At the time that Freddie was due for another appointment, Neil Cameron was the AMP. He was well
known for selecting the men he trusted, particularly if
he needed someone with drive and experience to handle
difficult situations. A recent defence review by the new
Labour Government had led to major cuts in the RAF
front line and an eighteen per cent reduction in manpower, which meant a painful redundancy programme
was in place. This inevitably impacted heavily on the
training programme of officers and airmen and women.

As a 'Cameron man', and with his recent experience
and success at Training Command and NDC, Freddie
was appointed director general of training (DGT) at
MOD, a post that allowed him and Anne to move back
into their mews house in Kensington.

DGT had a very wide remit for policy and plans
across the whole spectrum of training from recruit training to flying training, and from dog training to medical
training. There was also extensive and wide-ranging specialist training requirements; including post-graduate
courses within and outside the RAF organisation.

Arriving in the aftermath of the defence cuts, Freddie
was confronted with the need to change requirements,
and some policies, because of the decisions taken about
the number and type of operational squadrons, as he
observed:

Freddie and Anne are given a 'piped'
farewell as they leave Latimer.

> 'The trouble with front-line decisions is the im-
> pact they have on training cannot be turned on and off like a tap. It's a much more com-
> plicated arrangement, which goes right back to recruiting to meet manning targets, many
> of which change after major policy decisions.'

AMP had been tasked by the Air Force Board to find savings and make considerable reductions in the
training budget. Neil Cameron believed that the multi-engine pilot training task should be put out to
civil contract. Freddie and Cecil James, the assistant under secretary (personnel) (AUS(P)), had reser-
vations.

At the time, the RAF was acquiring the Jetstream to replace the Varsity for this task. The aircraft
were available but Freddie sought to have the minimum to meet requirements leaving the surplus to
be taken up by the Royal Navy for observer training. However, he was instructed to prepare an Air

Force Board Standing Committee paper to achieve the privatisation of the task. Freddie looked at what options existed, including visits to civil training organisations and foreign air forces to seek their advice. These aspects were incorporated into the paper, which was circulated through the Air Force Department. It received a mixed reception from Freddie's two-star colleagues and it soon became apparent that it was a non-starter, particularly as pilots at a critical stage of their career would, in effect, be 'outside' their parent service.

By this time, Neil Cameron had just been appointed CAS, Air Marshal Sir John Aiken having taken over as AMP. John Aiken had only been in post a few days, so Freddie and Cecil James sought a private meeting with CAS who listened to the arguments for using the Jetstream in RAF service and he was persuaded not to pursue the idea of privatisation further. Freddie, who had always admired Neil Cameron, believed this incident highlighted one of his great strengths. Although it was one of his cherished schemes, he was prepared to change his mind if the facts and arguments were compelling – and not shoot the messengers!

There was one final twist in this sensitive issue. John Aiken had been AMP for a few weeks when he asked Freddie what had happened to the policy for multi-engine pilot training to change his predecessor's mind as there was no indication anywhere. Freddie told him of the approach to CAS that Cecil James and he had made, an explanation which was accepted. As Freddie commented later, 'I fear that even when released, the files will not always tell the whole story'.

With his great interest in, and experience of, defence matters, Freddie was keen to establish a post of director of defence studies (D Def S) to promote the study of air power in all its military applications. He was aware that he would have some powerful allies in CAS and Air Chief Marshal Sir John Barraclough, the air secretary and a former director of public relations who had experienced the poor public awareness of the role and capabilities of the RAF. However, before the post could be established Freddie had to find an offset to pay for the new appointment and he identified a group captain post in the Education Branch.

Freddie was particularly pleased to establish the post of D Def S and it tied in with his belief that the RAF should not only be considered good operators but also good thinkers. An officer of the Education Branch, Group Captain Tony Mason, was appointed to the post in November 1976 and he was located at the RAF Staff College at Bracknell. CAS was determined that he should receive the full support of RAF commanders and he wrote to them with his instructions:

> 'In order to help provide a new stimulus to air power thinking throughout the air force, I have established a new post to be known as the director of defence studies.
>
> 'I attach a copy of the terms of reference, which indicate that the function of the director is to help promote the study of air power, not just at the Staff College, but throughout the whole service. I recognise that the task is a very large one for a single individual, but the first incumbent, Group Captain R.A. Mason, will hold the post for a considerable period, and my intention is that he should provide a source of intellectual challenge in this field by writing, lecturing widely and organising seminars and discussion periods.
>
> 'He will not succeed in isolation, and I therefore ask that you should make the appointment widely known throughout your Command and also alert your headquarters staffs...
>
> '...With your support, I am confident that Group Captain Mason will do much to make both the service and the public more alive to the importance of the air force's role in the defence of this country both now and for the future.'

In the early stages, Mason had a difficult task. Not everyone saw the need for such an appointment, not least because of manpower cuts elsewhere, and others questioned the choice of an officer who had no operational or front-line experience. That may have been so, but Mason possessed a powerful intellect and a great enthusiasm and knowledge for stimulating thought on air power issues, a topic he felt had been neglected both in and out of the service.

During his five years in post, Mason steadily established his credentials with the RAF, not least amongst the operators, and with the academic world. He won over the sceptics and developed a reputation as one of the country's foremost thinkers on the international application and theories of air power. Through his writings in RAF and academic publications and lectures to wide-ranging audiences, he encouraged an increasing number of intelligent young officers to think more widely about defence and international issues. Through his own efforts and work, Mason was responsible for the post of D Def S becoming recognised as a key appointment. It attracted some of the best brains in the RAF and many of Mason's successors went on to fill very senior appointments.

Some thirty years later, the post of D Def S has grown to be one of the most important and influential posts in the RAF and in the wider defence arena. The director now heads a small team whose remit is to promote thinking on the use of air power and to develop links worldwide. Tony Mason retired as an air vice-marshal before becoming a professor of war studies at Birmingham University and a regular commentator in the media on defence issues. Freddie always considered that the establishment of the post of D Def S was one of his most influential contributions to the RAF.

Towards the end of his time as DGT, Freddie was invited to see the air secretary, Air Marshal Sir Neville Stack. He was told that it was unlikely that there would be another job for him after his time as DGT. After discussing this disappointment with Anne, he decided to carry on rather than seek immediate retirement to start a second career. Soon afterwards, the post of UK Permanent Military Representative to the Central Treaty Organisation (CENTO) needed to be filled and Neil Cameron pressed for Freddie to be appointed.

So, after two years as DGT, a period that saw considerable change in the RAF's policy and plans for training its people, Freddie prepared to leave for an international appointment that would test his professionalism, patience and tact to the full.

Chapter Twenty-six

CENTO

In 1955 the Baghdad Pact was formed with Iran, Iraq, Pakistan, Turkey and the United Kingdom as members. In 1958, the United States joined the military committee of the alliance. Modelled on NATO, the pact committed the nations to mutual co-operation and protection, as well as non-intervention in each other's affairs. Its purpose was to contain any Soviet threat along its south-western borders and prevent Soviet expansion into the Middle East. Unlike NATO, the pact had no unified military command structure and there were few UK or US military bases in member countries, although the UK had large forces based in Cyprus.

On 14 July 1958, the Iraqi monarchy was overthrown in a military coup. Iraq withdrew from the Baghdad Pact, opened diplomatic relations with the Soviet Union and adopted a non-alliance stance. The organisation adopted the name CENTO and moved its headquarters from Baghdad to Ankara.

The 1960s witnessed considerable turmoil in the Middle East and Asia with Arab/Israeli and Indo/Pakistan conflicts. CENTO was unwilling to get involved in either dispute although Pakistan tried unsuccessfully to get assistance in its wars with India. This was rejected since CENTO was aimed at containing the Soviets, not India. The withdrawal of Pakistan from the Commonwealth following the establishment of Bangladesh caused further friction and Pakistan was to remain an uncomfortable and unenthusiastic partner. The situation in the 1960s was summed up in a Foreign Office memorandum:

> 'CENTO remains a weak organisation in constant need of moral and material bolstering by the United Kingdom and the United States. CENTO's weakness derives mainly from its dubious credibility as a military organisation and from the divergence in aims and policies amongst its members. The maintenance of the military credibility of CENTO depends, to a considerable extent, on the United Kingdom commitment of four Canberra squadrons in Cyprus…'

The thrust of this statement remained valid throughout the existence of CENTO. Furthermore, the Soviets presented a low military threat and this contributed to the lack of a joint focus of the national security priorities of regional member states. The Soviet establishment of closer links with Middle Eastern states, including Egypt, Syria, Libya and the Yemen, effectively 'leap frogged' the geographical barrier established by the member states and helped to undermine the stated aim of the alliance.

Freddie left for Turkey, on promotion to air marshal, on 25 October 1977 to take up his post at CENTO. He had bought a left-hand drive Ford Taurus and he and Anne were met at the frontier by their Turkish driver, Baha. He thumped it and declared, 'good strong car'. In the event, it needed to be in order to cope with Turkish roads.

With the assignment of RAF forces to the alliance from its earliest days, the post of UKPMD had always been filled by a senior RAF officer. The personal staff officers (PSO) were always army, which Freddie described as 'an inspired choice'. Two excellent officers served him, initially Lieutenant Colonel Hugh Diamond who later handed over to John Speight. His aide de camp (ADC) was Flight Lieutenant Ian Spalding and Freddie said of his personal staff, 'we were always in the right place with the right brief and the right dress for every occasion'.

When Freddie arrived in Ankara, the RAF's capability to support CENTO was in decline. For many years, the RAF had declared some Cyprus-based squadrons to the alliance. These had been replaced by two Vulcan squadrons but their withdrawal (as part of the cuts resulting from the 1974 Defence Review), followed by the Nimrods from Malta a few years later, took away the RAF's main military contribution, and capability, to the alliance. The review also reduced UK defence spending on non-NATO commitments. Withdrawals from Aden and the Persian Gulf had been completed and, for future exercises, UK participation in CENTO manoeuvres was put in the lowest priority category.

Despite the loss of the permanently-assigned RAF forces, annual exercises did continue but on a smaller scale. These included a naval manoeuvres, Midlink, a search and rescue exercise and a skill at arms competition. Exercises to test air defences did continue on a small scale but with very few RAF aircraft available to participate. These exercises had some merit but suffered from raid plans that were designed to avoid an individual country from 'losing face'. Hence, flight plans were submitted by attacking forces which allowed defending forces to achieve a successful interception. In addition, each country was jealous of its own sovereignty so 'hot pursuit' across borders was not allowed. Freddie attempted to persuade his fellow PMDs that such 'success' in interceptions was less important than their ability to improve tactics and procedures. Also, by a greater degree of integration of the air defence systems within individual countries, the overall deterrence capability of the alliance could improve. This could then lead to some cost savings, which could, in turn, be used for other areas such as schools and hospitals. Visits to the countries of the alliance gave the opportunity to use friendship and persuasion to try to improve deterrence to the Soviet Union.

The RAF withdrew from the main air defence exercise, Shahbaz, in 1977 on security grounds. In an attempt to offset the loss of RAF forces for CENTO exercises, the MOD sought ways to prevent a decline in RAF influence over the air forces of the regional nations without imposing too great a strain on resources. One proposal was to deploy Jaguars or Buccaneers from RAF Germany to Turkey under the NATO squadron exchange scheme to take part subsequently in Exercise Shahbaz. However, this foundered on a host of 'difficulties' put forward by the Turkish air force, based shakily on their insistence that CENTO and NATO deployments should be kept entirely separate.

Although it was frustrating at the exercise level, the failure to address policy issues was more worrying. In his 1977 annual report to the chiefs of staff, Freddie highlighted the greatest difficulty that faced any efforts to prepare appropriate contingency plans and to focus participating members' efforts on providing direct support. He wrote:

'The greatest single inhibiting factor in the alliance is the current lack of agreed political guidance for military planning.'

After outlining the historical background, he concluded:

'To summarise, the assumptions on which military planning was to be based were approved for 1961 only, although they continued to be used after that year. The Threat Paper was last agreed upon for a one-year period in 1963 and thus expired on 31 December 1964.

'In the face of the remorseless improvements and increase in Soviet capability, which still continues to grow, the CENTO alliance (unlike NATO) has taken no commensurate

Freddie (far right) hosts his fellow military representatives on a visit to the United Kingdom.

collective improvements towards deterring the threat from the same source. With the present national attitudes it would be unrealistic to expect any change in policy for the alliance to achieve more than the modest standing that it enjoys. CENTO's progress has been strictly marginal and with the differing national opinions as to the value and purpose of the alliance, no more is to be expected.'

This stark appraisal graphically illustrated the problems that beset CENTO.

The pattern of activities varied little over the next year. The economic and political difficulties faced by Pakistan and Turkey, and increasing demonstrations in Iran, frustrated many of the efforts to bring a greater purpose and cohesion to the alliance. However, some progress was being made by a political working group to draft a paper on the 'Situation in the CENTO Region' which led to a report on political guidance on which military planning, and the integration of existing national defensive plans, could be based. This sudden, and increased, interest stemmed, in part, from the increasing Soviet involvement in affairs in Afghanistan and the Horn of Africa in addition to its continued influence in the Middle East.

On a personal front, the beginning of 1978 brought satisfaction and great pleasure to Freddie's family and many friends, when HM the Queen conferred a knighthood on him and he was elevated to be a Knight Commander of the Order of the Bath.

During 1978 there was an increasing shift towards non-military co-operation and support. At the CENTO conference in London in April 1978, the UK and the US were in agreement that CENTO should focus on the economic development and not become a NATO-style alliance. With the increasing difficulties experienced by each of the regional members, Freddie wrote to CDS (Neil Cameron) in December 1978 and commented:

'Looking at the overall scene one cannot but ask how the West can best achieve the dual aim of regional security and maintaining the countries concerned within the Western sphere of influence. For their part, the regional members of CENTO appear to be seeking a greater political (and thus military) commitment from the United States and ourselves, followed closely by greater economic aid in the case of Turkey and Pakistan.

'Lastly, there is the effect of personal contacts, which I judge to be still most important. In the absence of anything more concrete to offer to the regional countries, perhaps the understanding, sympathy and support of the US and UK military still remains the best contribution.'

In January 1979, the annual PMDG visit to Pakistan took place and Freddie had the opportunity to meet most of Pakistan's senior military figures. At social events, and the formal dinner, Pakistan's commitment to CENTO was frequently emphasised but privately there were significant misgivings expressed, not least at the American failure to grasp the gravity of the situation in the region. Every effort was made to convince the Pakistan military of the advantages of Commonwealth membership and the dangers of flirting with China.

During this visit, Freddie met the head of state, General Zia-ul-Haq, and enjoyed a friendly discussion. When the general learnt that Freddie had never been to Gilgit, a Hercules aircraft was laid on and Freddie and Anne enjoyed a panoramic view of the Hindu Kush before landing at the old north-west frontier post.

No sooner had Freddie returned to Ankara, than events in the region gathered momentum rapidly. By now, he had completed two winters with the heavy smog in Ankara and was asked if he would be prepared to complete a third to which he readily agreed. However, it was not to be.

The demonstrations in Iran against the Shah reached a critical stage and in mid-January he left Iran for exile. The resulting power vacuum led to the return of the Ayatollah Khomeini and the royal regime finally collapsed on 11 February – Iran was declared an Islamic Republic on 1 April.

Early statements from Khomeini and the

Freddie meets Pakistan's President, General Zia-ul-Haq.

Iranian foreign minister indicated that Iran would leave CENTO. Within days, Pakistan warned its allies of a similar intention. The UK and US took the view that it was for the regional countries to determine the future of CENTO. During a visit by the Pakistan foreign minister to Iran on 8-10 March, the two countries decided to issue statements withdrawing from the alliance. These were followed by a similar statement from Turkey favouring an early dissolution of CENTO. At talks held in Washington on 15-16 March, the UK and US officials concurred with this view and subsequently a request was sent to the secretary general suggesting that he draw up plans to dissolve the alliance at an early date.

The run-down started in early April and the final PMDG meeting was held on 15 May without Iranian representation. A short and dignified ceremony enabled the remaining PMDs to pay tribute to their predecessors, the staffs, and achievements of the alliance. Freddie concluded his brief valedictory statement:

'The links forged in mutual interest and trust will not be forgotten, and the United Kingdom will continue to be concerned for the territorial integrity, peace, and freedom of the states in the area. We warmly reciprocate the wish expressed by the regional members to see friendly relations continue, and we shall maintain our close association with our hosts Turkey, to whom we express especial thanks, through membership of NATO.'

Freddie submitted a detailed report to MOD on the alliance; benefits gained, and difficulties encountered, over CENTO's twenty-four years of existence and included his views on its achievements. He acknowledged it would be difficult to prove but Soviet expansion in the area had not occurred and regional countries were given confidence to withstand Soviet political pressure backed by overwhelming force of arms. He went on to say that it was true that CENTO had tied up Soviet military forces that might otherwise have been directed elsewhere.

He drew attention to other aspects, particularly the opportunity for pervasive influence on the regional countries. He gave as an example, the help made to maintain Pakistan's western commitment over a long period of internal difficulties and doubt. In the isolation they were likely to feel, he believed it could be the right time to re-open the question of Pakistan's return to the Commonwealth. He also cited the CENTO cloak which enabled the UK to be sympathetic contributors to the problem of Turco-US relations before the lifting of the arms embargo. Indeed, the presence in Ankara of a western defensive alliance with its staff, officials and senior officers had all played its part in underpinning Turkish confidence in the west.

He concluded his final report:

> 'There is a continuing benefit into the future. The basis has been laid for greater economic and military co-operation amongst regional countries if the will exists. Additionally, the bilateral links between the UK and US, and the regional countries will facilitate our continuing influence and presence in the area at a time that it is most needed. If this had not been part of the normal CENTO scene, I judge that it would need a considerable political will in both countries and be a source of divisiveness in this important area. This, together with the maintenance of western ideas and contacts, may well be CENTO's greatest contribution long after it has ceased to exist.'

Finally, on 31 May Freddie and Anne left Ankara for the UK via Vienna to be briefed en-route on the current arms limitation talks.

Back in the MOD a spare air marshal was a useful commodity. Freddie was soon put to work on an all-embracing study of the three services and industry. The aim was to determine how existing resources, including civil and military manpower and industrial material, might better be utilised in support of the United Kingdom defence effort in a period of tension or during hostilities.

With a young officer of considerable potential from the other two services, they were able to ask a series of 'what if' questions and go on asking them. The resulting 'Sowrey Report' was endorsed by the chief of staff and forwarded to the secretary of state.

There was one other commitment that Freddie and Anne were asked to undertake as personal escorts to Chinese chief of staff Yang Yong, and his wife Lim Bin on their official visit to the UK. Whilst his wife was being taken round museums and London department stores, the general and Freddie spent many hours in cars (he did not like helicopters) with an interpreter. Having agreed not to discuss each other's political systems, they enjoyed each other's company in wide-ranging talks about what they were seeing. The idea of building Harriers under licence did not succeed (the primary reason for the trip) but both the Chinese visitors had a detailed and intimate experience of parliamentary democracy.

A round of farewells, including the honour of an audience with the Queen, brought to an end, in 1980, a career which had started forty years earlier. And so, for the first time in sixty-five years, the name of Sowrey no longer appeared on the active brief of the Air Force List.

EPILOGUE

Both Johnnie and Freddie followed in the tradition of the Sowrey family and were men of action. They were never going to settle to a mundane retirement and, for the next thirty years, life was a continuous round of work, projects and pleasure.

After retiring in July 1968, Johnnie supported his wife Audrey and her developing business, which she called Regamus. She obtained orders for her dress designs from high street shops but her Indian contacts failed her. Undaunted she set up a workshop at their home in Rutland, found Indian materials in Leicester, silks in Suffolk, organza in Switzerland and fulfilled the orders. Realising what mark up was being added by the London shops, Audrey bought her own shop in Beauchamp Place, Knightsbridge, and ran a very successful women's fashion business until retiring in 1988. Many of the icons of the day including the Begum Aga Khan, Diana, Princess of Wales and Jerry Hall shopped at Regamus.

In all this Johnnie became fully involved in every field, short of designing, sewing, selling or, presumably, fitting. An example of one of his minor tasks was delivering an outfit to Buckingham Palace for Princess Diana to wear in her engagement photographs.

The business was a success and enabled Johnnie and Audrey to buy a large house in Knightsbridge with a wing used as a workshop, and they moved from Rutland to London. Having enjoyed family holidays in the south of France, they bought apartments in the French Alps and the Italian Riviera, the latter being replaced by a house in Puget a few miles north of Nice. They enjoyed renovating and improving the houses.

Following his retirement Johnnie took up sailing again, keeping his yachts in Walton Backwaters, north Essex, made famous by Arthur Ransome. In addition to several crossings of the North Sea and English Channel, he cruised in his 42-footer to Kristiansand, and up Oslofjord, piloted by his old Norwegian friend, Hal Christensen. He came home via Sweden, Denmark and the Kiel Canal, finally

Johnnie and Audrey at their daughter Julia's wedding.

interminably zigzagging across the North Sea against adverse winds.

His stepson Gavin recalled many of their sailing adventures together:

'I have very happy memories of passages both in John's boats and mine. He was a ready crew and there were some magic occasions bringing a boat back from Weymouth via Dieppe and ghosting across the Thames estuary in the early morning under spinnaker at 5 knots, John cooking breakfast, with the pan sizzling away. We also made a passage from Palma Majorca to Porto Cervo, Sardinia, in a state of the art racing yacht, with Audrey and my family. In John's seventy-fifth year, we had a more rugged experience, a passage race from Falmouth to Cork in my 32-foot racing machine. We blew a spinnaker out before getting out of the Fal estuary, ran out of wind, dodged between rocks, avoided adverse tides off the Lizard, then suffered a very bumpy reach across the Irish Sea. John was bruised but uncomplaining.

'I also have happy memories of flying with John and he often bravely entrusted his life with me. He was thrilled to make many flights from Suffolk including trips to Bielefeld in Germany, Deauville, and to Cornwall. I was a rookie and John's presence was a great reassurance and boosted my confidence. He did most of the en-route piloting and it was immediately clear that he was absolutely on the ball and at home. There must have been times when he was itching to offer guidance, but the only time I remember was a gentle reminder that it would be better to lower the flaps on one landing.

'On a return flight from Alderney, low cloud as far as the Isle of Wight forced us to fly at less than 1,000 feet, not good if we had an engine problem. John remained completely unfazed – probably chicken feed by comparison with his previous experience.'

Johnnie's wife Audrey became terminally ill in 1992 and she died in September 1993. Later he married Lorna and they settled in Devon where he set about restoring a residential annex of their farmhouse.

He never lost his fondness for France and Italy, and the long drives to the Mediterranean coasts, a journey he continued to make until he was almost ninety.

He remained in good form up to his last bedtime with plans for an expedition to see his family in London and Suffolk. He had also planned an outing to the Lugger Inn at Looe to celebrate his ninety-first birthday and had his flight ticket booked to visit his daughter Mina in France in January 2011, but he died peacefully on 30 November 2010.

Within days of Freddie leaving the MOD in March 1980 on his retirement from the RAF, he started a one-year period as a visiting fellow at the IISS writing on the risks of terrorism on urban society. He commented on the transformation:

'One day I was taken to work in a shiny black car and given a cup of tea as I arrived, the next day I went to the IISS on the tube, worked with a Japanese diplomat, made my own coffee and everyone called me Fred.'

During his later years in London, Freddie and Anne had bought Home Farm in Heron's Ghyll in the High Weald area of outstanding natural beauty, and moved there on his retirement. The working farm with its Victorian (and earlier) buildings needed a great deal of restoration and they both set about the work with typical energy. The farm carried rights of common on Ashdown Forest and Freddie and Anne bought fifty acres of the adjacent ancient woodland. It was not long before he was invited to stand for election to the Board of Conservators. Over the coming years, he would serve for three separate periods of five years, elected by his fellow commoners.

The first ten years at the farm were spent in the renovation and restoration of the historic landscape of the parkland created by the poet Coventry Patmore. Since then work has been on environment conservation schemes and the management of pasture and woodland sympathetic to nature. A family partnership ensures close supervision with, virtually, daily involvement by nearby family.

With a childhood and a long career in the RAF, Freddie had a deep interest in the history of the service. During his time in Ankara, he had noted the way the other two armed services recorded their histories through societies and he felt that the RAF should do likewise. However, he also thought that it would be more valuable for such an RAF organisation to be more participative and offer opportunities to hear of the experiences of the wartime generation first hand and whilst they were still available.

He produced a paper setting out his ideas and sent it to the then air member for personnel but it was not the right time, and there were concerns that the service might have to 'bale it out' financially, so he let the idea drop. However, a few years later, the head of the Air Historical Branch, Air Commodore Henry Probert, suggested that he 'run it again'. Before a presentation at the Royal United Services Institute (RUSI) by the eminent military historian John Terraine, Freddie approached the chairman, Marshal of the RAF Sir David Craig (then chief of the air staff and later Lord Craig). Freddie briefed him on his ideas and asked for two minutes at the end to explain them. Full support was forthcoming and, with the involvement of the Air Historical Branch, the RAF Historical Society was launched in 1986 and a secretary and editor were appointed. Air Chief Marshal Sir Bing Cross was a strong supporter and bluntly told Freddie, 'it was your idea so you can be chairman', a post he held for the next ten years.

The society enjoys the full support of the Air Force Board, and has gone from strength to strength with a membership today of almost 800. It organises two seminars a year, held at the RAF Museum, and in addition to covering the major facets of RAF history, it also endeavours to cover areas that official historians have neglected. These events are published in the society's

Freddie dedicates the history room at RAF Honington in the memory of his Uncle Bill.

Proceedings, a journal that has attracted much favourable comment. For over twenty years, Freddie has hardly missed a meeting; he is the society's vice president and this could be his lasting memorial.

In September 1989, Freddie was the guest of the station commander at RAF Honington. After a tour of the airfield, he was invited to open the station's new history room, the 'Sowrey Room', named in memory of his Uncle Bill, Honington's first station commander.

Motor cars, particularly old ones, continued to fascinate Freddie throughout his retirement. He commented:

'Restoration of seriously old cars is an art not a science, and very personal. Every nut, bolt and ball bearing goes between your finger and thumb as you feel life returning to a previously inert collection of parts. Our 1903 Riley Forecar and 1901 6 ½ hp Darracq Tonneau have responded well having been in a loft above a demolished shop, used as a tractor or saw bench before being finally abandoned. Fifty years of intermittent years of the London to Brighton run have proved the point.'

With his son Peter sharing the driving, he completed the 2011 event as the oldest entrant and with the oldest competing car.

In 2004, Air Commodore Peter Dye, chairman of Cross and Cockade, the First World War Aviation Historical Society, launched an appeal for a memorial to be sited on the aerodrome at St Omer in memory of the men of the British Air Services who had served in northern France. Lord Trenchard and Freddie were invited to be the patrons and a fundraising campaign was started. Johnnie was very supportive and contributed to the appeal and commented, 'it is very appropriate that our family's service should be commemorated and have a fitting memorial'. The appeal was successful and on 11 September 2004, Air Chief Marshal Sir Brian Burridge, the C-in-C of Strike Command, and Lieutenant General Jean Gaviard of the French air force unveiled the memorial in the presence of many local dignitaries and a large RAF contingent. The unveiling of the memorial on 11 September coincided with the ninetieth anniversary of the first British aircraft to arrive at St Omer in September 1914. By the end of the war there were nearly 5,000 air service personnel serving at the base.

Both Lord Trenchard and Freddie addressed the gathering in English and French before 108-year old Henry Allingham, the last surviving RAF airman from the First World War, laid a wreath. The gathering was then entertained at a reception hosted by the mayor of St Omer.

Today, Freddie will often be found with his head under the bonnet of a car or rushing round the woodland on a quad-bike selecting the next area for coppicing...that is when he is not heading up to London for meetings and gatherings. His aim is to continue this through his ninetieth birthday and beyond.

Above: Freddie and his all-family crew complete the 2011 London to Brighton run. *Right:* The memorial at St Omer in memory of the men of the British Air Services during the First World War (Peter Dye).

Saint Omer

"In memory of those members of
the British Air Services and air forces
from every part of the British Empire
who served on the Western Front during
the First World War 1914 to 1918"

———•———

"A la mémoire des membres des
Forces Aériennes britanniques et des
armées de l'air de l'Empire britannique
qui ont combattu sur le front ouest pendant
la Première Guerre Mondiale 1914 à 1918"

———•———

"Erected by Cross and Cockade,
the First World War Aviation Historical Society · 2004"

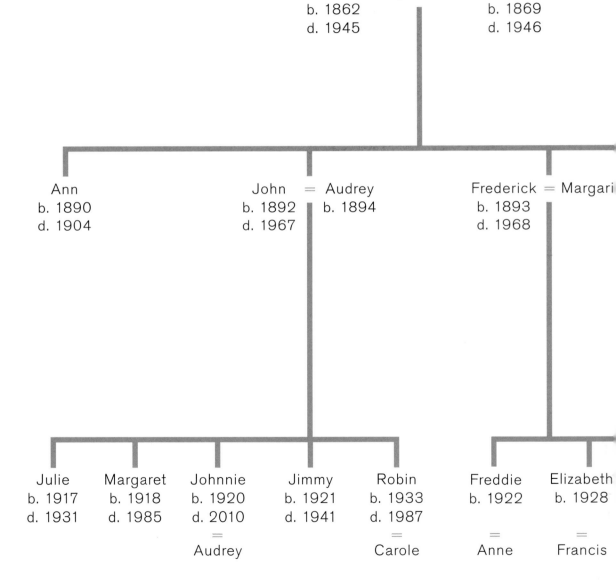

John William Sowrey = Susan Maria Chambers
        b. 1862   b. 1869
        d. 1945   d. 1946

Ann   John = Audrey   Frederick = Margari
b. 1890   b. 1892 b. 1894   b. 1893
d. 1904   d. 1967   d. 1968

Julie   Margaret   Johnnie   Jimmy   Robin   Freddie   Elizabeth
b. 1917   b. 1918   b. 1920   b. 1921   b. 1933   b. 1922   b. 1928
d. 1931   d. 1985   d. 2010   d. 1941   d. 1987
                        =   =   =   =
                     Audrey   Carole   Anne   Francis

THE SOWREY
FAMILY TREE

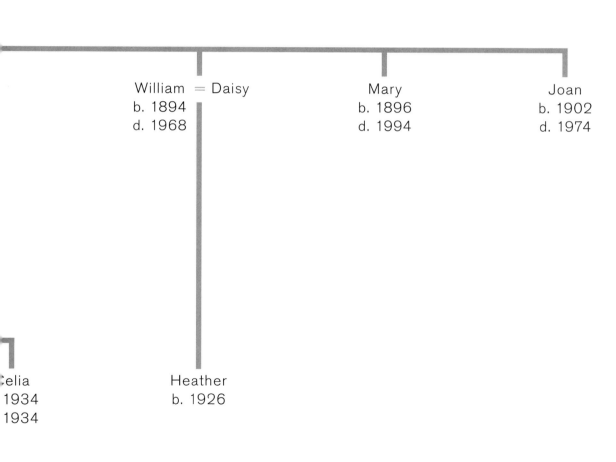

William = Daisy
b. 1894
d. 1968

Mary
b. 1896
d. 1994

Joan
b. 1902
d. 1974

Celia
1934
1934

Heather
b. 1926

BIBLIOGRAPHY

Absolon, Eric, *On the Edge of Flight,* Pen & Sword, 2012

Air Publication 125, *A Short History of the Royal Air Force,* Air Ministry, 1936

Air Publication 956, *Lectures & Essays, RAF Staff College 1922-23*

Air Publication 1105, *Iraq Command – Report*

Air Publication 1152, *Lectures & Essays, RAF Staff College 1924-25*

Air Publication 3003, *A Brief History of the Royal Air Force,* HMSO, 2004

Air Publication 3236, *Works,* Air Ministry, 1956

Allward, Maurice, *Gloster Javelin,* Ian Allan, 1983

Armitage, Michael, *The Royal Air Force – An Illustrated History,* Arms & Armour, 1993

Bowyer, Chaz, *Royal Flying Corps Communiqués,* Grub Street, 1998

Bowyer, Chaz, *RAF Operations 1918-1938,* William Kimber, 1988

Boyes, John, *Project Emily, Thor IRBM and the RAF,* The History Press, 2008

Boyle, Andrew, *Trenchard,* Collins, 1962

Brown, James Andrew, *A Gathering of Eagles,* Purnell, 1970

Bruce, J.M., *The Aeroplanes of the Royal Flying Corps,* Putnam, 1992

Burge, C. Gordon, *The Annals of 100 Squadron,* Bivouac Books, 1975

Burns, Michael, *The Queen's Flight,* Blandford Press, 1986

Cameron of Balhousie, *In the Midst of Things,* Hodder & Stoughton, 1986

Cherry, Niall, *Most Unfavourable Ground,* Helion & Company, 2005

Chorley, W.R., *Bomber Command Losses 1939-40,* Midland Counties, 1992

Cole, Christopher, & Cheesman E.F., *The Air Defence of Britain 1914-18,* Putnam, 1984

Corrigan, Gordon, *Loos 1915 – The Unwanted Battle,* Spellmount, 2006

Delve, Ken, *The Winged Bomb,* Midland Counties, 1985

Delve, Ken, *The Source Book of the RAF,* Airlife, 1994

Dunmore, Spencer, *Wings for Victory,* McClelland & Stewart, 1994

Fairbairn, Tony, *Action Stations Overseas,* Patrick Stephens Ltd, 1991

Franks, Norman, *RAF Fighter Command,* Patrick Stephens Ltd, 1992

Furse, Anthony, *Wilfrid Freeman,* Spellmount, 2000

Glubb Pasha, *War in the Desert,* Hodder & Stoughton, 1960

Golley, John, *Aircrew Unlimited,* Patrick Stephens Ltd, 1993

Guttman, John, *Spad VII Aces of World War I,* Osprey, 2001

Hanson, Neil, *First Blitz,* Doubleday, 2008

Haslam, E.B., *The History of Royal Air Force Cranwell,* HMSO, 1982

Hill, Wg Cdr Roderic, *The Baghdad Air Mail,* Edward Arnold, 1929

Hunt, Leslie, *Twenty-One Squadrons,* Garnstone Press, 1972

Hyde, Andrew P., *The First Blitz,* Pen & Sword, 2002

James, John, *The Paladins,* Macdonald, 1990

Jefford C.G., *RAF Squadrons,* Airlife, 1988

Jefford C.G., *Observers and Navigators,* Airlife, 2001

Jones, H.A., *The War in the Air,* Oxford University Press, 1931

Joubert, ACM Sir Philip, *The Third Service,* Thames and Hudson, 1955

Kahn, Walter, *A Glider Pilot Bold,* AFE, 2008

Kimber, James, *Son of Halton,* Thorley Publications, 1977

Laffin, John, *Swifter than Eagles,* William Blackwood, 1964

Lee, Sir David, *Flight from the Middle East,* HMSO, 1978

Leeson, Frank M., *The Hornet Strikes, The Story of 213 Squadron,* Air Britain, 1998

Liddel Hart, B.H., *History of the First World War,* Cassell & Co, 1934

MacCarron, Donal, *A View from Above,* The O'Brien Press Ltd, 2000

Mason, Francis K., *The British Fighter Since 1912,* Putnam, 1992

Mason, T., *The History of 9 Squadron,* Beaumont Publications, 1965

Mason, Tim., *The Cold War Years: Flight Testing at Boscombe Down,* Hikoki Publishing, 2001

Middlebrook & Everitt, *The Bomber Command War Diaries,* Viking, 1985

Morris, Joseph, *The German Air Raids on Great Britain 1914-1918,* Sampson Low, Marston & Co.

Neate, Don, *Scorpion's Sting – The Story of 84 Squadron RAF,* Air Britain, 1994

Noble, Bernard, *Properly to Test – The Early Years,* Old Forge Publishing, 2003

Onderwater, Hans, *Second to None,* Airlife, 1992

Palmer, Derek, *Fighter Squadron,* Self Publishing Association, 1990

Petre, F.L., *The Royal Berkshire Regiment Vol II,* 1925

Philpott, Bryan, *Challenge in the Air,* Model & Allied Publishing, 1971

Philpott, Ian, *Royal Air Force – An Encyclopaedia of Inter-War Years,* Pen & Sword, 2005

Pitchfork, Graham, *Royal Air Force Day by Day,* Sutton Publishing, 2008

Probert, Henry, *High Commanders of the Royal Air Force,* HMSO, 1991

Probert and Gilbert, *'128' The Story of the Royal Air Force Club,* RAF Club, 2004

Richards, Denis, *Royal Air Force – The Fight at Odds,* HMSO, 1953

Rimmel, Raymond, *Zeppelin!,* Conway Maritime Press, 1984

Rosier, Sir Frederick, *Be Bold,* Grub Street, 2011

Ross, A.E., *Through Eyes of Blue,* Airlife, 2002

Ross, Blanche, Simpson, *The Greatest Squadron of Them All, Vol II,* Grub Street, 2003

Saunders, Hilary St George, *Per Ardua,* Oxford University Press, 1944

Saward, Dudley, *'Bomber' Harris,* Cassell, 1984

Shores, Franks & Guest, *Above the Trenches,* Grub Street, 1990

Shores, Christopher & Williams, Clive, *Aces High,* Grub Street, 1994

Shores, Christopher, *Dust Clouds in the Middle East,* Grub Street, 1996

Shores, Christopher & Ring, Hans, *Fighters over the Desert,* Spearman, 1969

Singh, Sukhwant, *India's Wars Since Independence,* Lancer, 2009

Taylor, John W.R., *C.F.S: Birthplace of Air Power,* Jane's Publishing, 1987

Terraine, John, *The Right of the Line,* Hodder and Stoughton, 1985

Thetford, Owen, *Aircraft of the Royal Air Force Since 1918,* Putnam, 1995

Tunbridge, Paul, *History of Royal Air Force Halton,* Buckland Publications, 1995

White, Arthur, *The Hornet's Nest – A History of 100 Squadron,* Square One Publications, 1994

White, C.M., *The Gotha Summer,* Robert Hale, 1986

Wylly, H.C., *History of The Queen's Royal Regiment Vol VII,* Gale & Polden

OFFICIAL SOURCES AT THE NATIONAL ARCHIVE

Air 1/176/15/191/2

Air 1/176/15/200/1

Air 1/691/21/20/39

Air 1/694/21/20/100

Air 1/863/204/5/490

Air 1/922/204/5/892

Air 2/2759, 3429A & B, 10655

Air 5/214, 292, 862, 1287, 1288, 1293, 1294

Air 8/10, 2859-61

Air 14/41

Air 20/344

Air 23/6522, 6523, 6536, 6755, 7759, 7760

Air 24/459

Air 25/521

Air 27/19, 74, 278, 942, 1418, 2687, 2779

Air 28/370, 409, 788, 815, 1628, 1829

Air 29/789, 2356, 2365

Air 32/14, 15

Air 69/8

DEFE 113/1413

WO 95/2208

WO 339/1219

WO 339/11454

PAPERS, JOURNALS AND MAGAZINES

Aeroplane
Air Historical Branch Narratives
Comparative Strategy, Vol 28
Cormorant
Cross and Cockade
Flight International
Journal of the RAF College
London Gazette
RAF Air Power
RAF Historical Society Proceedings
RUSI Journal
The Aerospace Professional
The Air Force List
The Times

PERSONAL PAPERS

Flying Logbooks
Notes by F.B. Sowrey
Notes by J.A. Sowrey
Sowrey Papers, RAF Museum Hendon

INDEX

NB: The Sowrey family has been featured throughout. Hence it was felt prudent to omit any relevant entries in the index.

Also, ranks stated below are as per first mention in the book.

Personnel

234

Aircraft

General

Miscellaneous